# PERISH THE THOUGHT

PUBLISHER's NOTE: The review quote from *Change* on the cover of this edition is erroneously ascribed to Harvey D. Shapiro. The review was written by Doris Grumbach.

# PERISH THE THOUGHT

Intellectual Women in Romantic America,
1830–1860

## Susan Phinney Conrad

THE CITADEL PRESS
Secaucus, N.J.

First paperbound printing, 1978
Copyright © 1976 by Oxford University Press, Inc.
All rights reserved
Published by Citadel Press
A division of Lyle Stuart Inc.
120 Enterprise Ave., Secaucus, N.J. 07094
In Canada: George J. McLeod Limited
Don Mills, Ontario
Manufactured in the United States of America
ISBN 0-8065-0650-4

# Acknowledgments

I am much obliged to the staffs of the following libraries for their aid and cooperation: The Houghton Library, Harvard University; Manuscripts and Archives Division, The New York Public Library, Astor, Lenox, and Tilden Foundations; Inter-Library Loan Service, the University of Texas at Austin; and The Arthur and Elizabeth Schlesinger Library, Radcliffe College. Jeannette Cheek, former Director, and Barbara Haber, Librarian, The Schlesinger Library, deserve special thanks for bringing to my attention several figures and documents of great importance to this book.

I am indebted to Daniel Aaron, William L. O'Neill, Elspeth Rostow, and Donald Weismann for reading all or part of the manuscript and offering perceptive criticisms. I would also like to thank Sheldon Meyer, Susan Rabiner, and Ann Lindsay of Oxford University Press for their confidence in my work and their expert guidance during the publication process.

My greatest obligation is to William H. Goetzmann, of the University of Texas at Austin, who tirelessly advised me in the preparation of this work. My debt to him and his wife Mewes can never be adequately acknowledged. Finally, since "life is short

and kindred spirits are few," I would like to thank my husband
Karl for his companionship, criticism, and wise counsel.

S. P. C.

Washington, D. C.
February 1976

*To my Mother and my Father*

# Contents

*The world is not superabundant in intellect, even ranking that of men at the highest, and when women repine over the burdens of large endowments, it is a poor augury.*

—Elizabeth Oakes Smith

*It requires philosophy and heroism to rise above the opinion of the wise men of all nations and races, that to be* unknown *is the highest testimonial woman can give to her virtue, delicacy and refinement.*

—Elizabeth Cady Stanton

*Amidst the downward tendency and proneness of things . . . will you not tolerate one or two solitary voices in the land, speaking for thoughts and principles not marketable or perishable?*

—Ralph Waldo Emerson

# PERISH THE THOUGHT

# Introduction

*Oh, why was I born with so much sensibility, and why, possessing it, have I so often been called to struggle with it?*

—Abigail Adams

*Contemplation is the gravest sin of which any citizen can be guilty.*

—Oscar Wilde

Americans have always been uneasy about intellectuals of either sex and often unwilling to certify the sexual and intellectual credentials of American participants in the life of the mind. Waves of anti-intellectualism have periodically swept across this country during the two hundred years of its history, contributing to and reinforcing this strong cultural ambivalence toward the worth of intellectual activity. Indeed, intellectuals themselves and the middle class from which they most often come have best expressed this nagging uncertainty concerning the value of intellectual activity.

Although the noun "intellectual" was not yet current during the thirty years before the Civil War, men and women then engaged in intellectual work knew who they were, and among themselves expressed feelings characteristic of those doubts and uncertainties dogging American intellectuals into the twentieth century. The women in this group, as this study will attempt to show, felt especially uneasy because they were women pursuing an intellectual life. That today's female intellectuals are still not free of this second burden speaks directly of the persistent problem women intellectuals face.

Notwithstanding these common cultural handicaps that have marked American intellectuals since the founding of the nation and the double burden placed upon the American female thinker now and in the previous century, those American intellectuals—both male and female—doing their primary work before the Civil War should be considered as separate from those working after it. Only after the Civil War did American culture make its concrete commitment to that institutionally organized life of the mind, the American university, thus ensuring male intellectuals a base of power and influence and, possibly more important, a livelihood. Regardless of how uncomfortable they might feel in a university environment, it was, for them, a home. The rise of women's colleges, particularly that cluster in New England called "The Seven Sisters," would provide similar opportunities for women intellectuals later in the nineteenth century.

However, between 1830 and 1860, the period under discussion, intellectuals in America felt only the beginnings of the massive institutional change in higher education that would later transform American intellectual life. In this simpler but still perplexing time before the Civil War, a group of women, recognizable as a special social type with distinctive intellectual styles, did pursue a life of the mind. Although they did not experience many of the difficulties that would plague their post-Civil War and twentieth-century counterparts, they encountered their own obstacles and opportunities—some of which remain, some of which have vanished. They form America's first generation of intellectual women: this study is their story.

It is certainly not surprising that woman as intellectual has been ignored or misunderstood by cultural historians. Most people would rather *not* entertain the thought that she is a cultural type. It has been more comforting for historians of both sexes to explain her away according to numerous formulas, for neither mankind nor womankind—nor even scholars—can bear very much reality. The idea of an "intellectual woman," that favorite phrase of her enemies, haunted nineteenth-century American women who happened to be thinkers. As of today, both the scholarly and the popular mind still rely on common stereotypes to characterize women intellectuals. "Salon women," old-maid schoolteachers, "lady" writers, "headhunters," hysterics, headmistresses—all form a vast sisterhood whose members are identified as "intellectual women." Drab, aggressive, unnatural, unloved, and usually pitiful, they are often interchangeable with those domineering businesswomen, bureaucratic bores, and single-minded careerists in fiction, Hollywood movies, and TV commercials—who are seemingly invincible until their pretensions to authority are rendered ridiculous and their vulnerability is exposed.

Women's pretensions to intellectuality are likewise dismissed by academic and cultural gurus, formidable in their sincerity and their learning. For Erik Erikson, with his mystical doctrine of woman's "inner space," women think with their glands. In agreement, some contemporary feminists advocate rejection of the male intellectual tradition and the adoption of magic, art, and the intuitive wisdom practiced in ancient matriarchies. Some historians also prefer to present intellectual woman as irrational, neurotic, aggressively homosexual, intent on dominating everyone, like Mabel Dodge in Christopher Lasch's *The New Radicalism in America.*[1] The mere mention of Mabel Dodge conjures up an image of the "salon woman" whom Hemingway and others described as rank with ambition, presiding over menageries of social climbers and superstars in the hope that some of the talent of the assembly might rub off on her. This image of the "salon woman" as intellectual, or rather as pseudointellectual, has certainly prejudiced public opinion of such major figures as Gertrude Stein, called in a recent literary study, without a trace of irony, the "wicked virgin from Baltimore."[2] This stereotype of the woman intellectual is still the central character in a very cruel fairy tale.

That twentieth-century America can present such a united front, such a consensus against a typical intellectual woman, suggests that all those supposed changes in women's status that even television commentators like Eric Sevareid chuckle about now ("the ladies, God bless 'em") have yet to dilute resentment against the woman as thinker. Whether as psychopath, libertine, or purse-lipped defender of public morality, the intellectual woman remains a hostage to the nineteenth century, when all these images became part of literate America's repertoire of cultural stereotypes. Today, even Tom Wolfe cannot re-create her. His California girl, with her sensible and sturdy calves, is as stolid, earnest, and moralistic as "true women" of the nineteenth century were supposed to be, regardless of the fact that the teacher whom Wolfe describes is reading Eldridge Cleaver in reverential tones to her English Lit. class.[3] Each of these renderings of the intellectual woman rests on the supposition that, having limited intellectual ability, a woman will make insignificant intellectual contributions. Each thinking woman seems to be, in W. H. Auden's terms, both boring and a bore.

The tension between the terms "intellectual" and "woman" reflected in these stereotypes represents semantic as well as historical confusion and controversy. Even when considered separately, both words are so extremely difficult—if not impossible—to define precisely that it is necessary to describe how I have chosen to use them. Although both terms have had long-term associations with woe and suffering, "intellectual" was not in usage as a noun until the last decade of the nineteenth century.[4] To establish that the women I have included were intellectuals, I have used this working definition: Intellectuals are those individuals who willingly pursue and master a portion of their culture's extant body of knowledge, which body is changed by their subsequent analyses, interpretations, revisions, and additions. For consideration in this study, intellectuals must have left a record of their participation in this process of change in a communicable form. They must be part of the "hard core creators of culture," as distinguished from "distributors" and "applicators," whose primary functions, interests, and skills lies in the transmission of existing knowledge.[5]

So many American women have acted as custodians, promoters, and enthusiasts of culture—often with a capital C—that I find it especially important to distinguish between these women and those qualifying under my definition as intellectuals. For similar reasons I have maintained a distinction between women reformers, radicals, and activists not engaged in intellectual activity, and women who have made intellectual contributions to social thought. Only the latter belong in this book. In addition, popular misconceptions of feminism make it doubly important to keep a definition of "intellectual" in mind. Two common assumptions—that every feminist is an intellectual and that every woman intellectual is a feminist (or thinks only in terms of women's rights, roles, etc.)—have hopelessly obscured the accomplishments of women and arbitrarily restricted the range of their interests. A feminist intellectual makes contributions to feminist thought, without necessarily adopting an activist stance. Most feminists are not intellectuals; they are engaged in distributing and applying the theories of others to specific social problems. Although women have been astute analysts and critics of woman's role, they have obviously also found other aspects of life and thought equally interesting. One of the major tasks confronting American intellectual women in the nineteenth century was to move from that narrow area of exploration contemporaries called "woman's sphere," to broader intellectual vistas.

An intellectual's mark can be left on any "field" that calls for new hypotheses, speculations, interpretations, and generalizations. Data most conducive to intellectual activity has a quality that William James called "tough absurdity," a density and complexity that invites or defies one to notice discrepancies between ideas and experience and, accordingly, to generate intellectual change. To become engaged in this process, and skilled in their chosen areas, intellectuals do not necessarily have to pass through institutions of higher learning or be affiliated with other institutions; they need be "professionals" only in the conscious mastery of their subject that characterizes professional work. This distinction is especially important with reference to women intellectuals of this period, to whom many professions, supposedly congenial to intellectual activity, were closed. Intellectuals are most easily distinguished from other people by their commitment to critical inquiry, analysis, synthesis, and discovery, without regard to institutional affiliations.[6]

To define "woman" is, of course, more difficult. Although female physiology is now the object of intensive research and revision, the most basic physiological characteristics of women are obvious and ordinarily not subject to historical change. The cultural makeup of women is likewise going through its own intensive investigation. Anthropological research to date suggests, not surprisingly, that cultural articulations of female roles, however varied they might seem, are usually closely identified with woman's biological function as childbearer and nurturer of the young. Moreover, anthropologists have found that even in primitive societies in which women play prominent and powerful roles not associated with their maternal function, they have never assumed the highest posts of authority.[7] At some stage in each society women always become Simone de Beauvoir's "second sex."

The specific societal influences on women operative in mid-nineteenth-century America have been precisely analyzed by the cultural historian Barbara Welter, who calls the nineteenth-century feminine ideal "the cult of true womanhood."[8] This particular interpretation of woman's nature and social role grew out of a complex of then-current attitudes, beliefs, and conventional wisdom in which the virtues considered truly feminine were submissiveness, piety, purity, and domesticity.[9] These traits also defined the intellectual nature of a "true woman" and constituted her essential "genius." I will explore in this study how women as intellectuals interpreted this ideology and how they attempted to transform it after they were so profoundly influenced by the new intellectual orientation of romanticism.

The period covered in this study, 1830 to 1860, forms an intellectual unit, for it was during these years that the Romantic revolution transformed the cultural life of America as well as Europe. Romanticism suggested a new formula for the universe, an organic interpretation of nature, the cosmos, and humanity, which seemed to invite the participation of women in its expansive and always expanding vision. According to Morse Peckham's convincing interpretation, the Romantic revolution took hold in the late eighteenth century when a few European intellectuals became convinced they had discovered a new vantage point from which to investigate the universe and all existing knowledge. Theirs was a truly new metaphysic, argues Peckham, for romanticism was the first "self-conscious" world view. "The new way of thinking, the Romantic way, looked at itself from right angles; saw itself creating a world view . . . ." [10] This act of creation, newly valued as the highest function of the human mind, was accordingly defined as the ability to perceive all aspects of experience and knowledge symbolically, in terms of the analogies and correspondences suggested by nature's organic processes. The man of feeling, the most sensitive observer, was the new hero; and the artist, manipulating language or paintbrush to create new symbols, was the most sublime and transcendent example of that sacred self-hood upon which romantics bestowed ultimate value. "The great man is the one who, by experiencing within himself the failure of the old symbols, perceives that new symbols must be created." [11] Among the myriad interpretations of romanticism, these emphases appealed most to women intellectuals in antebellum America.

Like most American romantics, women intellectuals affected by this new orientation were not overly concerned with the technicalities of German philosophy, Kant's metaphysical system in particular, upon which many European and English romantic works were based. [12] Americans preferred to consult, in the original, in translation, or through English interpretations like those of Coleridge and Carlyle, romantic thinkers who had discredited that cold "Reason" associated with the Enlightenment tradition, and enthroned imagination, empathy, and intuition in its stead.[13] These qualities were, of course, the very traits traditionally associated with woman's nature. Moreover, American romantics placed a heavier emphasis than did Europeans upon the morality and social vision of their heroic artists. For these Americans, art was ideally a redemptive and regenerative, not a socially destructive, act. Although the idea of the alienated artist favored by many European romantics appealed to women experiencing a similar alienation from many aspects of cultural experience, American women intellectuals preferred, as did William Ellery Channing, to define the role of the alienated artist or thinker out of existence.[14] Only Margaret Fuller flirted with the possibilities of alienation, but she too finally rejected them, preferring the role of artist and thinker as social redeemer.

These American interpretations of romanticism had what Goethe would have called "elective affinities" with "the cult of true womanhood." Although that "cult" was reasoned down from Enlightenment concepts of order and symmetry— mechanical and uniformitarian assumptions about the nature of mind, society, nature, and the cosmos—three of its four cardinal virtues would, at least from a philological standpoint, reappear as part and parcel of romanticism. Both the *piety* and *purity* demanded of women by the mid-nineteenth-century code were characteristic of the moral focus of the romantic orientation and of its sacred mode of symbolic perception. Since perception was, in part, an "attitude" and "habit of wonder," a nonaggressive act of appreciation and observation,[15] perception seemed appropriately *passive* and, therefore, feminine. Thus, romanticism not only seemed compatible with those definitions of female virtues accepted at the time but also seemed supportive of these virtues as positive male attributes. Although the romantic emphasis was, finally, on the human as *homo symbolicus,* having relocated the source of value and order from the external world to the perceiving self, investing it with an almost divine authority,[16] it was possible for women to begin romantic journeys without sensing that true romantic self-hood might prove to be as incompatible with the tenets of "true womanhood" as any other theory of personal accomplishment had been. Consequently, in antebellum America, romanticism, by seeming to offer a new and vital synthesis of womanhood and intellect, lured women into genuinely intellectual roles. Although, like most intellectuals in the nineteenth century, they did not see the problems inherent in the romantic orientation, their work reveals that their extravagant hopes for creating a new ideal of womanhood were dimming on the eve of the Civil War.

Regardless of its failings and the new dilemmas it created, romantic thought did encourage women, on the basis of their "ideal femininity," to embark upon a life of the mind and a quest for their own identity and individuality. The work of the most significant women intellectuals during this period reflects that orientation. Romantic tenets induced women to explore their own history, to develop a feminist consciousness, and to write literary and aesthetic criticism based on the romantic movement's major literature—often translating those works for the public or for the men in their circles who could not read the German language. Thus, the romantic revolution was directly responsible for the emergence and achievements of America's first generation of women intellectuals.

The concerns of women, like those of most thoughtful Americans in this period, were an "absorption with knowledge," "a thirst for the unique," [17] and a quest for a new form of personal and cultural identity, all of which illustrate the major preoccupations of romantic thought. Women, and everyone and everything else, seemed increasingly complex and problematic—and not just to intellectuals. Mechanical conceptions of the mind of woman and its limitations were rejected as inadequate bases for characterizing the experiences or aspirations of those women who, conscious of their dilemma, had begun to see themselves from a different perspective. These seemed to suffer, as Abigail Adams had, from "an excess of sensibility"; they struggled, however, not to restrain but to

---

The most recent attempt to confront the contradictions between self-hood and traditional femininity is, of course, the contemporary feminist movement, many facets of which reveal the continuing power and relevance of the romantic orientation.

release it. One outlet of self-expression for intellectuals and other Americans of both sexes was participation in the debate on the reconciliation of intellect and femininity, an important aspect of the larger "woman question" which became an almost obsessive cultural concern in the 1830s. Conducted at first according to intellectual concepts derived from the previous century, the debate continued throughout the nineteenth century, and still continues. In Chapter One, I have tried to recapture a sense of the often maddening confusion that this cultural debate generated in pre-Civil War America and to present a panorama of American attitudes toward the idea of an intellectual woman and the intellectual potential of the American women.

Between 1830 and 1860 American women as intellectuals formed a distinct social type; and not merely because they absorbed and confronted the same cultural assumptions about women. Most women still do, regardless of nationality. A specific set of historical circumstances created the mid-century American intellectual woman and distinguishes her from her post-Civil War and twentieth-century counterparts. The woman intellectual occupied a shifting, even constricting, social terrain in Jacksonian America, which was for her a land of "shrinking opportunities." [18]

Intellectual women were predominately daughters of professional men, yet expanding professional opportunities in the period were not becoming available to them. The response of women intellectuals to the idea of opportunity was modeled upon the professional orientations and ideals they had absorbed from their fathers. America's first generation of intellectual women all discovered that some form of intellectual activity was the only way they could live up to these ideals of learned excellence and ability, the only way to unite their experience as Americans with cultural definitions of the American woman and her sphere. After the Civil War, professional opportunities for women expanded slightly, and many American universities as well as new institutions of higher learning created especially for women opened their doors to the American woman. In antebellum America, however, only one intellectual covered in this study had what could be called a college education. And she pronounced it hopelessly inferior to what she had learned at home.[19] The accredited role of "female scribbler" was also unappealing to young women with truly intellectual ambitions and abilities. As intellectual talent severed the intellectual woman from the sphere of the "scribbler," social status sealed her off from the world of female factory workers. Thus, the intellectual woman in mid-century America had to find, even create, a territory of her own and defend it accordingly.

America offered an intellectual role to its most fortunate and articulate women in the same spirit of ambivalence and doubt in which it held out that possibility to men. Absorbing these attitudes marked and often marred the American intellectual of either sex, yet women had to confront a special complex of beliefs reserved for their sex alone, the dictates of the "cult of true womanhood," and attempt to reconcile these with their intellectual lives. Regardless of America's inability to decide what value, if any, to assign to intellectuals of either sex, women had to prove (as they still do) not only that they were capable of thinking but that intellectual behavior would not "unsex" or unfit them for truly feminine pursuits.

Throughout this book I have attempted to maintain a dual emphasis upon the intellectual and social orientations of women intellectuals, relating their work to the main currents of intellectual history and analyzing their thought and behavior in terms of American society's shifting aspirations concerning "woman's sphere," and in terms of the alterations in female roles in mid-nineteenth-century America. This study is, I believe, of significance to women's studies, not because the intellectual woman is the highest and most sacrosanct female being in the scale of civilization, but because no one has yet placed American women within the context of intellectual history or investigated the achievements and social roles of female intellectuals except in the most superficial, frivolous, or dogmatic fashion. Therefore, I offer this book to the field of women's studies and the spirit of relentless exploration and discovery that defines its nature and its future.

# (1)

# Mapping a Country of the Mind

## 1830-1860

*To do nothing at all is the most difficult thing in the world, the most difficult and the most intellectual.*

—Oscar Wilde

*Women live like subjects of a bureaucracy in which they must read interminable and triplicated forms, whether or not they agree to sign them in the end. Their self-consciousness grows with their reading, so that educated women tend, by twenty-seven, to walk about like sensate editorials on the Woman Problem. They are not allowed to escape the sense of species, they are like giraffes reading Lamarck every morning before they stretch their necks.*

—Mary Ellmann

*Where can I hide till I am given to myself?*

—Margaret Fuller

Nineteenth-century America drew from its complex and often contradictory Enlightenment heritage the words with which to characterize the mind and social role of the American woman. This vocabulary of concepts and images—the "cult of true womanhood," [1] the "bluestocking," and arguments for the intellectual and social equality of women—illustrated a fun-

Catharine Beecher
*The Schlesinger Library, Radcliffe College*

Sarah J. Hale (below left)
*The Schlesinger Library, Radcliffe College*

Harriet Martineau (below right)
*The Schlesinger Library, Radcliffe College*

damental Enlightenment principle, man in uniformity with nature's order. The definition of "true womanhood" rested upon common agreement that virtue, innocence, and submissiveness were the positive attributes of womanhood. These virtues both symbolized the order of nature and placed women securely within its hierarchy, giving them a definite place in the "Great Chain of Being." [2] This place was the domestic sphere, whose harmony reflected that of the cosmos.

Within the fixed orbit of the domestic circle, woman was the perfect complement to man. Her emotional nature and elegant accomplishments made life less severe for that eighteenth-century hero, the man of reason and common sense.[3] Like all phenomena in the "Great Chain," women were firmly rooted in a social context through the primary assumption of Enlightenment thought that "the structure of mind was identical with the structure of nature." Accordingly, "adaptation of the organism to the environment" became the "basis of all scientific and moral decisions." When translated into social theory, Enlightenment theory presented a symmetrical model of the good society which "sought to line up mind, society and nature into one unitary system." [4]

Originally the "bluestocking" had also been a reflection of perfect symmetry, a symbol of social and intellectual elegance, balance, and proportion. First used in the 1750s, the term referred to men and women of wit, knowledge, and advanced opinions who frequented houses where the social display of knowledge was cultivated as a fine art. The origin of the epithet, whether French or British,[5] was attributed to individuals who wore informal clothing rather than the orthodox black-stocking type and delighted in a correspondingly unconventional discussion of ideas. To "wear your blues" became a metaphor for an evening of brilliant conversation, and the term was soon reserved for the women who held salons and for the female members of these cultural coteries. To Dr. Johnson, Mrs. Montagu was the "Queen of the Blues" in England—the hostess who gave the most splendid evenings. Mrs. Hannah More, a member of the inner circle, recorded the history of the group in her long poem *"Bas Bleu."* Both Mrs.

Elizabeth Carter, author of a much admired translation of the works of the Greek stoic philosopher Epictetus and considered the most learned of all, and Mrs. Chapone, author of several guides for young women, with instructive titles such as *Letters on the Improvement of the Mind*, were often cited as examples of ideal femininity.

The stunning literary success of Samuel Richardson's epistolary novel, *Clarissa Harlowe*, suggested to women writers outside the original "bluestocking" circles that the novel, if it preached the moral values of true femininity to England and America's rapidly growing reading public, would assure a large and receptive audience. Mrs. Ann Radcliffe, the originator of the gothic novel, terrorized her readers with supernatural tales, only to reassure them with a final rational resolution, thus preserving the delicate balance of the Enlightenment synthesis.

At the end of the eighteenth century, Mary Wollstonecraft's stormy life, her illicit love affair, and her pioneering feminist tract, *A Vindication of the Rights of Women* (1791), shocked many of her contemporaries, both intellectually and morally; Horace Walpole denounced her as a "hyena in petticoats." Her essay urged that the Enlightenment's defense of social and intellectual equalitarianism be extended to include the natural rights of women. If reason was a natural and universal human attribute, she argued, identical in all men and equally distributed among all cultures, women must also possess it. If they did not, such an exception weakened the "Great Chain of Being" argument and threatened that uniformitarian ideal. Mary Wollstonecraft had found the role of "bluestocking" too confining. To her daughter, Mary Shelley, neither the order of nature nor the natural rights of women were clear. The life of reason had explained nothing to Mary Shelley: her vision of that life was Frankenstein's monster, representative and symbol of a botched civilization.

In her French salon, Mme de Staël, the daughter of a Swiss banker, entertained *philosophes* who discussed the revolutionary principles designed to destroy the Old Regime; yet, for many French women of the salon, she herself was more disturbing than the ideas entertained by her circle. Mme de Genlis found her "ill-bred" and a "most embarrassing woman." [6] Unlike her creator, the heroine of Mme de Staël's novel *Corinne* conformed to the ideal feminine model of the eighteenth century and to the French code of politesse. Not intellectually aggressive nor artistically original, she was an *improvisatrice* who brought out the wit in others and made them feel at ease. In Italy Corinne at last found a congenial intellectual and social climate in which to dramatize—and thus create—her own identity. If she is viewed as the fictional projection of her creator, Corinne, in her conventional role as *improvisatrice*, reveals that Mme de Staël preferred to envision herself as a representative of the salon and its code of politesse, which many contemporaries felt she had flagrantly violated. After the French Revolution Mme de Staël left Corinne far behind and set out for Germany to investigate personally the romantic spirit and meet its chief spokesman. During her journey in 1808 she paused in Vienna, where her notorious visit was long remembered. The horrified Prince de Ligne, field marshal of Russia and Austria, later damned her in a series of elegant reversals:

> She has more imagination than intelligence, and more intelligence than learning . . . . She makes pronouncements, decides everything, accumulates error upon error, and ends up by not knowing what she is saying when she talks about the arts, of which she is ignorant, and of religious feeling, which she sees in everything. Her Christianity makes one wish to be a pagan, her mysticism makes one prefer matter-of-factness, and her love for the extraordinary makes one appreciate everything that is common and vulgar. [7]

Liberated from the confines of the salon, Mme de Staël symbolized the vigor and energy of the romantic temperament. Spreading a new gospel of art and self-hood, she exhibited an extraordinary and terrifying forcefulness. Her experiences in the French Revolution had taught her—no matter how reactionary the consequences of that experiment were—that, as she put it, "intellect does not attain to its full force unless it attacks power." [8] Transferring her loyalties to the Romantic revolution, she helped destroy the order and symmetry of the eighteenth-century world view and its image of an intellectual woman as "bluestocking." By the middle of the nineteenth century even the staunchest advocates of women's rights blanched at that word—pedants and libertines danced in their heads whenever they heard it.

## 1. Intellect and Femininity:
*American Strategies of Reconciliation*

Between 1830 and the Civil War, the American debate over intellect and femininity was conducted according to Enlightenment principles. Most supporters of "true womanhood" who argued for an enlarged "woman's sphere" attempted to graft the gift of reason onto their model of femininity. Sometimes the results seemed as ludicrous as Mary Shelley's monster. In rejecting these creations, feminists pointed out the real discrepancies between feminine ideals and social realities and often argued their case in the very same Enlightenment terms.

New institutions for women's higher education, designed to produce an authentically American woman, also reflected the eighteenth-century heritage. Many women writers—whom Nathaniel Hawthorne called "that damned mob of scribbling women" [9]—deliberately avoided the use of reason and produced works totally within eighteenth-century traditions of female sensibility and sentimentalism. The domestic novelists and those who argued against the education of women still shared common assumptions about the limited capabilities of the feminine mind and evaluated female intellectual pursuits by how directly they manifested accredited feminine virtues. Whether the quality of rational intellect was or was not included in the concept of "true womanhood," that concept was itself an amalgamation of the many myths of order and stability Americans derived from the Enlightenment and applied to the chaotic experience of the nineteenth century.

The equalitarian rhetoric of educators and promoters of women's education was a source of comfort for many men and women caught in the midst of rapid social change. These techniques of reconciling old and new, past and present, of voicing new and often conflicting aspirations, reflected, however, a broader cultural strategy, which Marvin Meyers has named "the Jacksonian Persuasion." [10] As America moved into a more complex phase, Andrew Jackson became in the public mind a vivid image of an old American ideal—the eighteenth-century Jeffersonian yeoman. He seemed to promise that his program for a great society would restore and re-create the lost world of the plain republican—a simple and ordered world that encouraged individualism and enterprise. "Venturous conservatives," concerned with economic upward mobility, could, by subscribing to this persuasion, view their culture through the lens of the past and describe new aspirations in old and reassuring metaphors. Persuaded Jacksonians saw themselves as participants in a vast drama of restoration to a simpler way of life; and they were thus able to reconcile the often conflicting claims of idealism and opportunism.

The Jacksonian Persuasion itself reflected the impact of romanticism upon American culture and the source of its appeal. The heroic impulse inherent in romantic thought and the emphasis upon individualism suggested a method of recapturing the basic values of the Founding Fathers, of revivifying the original spirit of the American Republic. This political expression of romanticism was mirrored in the thoughts, writings, and political strategies of women seeking to find their role in a rapidly growing, expanding American culture.

Most participants in the debate over women's intellectual nature were expectant achievers and "venturous conservatives." Both the "woman of genius" ideal and arguments for intellectual equality supported optimistic analyses of the American woman's mind and social role. As a "woman of genius" she was not a threat to the social order but a participant in a glorious restoration of ideal femininity. If a more distinct variety of intellectualism had become part of her great expectations, it too could be adapted to the American scene. As an illustration of the Jacksonian ideology of equality, the territory of the intellect was supposedly a neutral domain, open to all who wished to enter. Women could ideally move forward into this new terrain and become more and more feminine as a result of their travels in that country of the mind. The mind and virtue of the American woman were synonymous for all who engaged in these strategies of reconciliation: intellect severed from virtue and duty, however, was unthinkable.

As the century progressed, the literature on the nature of femininity proliferated, offering a bewildering variety of opinions and analyses designed to effect a compromise between intellect and "true womanhood." In *The Young Lady's Companion* (1839), Margaret Coxe, using the epistolary form favored by eighteenth-century "bluestockings," apologized for writing another book on women but separated her contribution from earlier ones by its source of inspiration. This first "manual for ladies" to come out of the western states was designed to represent that "interesting portion of our Union—untried ground for authors of works professedly prepared for young ladies"—and designed to restore a religious perspective that Coxe felt other authorities on the woman question had abandoned. Emphasizing that the role of woman and the question of her education were far more complex than many were willing to admit, Coxe found that the most conspicuous change in the education of women during her century was "that which has made the study of the dead languages, and any modern ones, to occupy so prominent a place in the time and attention of the *mass* of young ladies." Coxe provided a home-study course, a "great design of education," emphatically Christian, which was based upon discipline, order, and the "habit of intellectual activity" as a corrective to the superficial education most women received.[11] Although knowledge had become too complex for a single mind to comprehend all its rapidly proliferating branches, women were still trying to survey all knowledge and, as a result, their mental future looked bleak to Coxe:

The science of healing is divided into three distinct branches; and, in the practice of surgery alone, how many are the subdivisions! But woman, ambitious, aspiring, universal, triumphant, glorious woman, even at the age of a school-boy, encounters the whole range of arts, attacks the whole circle of sciences. But the misfortune does not so much consist in their learning every thing, as in their knowing nothing; at least nothing well. [12]

Coxe's alternative system of education outlined a methodical strategy for mastering languages, history, geography, and natural science, "amidst the multiplicity of pursuits to which the attention of young ladies of the present day is directed." First, women must develop their intellects systematically, for they have been "little accustomed to pursue close reasoning, and to concentrate the attention on any subject." These habits will give "ballast to the mind, and discipline and prepare it for future trials." [13] Next, women should acquire a sound factual foundation, which will serve as a springboard to intellectual activity. Coxe described the life of the mind without reference to sex, without outlining a particularly feminine version, and assumed that women were capable of thought. She saw no conflict between intellect and femininity and implied that their union would make women happier. Even on rainy days the thinking woman would have something to do. Implicit in her book is an intellectual paradise in which more and more American women would learn to "exercise the faculties in generalizing, drawing conclusions from given premises, and forming opinions upon subjects of the highest importance to them as intellectual and moral beings. . . ." [14] Coxe seemed unconcerned that other authorities had concluded that women were either incapable of thinking or of cultivating the intellect without losing their femininity. The vision of this obscure writer was representative of a fragile yet carefully fashioned synthesis of intellect and femininity wrought by more famous cultural spokesmen—and spokeswomen. Dissenters from this compromise, including "female scribblers," saw conflict where Coxe did not and sought to discredit the idea of woman's intellectual potential.

Most cases against educated or intellectual women used science to prove that the experiment was doomed to failure. [15]

Few were so direct as an article in the British *Saturday Review*, quickly reprinted in *Littell's Living Age* (1860). It stated categorically, without any appeal to scientific evidence, that "the great argument against the existence of this equality of intellect is that it doesn't exist." [16] Experts from a variety of "disciplines" offered more substantive proof of the mental inferiority or incapacity of women. As Barbara Welter has written, the "natural laws" of anatomy, gynecology, even phrenology, were employed to reinforce God's laws. Woman's true relation to the intellect was to dissociate herself from it completely and to cultivate "what have sometimes been termed the passive virtues, fortitude, submission, patience, resignation." [17] Many clergymen, doctors, and journalists argued that an intellectual woman was a contradiction in terms; many found it necessary to warn women not to pursue a life of the mind. Equipped as they were with underdeveloped, tiny brains and overdeveloped nerves, any stimulation of the former might set women off. Their delicate constitution must be carefully guarded, for it was capable of self-destruction at the slightest provocation. The results of a college education would, accordingly, be disastrous: the college woman would be a deformation of nature and a mental and physical wreck. The experiment was absurd in the first place, since a woman, with her limited mentality, could not do college work. Reverend John Todd's jeremiad predicted the swift decline and death of a college woman:

> As for training young ladies through a long intellectual course, as we do young men, it can never be done. They will die in the process . . . . She must be on the strain all the school hours, study in the evening till her eyes ache, her brain whirls, her spine yields and gives way, and she comes through the process of education, enervated, feeble, without courage or vigor, elasticity or strength. Alas! must we crowd education upon our daughters, and, for the sake of having them "intellectual," make them puny, nervous, and their whole earthly existence a struggle between life and death? [18]

Dr. Alexander Walker's *Beauty* (1844) indicated how to avoid this dire fate and divided woman's fearful symmetry into three parts: "Beauty of the Locomotive System, Beauty of the Nutritive System, and Beauty of the Thinking System." Although in his taxonomy the Beauty was part thinking animal, this third category was "less feminine" and should always be subordinate to the "nutritive system," since "it is not the intellectual system, but the vital one which is, and ought to be most developed in woman." [19]

The work of women whom Hawthorne classified as "scribbling women" reflected the assumptions of those who pronounced the female mind inferior. In the late eighteenth and early nineteenth centuries, such works as Susanna Rowson's bestseller, *Charlotte Temple* and Sarah S. B. K. Wood's *Julia and the Illuminated Baron* had imitated and reduced the sentimental tradition perfected by Samuel Richardson to its simplest terms. Emptying this genre of all ambiguity and the complexities of psychology, these women novelists—and many others like them who took up the pen—stressed the purity and moral superiority of women without subjecting their virtue to conflict, temptation, or analysis. Many domestic and sentimental novelists went so far as to remove the seducer from the novel of seduction, thus robbing the Richardsonian formula of its power. Technically and thematically nonintellectual, and often blatantly and joyously anti-intellectual, many novels portrayed male scholars and artists as dangerous villains over whom the feminine virtues of purity, piety, and domesticity always triumphed.[20] The home, with its attendant duties, was the "female scribbler's" major theme. It was a wonderful place, never destitute of culture, sensitivity, and good company; and the women who wrote about domesticity stressed that it received top priority in their own lives and ever served as a catalyst for literary creativity.[21]

By 1820 one third of all American novels had been written by women. From 1830 to the Civil War, the works of Mrs. E. D. E. N. Southworth, Caroline Kirkland, Catharine Sedgwick, Susan Warner, and Caroline Lee Hentz—to name only a few of the most widely read novelists—drove more pessimistic analyses of human behavior, such as Nathaniel Hawthorne's, to the outskirts of literary popularity. Denouncing these domestic novelists for their feebleness, Hawthorne declared that they had left out all human life. Unlike Herman Melville and his fictional projection, Bartleby the Scrivener, the "female scribbler" continued to "copy." The pure sensibility of woman, the central tenet of these novels, defined the nature of the female intellect as well. Having chained the mind to the hearth or literally swept it under the rug, this conception of "the woman of genius" effectively dispensed with the life of the mind and accordingly reinforced the popular notion of woman's basic anti-intellectualism. The most famous domestic novel, Susan Warner's prose epic, *The Wide, Wide World* (1850), presents a most circumscribed universe, devoid of intellectual content.

Novelists were not the only "female scribblers." Essayists and poets, like Lydia M. Sigourney, the "sweet singer of Hartford," employed the same cloying themes and used the more floral aspects of nature as analogues to the exquisite female sensibility. They found a ready market for their wares in the lavish and ornate gift books and ladies' albums so popular in the nineteenth century, as well as in the more austere ladies' magazines. Whether in verse or prose, they wrote according to undeviating formulas. Poetic "women of genius," in their strict allegiance to rhythmic inflexibility, exhibited an insensitivity to the possibilities of language and poetic form in a century devoted to formalistic exploration. As a result, their poetry is as monotonous as the forms they employed, and their often uncomprehending use of language indicates their minimal artistic ability.

Since, through her chosen theme of domesticity, the "female scribbler" was still a "true woman" who merely brought "the home *into* the market," she could continue writing—for money—without having to consider disparities between her behavior and her concept of femininity.[22] She was not seen as standing in overt competition with men in the literary business, since the more obvious forms of ambition and self-assertion were now converted into domestic and feminine virtues. In addition, the lives and works of these "women of genius" were designed to elicit praise for not exhibiting any evidence of professionalism. The status of sublime amateur accordingly assured them of their true femininity. Theirs was an unconscious and compulsive art, untouched by intellectualism or artifice. The popular Southern novelist Caroline Lee Hentz described the artistic process of the "female scribbler" in *Ernest Linwood* (1856) as a mere transcription of reality and sincerity:

> Book! Am I writing a book? No indeed! This is only a record of my heart's life, written at random and carelessly thrown aside, sheet after sheet, sibylline leaves from the great book of fate.[23]

## 2. Woman's Intellect and Education:
*A Search for Symmetry*

Attempting to reconcile intellect and femininity in a more conscious and systematic manner than had the "female scribbler," educators devised strategies that would, it was hoped, produce ideal American women. They frequently argued that women had a distinct sensibility and social role as well as an intellectual potential equal to that of men in order to make doubly sure that the idea of an educated woman would conform to American ideals. Before the middle of the nineteenth century, female education was limited to the daughters of the prosperous. Academies had taught the elegant arts according to eighteenth-century precepts. Embroidery, painting, instruction in French, singing, and playing the harpsichord composed the usual curriculum.[24] Between 1830 and 1860, new educational experiments in women's seminaries and colleges were designed to create or maintain a perfect balance between the intellect and feminine nature. Promoters stressed that both femininity and intellect should be nurtured and developed in a systematic manner; both were learned responses, skills that resulted from the educational process itself.[25] The rationale and rhetoric employed by educators relied upon eighteenth-century principles of rationalism and scientific procedure to discredit another eighteenth-century ideal—that of the elegant woman with her frivolous habits and accomplishments—who had no function in mid-nineteenth-century America. A new age demanded a new woman, equipped with reason, knowledge, and the scientific skills necessary to domesticate the continent.

Although the triumphant institutionalization of women's higher education did not take place until after the Civil War, a series of pioneering steps were taken between 1830 and 1860 that constituted a progression toward the goal of an educated woman and the college ideal. The period witnessed the transformation of the female academy, the rise of the public school system and of teacher training schools, the beginnings of collegiate coeducation in the West, and the establishment of several women's colleges designed to award the B.A. degree and to give women an education equivalent to that available to men. These developments were social consequences of many disparate cultural stimuli: the increasing prosperity of a proto-industrial economy centered in New England, the torrent of population pouring westward into the Ohio River valley and Great Lakes region, the expansion of the political Union with the entry of numerous western states, and the impact of the Jacksonian ideology with its emphasis on equalitarianism. Even less dramatic developments such as the availability of labor-saving devices like the cooking stove and the sewing machine increased the percentage of American women with at least a margin of leisure with which to pursue literacy and other previously restricted cultural pursuits. These reading women provided enthusiastic support for "female scribblers" and ladies' magazines. Jacksonianism and literacy combined to encourage the concept of universal education, which correspondingly attracted a growing number of supporters. Although the ideal was far from being realized before the Civil War, the beginnings of the public school system and the accompanying need for enlightened teachers opened the profession to women. With a new purpose they pursued higher education, often in the new teacher training schools designed to meet the demands of the growing number of secondary schools.

Among the educational institutions for women before the Civil War that claimed to be collegiate enterprises and offered degrees were Georgia Female College (1836), Georgia's Mary Sharp College (1850), Illinois Conference Female College (1854), and New York's Elmira College (1855). Elmira, anxious to avoid describing its women as "freshmen," substituted the archaic and awkward term "protomathian." [26] In addition to their self-consciousness and questionable collegiate status, these educational ventures—like all colleges in the period—faced serious financial problems. Additional problems, however, were created by uneven educational backgrounds of applicants that necessitated flexible entrance requirements and affected women's colleges more deeply than men's institutions. In the paradoxical position of having to prepare students for college-level work while these same students pursued their B.A. degrees, the women's colleges compromised academic standards out of necessity.

In 1841, Oberlin College in Ohio awarded the B.A. to three women, the first degrees unquestionably equal to those granted men. When Oberlin opened its doors in 1837, coeducation was almost nonexistent in the East. Commenting obliquely on that deficiency, Philo Stewart, the co-founder of the college, described the experiment as necessary for the salvation of the Republic: "The work of female education must be carried on in some form, and in a much more efficient manner than it has been hitherto, or our country will go to destruction." [27] Several new colleges and universities admitted women: Hillsdale (1844) and Antioch (1853) in Ohio; the University of Deseret (1850) in Utah; and the University of Iowa (1855).

Although these were the only institutions that granted women college degrees before the Civil War, teacher training schools—"normal schools"—and several seminaries offered an equivalent to college women. Emma Willard's Troy Female Seminary (1821) was the first to replace the traditional offerings of women's academies with a rigorous program of instruction. The first woman to teach physiology, Willard also devised novel teaching methods to present algebra, solid geometry, trigonometry, geography, and history to her female pupils.

Transcending its beginnings as a seminary, Mount Holyoke (1837) served as a model for the most successful of the eastern women's colleges that were established after the Civil War. Holyoke's demanding curriculum made no provisions for domesticity; however, the founder's well-known biases and her goals for young women were sufficient to allay fears that students might be unsexed by their stay there. Mary Lyon hoped to educate women for a useful, productive, and Christian life—a life of benevolent activism that used knowledge only as a means to the end of right action. Reflection, far from an end in itself, must be transformed into conduct, for, as Lyon stated unequivocally, "The intellectual miser is an object of contempt." [28] As a young girl, her love of learning and her intellectual energy and aspiration were saved from confusion and placed into an ordered, utilitarian perspective:

> In my youth I had much vigor—was always aspiring after something. I called it loving to study. Had few to direct me outright. One teacher I shall always remember. He told me education was to fit one to do good. [29]

She tersely summed up her goals in teaching young women: "They should live for God and do something." [30] As one of her pupils described Mary Lyon's program, "her first aim was to make us Christians; her second to cultivate us intellectually." [31] Life and thought must be interchangeable, marked by rigor, discipline, and duty. She advised the girls to be "thoroughly systematic in the division of your time and duties." [32] They should even "learn to sit with energy," she declared. The mind was a machine to be worked with industry and careful planning: "Bring the mind to a perfect abstraction and let thought after thought pass through it." [33]

Catharine Beecher, perhaps the most powerful force in women's education in the mid-nineteenth century, essentially agreed with Mary Lyon's pedagogical philosophy; domestic science, however, played a major role in Beecher's grand system. The daughter of Lyman Beecher, one of the most influential Presbyterian ministers in New England, Catharine Beecher opened the Hartford Female Seminary in 1824. Pupils were charged extra fees for learning music and dancing because Beecher considered all forms of artifice to be superfluous if not subversive to the Republic and its pillar of strength, the American woman. An advocate of the "imperial" style of American femininity, Catharine Beecher believed that the American woman had a powerful mission and social role much too significant to play without sufficient preparation.[34] Westward expansion demanded able and educated women to domesticate and civilize the frontier. An early advocate of "go West, young woman," Beecher saw the West as a great test and opportunity for women and geared the curriculum at Hartford to meet it. Beecher herself participated in the westward migration and became the head of the Western Female Institute in Cincinnati in 1832. Her many published works served the same function as her educational ventures. These guides to informed domesticity and femininity—*Hearth and Home, Physiology and Calisthenics,* and *The American Woman's Home* are a few examples— provided a sense of security and certainty. Each of Beecher's works promoted simultaneously the sacred nature of woman and her home as well as the more secular notion of the woman as scientific manager of the home.

For Catharine Beecher, teaching the young was a feminine calling equal to motherhood—to combine roles was to achieve complete sublimity. The psychology of perception and common sense dominant in that period supported and sustained Beecher's ideal of the woman teacher. Psychological theories derived from John Locke characterized the mind of an infant as a tabula rasa—a blank slate upon which the impressions of the child's senses were irrevocably etched. The Lockean analysis of the mind had immense social implications for women, and Beecher pursued them to their most glorious conclusions. If the minds of children were the purest illustrations of the tabula rasa, those first impressions and ideals that the mother and teacher implanted would establish the character and intelligence of the child for life. The same process had formed the mind of woman. The result was a distinctly feminine intellect which, if nurtured correctly, could become female genius and an effective social force. The mental qualities distinctive to a woman were "her lively imagination, her warm sympathies, her ready invention, her quick perceptions." These habits had been encouraged in women from birth and should be developed further by education. Moreover, for women to realize their true femininity, they must cultivate the "more foreign habits" traditionally associated with masculine minds: "patient attention, calm judgment, steady efficiency, and habitual self-control, must be induced and sustained." [35]

This dual development was the core of Beecher's ideal program for the education of women. The balanced cultivation of intellectual faculties and practical skills led the individual ever outward to the virtuous, useful, and powerful role of redemptor and restorer of American society. A mother and/or teacher would pass her training on to the young and thus train other teachers. The process of forming minds and character by personal example and method constituted an orderly social blueprint for the future of the Republic. Thus, she asserted, "a regular and systematic course of education [could] be disseminated through the nation." If intellectual attributes were adapted to the social role and nature of women, the strength and virtue of both America and the American woman would be assured. The social power of women would become so great that they would form a "Pink & White Tyranny more stringent than any earthly thralldom." [36] Catharine Beecher relished that possibility.

In dangerous opposition to Catharine Beecher's ideal was the cultivation of intellect for its own sake. That perversion was a threat to the progress and power not only of America and American women, but of all humanity. For Catharine Beecher, the order and virtue of self, society, and the cosmos hung in the balance as the debate over the role of intellect was waged in the novel educational experiments of her century:

And the great crisis is hastening on, when it shall be decided whether disenthralled intellect and liberty shall voluntarily submit to the laws of virtue and of Heaven, or run wild to insubordination, anarchy, and crime. The great questions pending before the world, are simply these: are liberty and intelligence, without the restraints of a moral and religious education, a blessing or a curse? [37]

For her these great questions were clearly rhetorical, and Beecher's blueprint for the future—the correct education of women—was designed to save America from the dangers of intellect sundered from virtue and duty. Only then, she declared, would "females . . . cease to feel that they are educated just to enjoy themselves in future life, and realize the obligations imposed by heaven to live and to do good." [38]

### 3. Intellectual Equality and "True Womanhood":
*A Fragile Synthesis*

Defining woman's intellectual equality by appeals to Scripture and history was a frequent tactic of those supporters of women's higher education who were not directly involved in building these new institutions. Many male and female enthusiasts cheerfully endorsed the intellectual equality of women in ladies' magazines and other major periodicals. Although these writers were freer to explore the justifications of intellectual equality than were most educators, few wished—or dared—to contemplate a life of the mind unleashed from social utility or ideal femininity. Most were as frightened as Catharine Beecher by such a possibility. Those who ventured to speculate on the implications and consequences of intellectual equality, including the idea of an "intellectual woman," often drew back in confusion, refusing to make judgments until more data had been gathered. This note of uncertainty, papered over with grandiose rhetoric, haunted nineteenth-century America. To state the case for woman's intellect and gaze toward the future seemed for many writers the best way to avoid confusion.

With the rise of the feminist movement the argument for intellectual equality proved to be a good strategy for evading the issue of social equality. Antifeminists could easily grant woman a mind equal to man's without having to confront social reality if they conceived of the life of the mind as distinct from the rest of American life. Or if, like Beecher, they envisioned the educated woman as mother/teacher, order still reigned; since woman remained in her place, the music of the spheres played on. Feminists refused to abide by this consensus, applying the principle of intellectual equality directly to the American woman's social role, arguing that this doctrine justified her participation in all areas of American life. The size and vigor of their formidable opposition, including the clergy, press, and public, illustrated that under that comforting popular rhetoric about woman's intellectual potential lurked the darkest suspicions imaginable, that the very idea of an "intellectual woman" was a threat to the Republic. Yet, woman as thinker was not unthinkable if one did not translate the doctrine of intellectual equality into social terms or use it to argue for new social roles.

Perhaps the century's most rhapsodic account of the possibilities of female intellect was an article in *The Ladies' Magazine* entitled "Man's Mental Superiority Over Woman, Referrable to Physical Causes Only." [39] The anonymous author appealed to reason and common sense, to philosophy and Scripture, to state the case for intellectual equality. The "Universal Parent" designed both men and women in his own image and impressed upon both sexes, both "heaven-born intellectual natures . . . the *same* seal of immortality." Even to suppose that "there is a distinction of sex in the world of mind" was absurd; "the very idea of *mental inferiority*" was highly improbable, especially since history afforded such "splendid portraitures of female intellectual preeminence." Intellectual women of the future, however, would surpass them all. In the past even the greatest female minds had been checked by opposing forces, by "a dark tissue of unpropitious circumstances, and the prejudices of man." In the future—with impediments to marriages of true minds removed—the author foresaw in an ecstatic vision of harmony, "the innate sublimity of the female intellect, assuming its just rank in the world of mind, and companionlike, careering in happy unison with the proud spirit of man through the regions of literature and science . . . . " In concluding, the author returned to earth briefly to cover the supposed subject of the article and stated unequivocally that man is merely physically superior to woman and is so endowed in order to protect and defend her, perhaps in order that she may better pursue a life of the mind with him. On a cosmic plane, American men and women might someday be true American scholars, soaring together to the heights of knowledge.

"Whence arise the jests and the jeerings in relation to the intellectual character, the weakness, irresolution, want of purpose, with which the fairer portion of the creation have been stigmatized?" asked a *Ladies' Magazine* article entitled "The Intellectual Character of Woman." [40] The author, "N.G.P.," thinking that questions concerning the relationship between intellect and femininity had been settled, was discouraged that the prejudiced and unenlightened still "point at the general development of female intellect, and with a sort of triumphant exultation, enumerate the achievements of *female* mind, in a narrower and more contracted field, than that in which the exertions of manly mind have been made." While endorsing intellectual equality, "N.G.P." qualified it on the basis of the "diverse habits" of men and women—woman's faculty of perception was more developed and that of concentration less so than a man's. Consequently, one could not make generalizations about the mental capacity of women until equal conditions for their intellectual development had prevailed at length. Meanwhile, it was unfair to "institute a comparison between those of the one sex, who are within the temple of science, and those of the other, to whom the doors have been closed." "N.G.P." firmly believed—notwithstanding the possible equivocality of the results—that the methods of ensuring a state of intellectual equality and of observing the consequences with precision were clear, indisputable, and identical for both sexes:

> We must lead them both to the steep ascent. We must observe
> their progress with vigilance. We must watch the aberrations of

each at the call of the passions, and detect the first deserter to the bowers of pleasure. We must give to each the same advantages of birth and fortune; the same opportunities for intellectual culture. We must not divest them of the estimation which they now hold in society, nor intimidate the intellectual progress of the one, by stigmas and reproach, while the other is cheered and assisted by the admiration and encouragement of partial friends. We must open to each indifferently, the halls of academic learning; of judicial science and legislative wisdom, before the question of intellectual inferiority can be completely and satisfactorily settled. . . .

After such a display of confidence, "The Intellectual Character of Woman" ended on a note of uncertainty, as if its author felt that the intellectual abilities of women might be found wanting after all. Although only abundant evidence and time would allow one to "give currency to the calumny on female intellect, and to assert without fear of contradiction their mental inferiority," the author prematurely awarded women a traditional consolation prize: "Let her not be ashamed to shine with reflected light." If women should not "seek the paths of originality, or strike out new theories and doctrines" they could still be "contented, like Ruth, to glean in the field after the reapers, who doubtless will have let fall much, although not on purpose for her.' " The author had come full circle: "The Intellectual Character of Woman" was consequently a tautological concession to the views the author wished to oppose.

Proponents of women's intellectual development found that humor was not the exclusive property of their adversaries. It could be used against their adversaries, and it could also alleviate that sense of uncertainty and depression that thinking about women often generated. Cincinnati's *The Ladies' Repository, and Gatherings of the West,* a journal devoted to woman's intellectual and spiritual cultivation, printed many involved analyses of the mind, of intellectual activity, and of woman's nature. Many contributors seemed to enjoy confronting and ridiculing " . . . that 'objection that good, sound, substantial knowledge in women prevents their attending to their domestic duties of wife, mother and friend.' " [41] In "Female Education," Caleb Atwater—the founder of Ohio's public school system—presented a most amusing tour de force. If learning, "even profound learning, can blot out connubial love . . . " just think of what ignorance could do, argued Atwater, as he gleefully reversed the arguments of his opposition. "Can ignorance give its Cimmerian votary order, method, prudence, discretion, industry, frugality, love, affection, and all the domestic virtues?" Certainly not. For Atwater, the maxim " 'that we cannot have *too* much of a *good* thing' " did not apply to ignorant women. Forty-year-old women were frequently more ignorant than boys of twelve:

> Even the lovers of ignorance in women, will hardly dare to argue in favor of such a disparity of knowledge . . . . For the consolation, however, of men, who fear that our system of female education will soon become so perfect that they cannot find ignorant women enough for wives and companions . . . , we can assure them that we do all we can to educate them, yet there will always be ignorant women enough for all such men. We hope this idea will console them.

Atwater urged more sensitive minds to consider the powerless state of woman's subjection. Reflective men would accordingly acknowledge "that the happiness of such women must be drawn from their own minds," and realize that the question of the relative happiness of the educated and the ignorant woman was merely rhetorical. Perhaps playing upon his readers' vanity, Atwater stressed that only "pompous men, who fear women as their rivals in knowledge, prefer ignorant women . . . . Men of liberal minds and true politeness, prefer, enthusiastically prefer, a learned woman as their wife, companion and friend, and for the mother of their children."

Atwater stressed that women should receive the same education as men and based his argument and his educational program upon the principle of intellectual equality. A subsequent article on "Female Education" noted that objections to this principle "might have passed in the dark ages, when ignorance was supposed to be the mother of devotion, but it will not do for the nineteenth century." [42] In a similar spirit, *The North American Review* outlined the historical progression of women through the Dark Ages to the glorious present. Since the discovery of America, the "social position of the female sex . . . has been modified by two new facts, the progress of intellectual refinement and of the useful arts." [43] Intellectual cultivation and equality would not, however, lead woman away from her true relationships with man and society:

> Hers be the domain of the moral affections, the empire of the heart, the co-equal sovereignty of intellect, taste, and social refinement; leave the rude commerce of camps and the soul-hardening struggles of political power to the harsher spirit of man, that he may still look up to her as a purer and brighter being, an emanation of some better world, irradiating like a rainbow of hope, the stormy elements of life. [44]

This august journal, a bastion of the New England mind, could easily endorse woman's intellectual potential since it simultaneously severed the mind from American life. Consequently, it would have been more difficult to deny than to affirm woman's "co-equal intellectual sovereignty" in such an ethereal realm. [45] Yet, not wishing to leave this mental terrain uncharted, *The North American Review* published accounts of what it considered representative women, and all of them reflected the journal's distinct preference for the "female scribbler" as an ideal intellectual woman. Essays ranked Lydia Sigourney with England's best literary women and warned their readers of Mme de Staël's fall into that den of corruption, power politics—a great mind, and a great woman, lost to history.

Like *The North American Review*, Sarah J. Hale, upon becoming editor of *The Ladies' Magazine* in 1828, also offered grandiose syntheses of intellect and true womanhood. Yet even her own rhetoric and hopeful predictions for the future could not deceive her of the facts. If it was so easy for a "true woman" to be a thinker without losing her femininity, why did the woman author, for example, receive such bad press? Why was it so difficult to make her seem respectable? In her series "Authoresses," Hale concluded that the fault lay not in the literary talents of the woman author but in public opinion: society, blinded by prejudice, saw every "authoress" as a dread "bluestocking" who was "unamiable and unuseful," pretentious and pedantic—ruined by her intellect.[46] Hale decided to take on herself the mission to destroy this image, to banish the vile "bluestocking" from the American idiom. Like Catharine Beecher, Hale recognized that the answer lay in education. Higher education was "that theatre where the abilities of woman are to be developed." She envisioned America as a vast laboratory for the testing of the compatibility of intellect and femininity. The ultimate outcome of this experiment would be of momentous importance to "the happiness and order of society, and even the character of our country."

Meanwhile, an appeal to the past was completely unsatisfying to Hale. She found that, regardless of the significance of women's achievements, the historical record was bare. The fact that history did not seem to register woman's existence made Hale question the basic order of the universe. To be able, somehow, to uphold that structure of belief was the greatest challenge facing the American woman, a challenge Hale felt she must meet successfully. With a good education and an opportunity for using it in the schoolroom—which she called the thinking woman's "temple of fame"—the American woman, like Beecher's teacher, would steer a middle course, maintaining her own balance and that of society and the cosmos as well. Neither stupid nor too learned, this "new woman" would "converse sensibly without the charge of pedantry, and be intelligent without the appellation of a *blue*." "Rational" and "useful," she would "not disappoint public expectation." [47] Hale found it difficult to be more specific about her new woman, having tried unsuccessfully to draw a fictional diagram, contrasting *bas* and *bleu* as equally unattractive examples of femininity. In this schematic and unresolved account, *bas* stands for the witless "belle," *bleu* for the pedant, a "would-be literary lady" whose "affectation was all the claim she had to genius." Poised between them, a suitor finds both women equally repelling and concludes only that "though learning might make a woman excessively disagreeable, yet she might be excessively disagreeable without it." [48]

In a review of *Bluestocking Hall*, Hale, identifying the term with feminism as well as pedantry, warned readers unsympathetic to "women's rights" that they might find this novel dull. As she recounted the plot, the male protagonist, expecting the worst—"with fearful apprehensions of being addressed only in 'words of learned length, the technicalities of chemistry, or the barbarous nomenclature of botany' "—was surprised to find in that dread "bluestocking" citadel "true women" of "taste, intelligence, and piety." [49] Although this novel had attempted to rehabilitate the "blue," Hale joined the backlash against her, deliberately using the epithet to illustrate what the American woman who cultivated her mind would *not* be like. For Hale, the image of the "bluestocking" had obviously lost its connection with wit and the life of the salon; the pedant and social bore had taken the field. Nobody liked a "bluestocking," and nobody wanted to be one.

For Hale the image of the female thinker as "bluestocking" had all the qualities still associated with the idea of woman as intellectual. The salon's heritage was the "headhunter," a collector of celebrities, art, and culture. Original English "bluestockings" had often been experts on ideal femininity; women thinkers were thus to be, almost by definition, thinkers about women. Outside the original "bluestocking" milieu, explicit feminists, rebels like Mary Wollstonecraft, were soon castigated as "blues," despite their more legitimate claims to being wider-ranging pursuers and purveyors of then-current ideas. Promoters of true womanhood ransacked history, selecting the most lurid examples of "monsters," "non-women," and "perverts" who had broken all natural laws and disqualified themselves as women. Feminists with irregular lives were favorites, for they provided a neat package of all the vices. Supporters of a distinctly feminine genius had collapsed the intellect into feminine virtue; a popular contrasting image, the "blue" as "free-thinker," was identified with sexual deviance and corruption. Although the "bluestocking" was a "free-

thinker," she was, according to the stereotype, always thinking about women, women's rights, and sex in some eccentric
and neurotic manner. And, in the absence of pathology, pedantry always sufficed. In addition, as in Hale's analysis, the
"blue's" intellectual and sexual credentials were constantly
called into question: the intellectual woman was a pseudointellectual.

In spite of Hale's campaign against the "bluestocking," Harriet Martineau described America as the home of the "blue."
After only ten days on American soil she had already encountered "three outrageous pedants, among the ladies." [50] During
the rest of her 1834 tour she searched all over America for
"real" intellectual women, only to find more and more pedants
and pretenders—"a greater variety and extent of female pedantry than the experience of a lifetime in Europe would afford." She watched them passively absorbing foreign languages, converting the most cursory and informal exchanges
into wildly abstract meditations. Martineau concluded that the
same phenomenon accounted for the absence of intellectual
women and the ostentatious presence of pedants: " . . . the
intellect of woman is confined." Judging America by its treatment of women, she could hardly call it a civilization. The
status of women in the New World was truly paradoxical.
With scant educational opportunities and marriage as the
American woman's only "mental" goal, with "her morals
crushed, her health ruined, her weaknesses encouraged, and
her strengths punished, she is told that her lot is cast in the
paradise of women. . . . " Martineau reasoned that the idealized status of American women was founded on "chivalry,"
that "indulgence" was her "substitute for justice." Consequently, she declared that all American women were pris-
oners of sex.

American feminists were advancing similar arguments in
the 1830s; when they began to hold women's rights conventions—the first at Seneca Falls in 1848—press, public, and
clergy mercilessly and often comically smeared them as a gag-
gle of unsexed, unhappy, and unhinged "bluestockings."
Press coverage of these conventions reveals how automatic it

had become to equate feminist, "bluestocking," and "intellectual," and in one stroke to destroy the intellectual and sexual credentials of these women, unmoored and listing, eager for battle, far "OUT OF THEIR LATITUDE," as the Albany *Mechanic's Advocate* headlined these first meetings at Seneca Falls and Rochester. It seemed like a ghastly replay of the Wollstonecraft saga on a larger scale: "The hyena in petticoats" had multiplied and, bent on "insurrection," looked forward to "the reign of petticoats," ranting "Bluestocking Effusions." [51] Announcing the 1852 Syracuse National Convention, the *Syracuse Daily Star* left the women their femininity and unsexed their male supporters instead, feeling perhaps that this felicitous simile could easily discredit the entire proceedings: "The blues are as thick as grasshoppers in hay-time, and mighty will be the force of 'jaw-logic' and 'broom-stick ethics' preached by the females of both sexes." The *Daily Star*'s coverage of what it called the "Tom Foolery Convention," that gathering of "brawling women and Aunt Nancy men," emphasized that the participants belonged to the lunatic fringe of American life—" 'isimizers' of the rankest stamp, Abolitionists of the most frantic and contemptible kind." The paper questioned their Christianity and pronounced feminist oratory "gabble," a "mess of corruption, heresies, ridiculous nonsense and reeking vulgarities which these bad women have vomited forth for the past three days." [52]

Surveying the "farce at Syracuse" from the metropolis, the *New York Herald* asked and answered for its breathless readers that proverbial question that was so to perplex Sigmund Freud:

> Who are these women? what do they want? what are the motives that impel them to this course of action? The *dramatis personae* of the farce enacted at Syracuse present a curious conglomeration of both sexes. Some of them are old maids, whose personal charms were never very attractive, and who have been sadly slighted by the masculine gender in general; some of them women who have been badly mated . . . and they are therefore down upon the whole of the opposite sex; some, having so much of the virago in their disposition, that nature seems to have made

a mistake in their gender—mannish women, like hens that crow; some of boundless vanity and egotism, who believe that they are superior in intellectual ability to "all the world and the rest of mankind". . . .[53]

The fact that the *Herald*'s classification of feminine types, or stereotypes, remains—without alteration—the most popular approach to "understanding" feminists and/or female intellectuals gives one a sense of the power these stereotypes must have had in the nineteenth century. After concentrating on the pathology of feminism, the *Herald* dismissed most of the feminists as "flimsy, flippant, and superficial." [54] When the famous "Mob Convention" met in New York the next year, the *Herald* printed a slightly different version of its character analysis of the women at Syracuse: ". . . entirely devoid of personal attractions," disappointed in love or frustrated by attempts to become men, these "rampant women" were both "unsexed in mind" and unable to think coherently. Having lost (for obvious reasons) the respect of their husbands, if they had spouses in the first place, these errant women were traipsing about the country, "boring unfortunate audiences with long essays lacking point or meaning." [55]

The antifeminist press—most papers in the United States— demonstrated how easy it was to destroy that compromise between intellect and "true womanhood" so carefully fashioned by educators, journalists, cultural arbiters, and by the dread feminists themselves. For their opponents, feminists served as proof that the reconciliation of intellect and femininity was impossible. Female enemies seemed particularly fond of dismissing advocates of women's rights as "intellectual women," adding, "Oh, they are monsters!" [56] Sarah Hale's new woman, neither *bas* nor *bleu*, was, like the idea of national character, an elusive concept, a synthesis as fragile as that of the nation. To unite "true womanhood" with the intellect was as difficult as to reconcile the concepts of nationalism and sectionalism, that unresolved conflict over which America would subsequently go to war. In 1860 the results of the debate on women and the life of the mind were as indeterminate as the future of the

Republic: the question seemed suspended by the thought of war. The unity of America as well as the relationship between the intellect and the role of the American woman had yet to be decided.

Amid the confusion of her times Sarah Hale returned to history to insert that missing link—woman. To establish that women belonged securely in the history books of each generation might bring clarity and a sense of stability to the present. Compiling her massive *History of Woman's Progress from the Beginning to A. D. 1851* (1851), she soon encountered an insurmountable problem: Although she dismissed most feminist contemporaries, she had to include several women whose lives and works threatened both her ideal of woman and her notion of progress. Forced to confront Margaret Fuller, whom many called America's Mme de Staël, Hale blanched at such a specimen, so highly irregular, so asymmetrical, so recalcitrant to synthesis or any idea of order. Hale's "great chain of female being," a linkage of "true women" throughout time, seemed to weaken under the force of entries like Margaret Fuller, whose own attempt to unite mind and femininity made Hale fear that chaos, not progress, might be the law of the future.

# (2)

# "The Beauty
# of a Stricter Method"
## Margaret Fuller, Interpreter of Romanticism

*Each morning prayed I when I awoke, 'dear God, why was I born?' and
now I know; that I may not be so senseless as the others are. . . .*
—Bettina von Arnim, *Die Günderode*
Margaret Fuller, translator

*If thou keep these laws, thou shalt have a leader's eye, or live always in
the mountain, seeing all the details, but seeing them all in their place and
tendency. . . . And thou shalt serve the God Terminus, the bounding Intellect, and love Boundary or Form; believing that Form is an oracle which
never lies.*
—Ralph Waldo Emerson, *Journals*

*I think constantly of Goethe while I see life overflowing thought as soon as
it has expressed it.*
—Margaret Fuller

*Could but love, like knowledge, be its own reward.*
—Margaret Fuller

*The great critic is not merely the surveyor but the interpreter of what
other minds possess.*
—Margaret Fuller

Margaret Fuller
*The Schlesinger Library, Radcliffe College*

Margaret Fuller
*The Schlesinger Library, Radcliffe College*

## 1. "How Is It That I Seem To Be This Margaret Fuller?"

In the 1830s Sarah Josepha Hale, a powerful arbiter of American femininity even before she became editor of *Godey's Lady's Book*, drew many intellectual maps for women and warned them not to leave the terrain she had charted:

> The path of poetry, like every other path in life, is to the tread of woman, exceedingly circumscribed. She may not revel in the luxuriance of fancies, images and thoughts, or indulge in the license of choosing themes at will, like the Lords of creation.[1]

As if in defiance of this command, Margaret Fuller ventured forth into the terra incognita of romanticism, leaving, according to Hale, religion and femininity far behind. She was a graphic illustration "that the greater the intellectual force, the greater and more fatal the errors into which women fall who wander from the Rock of Salvation, Christ the Savior."[2]

Harriet Martineau, that "godless" Englishwoman, and Horace Greeley, Margaret's employer at the *New York Tribune*, concurred in the opinion that an earlier marriage and a family would have redeemed Margaret to society and "cleared her mind of much cant and nonsense."[3] Margaret and her friends, Martineau recalled, "fancying themselves the elect of the earth in intellect and refinement," sat idly in Boston, discussing Kant, Goethe, and Greek mythology while "the liberties of the republic were running out as fast as they could go."[4] Although Fuller would later vindicate herself from charges of pedantry and other worldliness by participating in a revolutionary struggle on foreign soil, her intellectual excesses were never forgotten.

These assessments of Margaret Fuller reveal how outlandish the idea of an intellectual woman seemed to her contemporaries; conventional arbiters of femininity as well as radical intellectuals found her a curiosity. To them Fuller was neither a "true woman" nor the kind of intellectual most needed in America. Something in her character seemed askew. Difficult to classify, she was often banished to a shadowy and shifting territory. Edgar Allan Poe described hers as a third world—

"there are men, women and Margaret Fuller." [5] At best she was a puzzle that stymied her contemporaries and later generations; at least she was a pretext for discussion and analysis. Henry James, haunted by her memory, could not decide whether she had been a "somewhat formidable bore, one of the worst kind, a culture-seeker without a sense of proportion," or "a really attaching, a possibly picturesque New England Corinne." [6] As both illustration and representative of the "reign of wonder" that was romanticism, her very existence and rise to prominence indicates that the landscape of American thought changed during her lifetime. As a participant in the transformation, Margaret Fuller saw herself as a symbol of intellectual womanhood—"chosen among women" to "act out her nature." [7]

After Margaret Fuller died in a shipwreck in 1850, Thomas Carlyle wrote to Emerson about her tragic and often heroic history—"wild as the prophecy of a Sibyl." [8] Present when Margaret Fuller "accepted the universe," Carlyle had retorted, "By Gad, she'd better!"; now he seconded Emerson's description of her "mountain *me*," a unique ego of astonishing proportions, rather like Carlyle's own: "Such a pre-determination to *eat* this big universe as her oyster or her egg, and to be absolute empress of all height and glory in it that her heart could conceive, I have not before seen in any human soul." [9]

Margaret's father and all those other Fuller men before him would have called an urge within them to dominate experience a natural ambition. To accept the universe and a small niche in it for oneself was unthinkable for a New England Fuller. Forced by her father to pursue and master a rigorous course of study essentially superior to that given Harvard men at the time, Margaret Fuller felt that all New England had conspired to make her the "formidable bore" that Henry James later mentioned. She nearly became, as he phrased it, a "culture-seeker without a sense of proportion"—engulfed by the spirit of romanticism. How she developed from a learned enthusiast and inspired conversationalist to a major interpreter of romanticism is the story of the making of an intellectual woman—one who, insisting on her femininity, attempted to make it something rich and strange.

In a century devoted to a sublimely nonsexual ideal of femininity, Margaret Fuller did not lose her sexual energy. She was certainly not the "female eunuch" that Germaine Greer later insightfully defined.[10] Her life and work were heroic attempts to integrate sexuality and intellect, and this strategy made her rather unique among New England intellectuals. To them her sexuality was more threatening than her mind. To Ralph Waldo Emerson she was indeed a dark lady whose presence made his becoming a "transparent eyeball"—a romantic image for symbolic perception—most difficult. Most men fled in terror from the honesty of her passion. In the repressive environment of New England, she found in the lush organicism of romantic thought and its dialectical interplay between world and spirit, real and ideal, outlets for her intellectual and sexual energy and new ways to resolve that ancient tension between mind and body. Almost every sentence she ever wrote is fraught with active, assertive, dynamic, sexual imagery that is intensely phallic.

Although Fuller is usually caricatured as a "bitch castrator" who became an intellectual because she could find no man to love her, it is time to see her as she saw herself and to admit that life and thought cannot be explained away so easily. Margaret Fuller was rather like an Elizabethan lost in the nineteenth century, a woman of zest and energy who always searched for her ideal, Sir Philip Sidney, the last man she felt to have lived successfully the life of thought and the life of action at the same time—the last to integrate body and spirit.[11] Her contribution to that favorite American genre, the list of negatives with which one describes the American experience, reflects her disappointment and her values: America had no women, no art, and no men. Her goal was to rectify that situation.

## 2. "I had no natural childhood."

To the educationist Horace Mann, whose tastes were confined to women of symmetry, Margaret Fuller was insufferable, not merely because she was an intellectual woman but because she was a quintessential Fuller who "combined the disagree-ableness of forty Fullers." [12] Thomas Wentworth Higginson, that famous Renaissance man of New England—minister, re-former, romantic—concurred in Mann's assessment of the Fuller character. He remembered those five Fuller men, Margaret's father and his brothers—all lawyers—as equally and almost interchangeably irritating. Their formidable "uniformity" was responsible for "their being liked and disliked—especially the latter—in a body." To Higginson they were "men of great energy, pushing, successful, of immense and varied information, of great self-esteem, and without a particle of tact." [13]

Fullers always worked against the grain, in the name of principled action. Compelled in particular to fight against all forms of social corruption and tyranny, they were born for defiance, and their assertions often seemed deliberately de-signed to tempt fate to strike them down. Fullers did not shrink from staking their lives on their principles, and they were especially fond of gratuitous gestures that might destroy them personally without necessarily furthering the cause of justice. [14] The importance of being earnest was its own reward.

Margaret's father was the firstborn and the namesake of his father, the Reverend Timothy Fuller. The minister's son would have received first honors in his Harvard class of 1801 if he had not participated in a student riot. Fully aware that he would lose first place, young Timothy decided that the justice of the student's cause was more important than his own class rank—he came in second anyway. His father had suffered more direfully for his principles. The elder Timothy (Harvard, Class of 1760) outraged his first congregation in Princeton, Massachusetts, by insisting, publicly and incessantly, that the idea of an American revolution had been conceived too hastily—that it should be postponed until a more propitious time. Accordingly dismissed from his church in 1776, he returned after the revolution; his parishioners and neighbors then sent him to the state constitutional convention. Steadfastly voting against ratification, he denounced the Constitution for its recognition of slavery.

The younger Timothy had a longer and more distinguished career in state politics, although his views closely paralleled his father's. Successful and self-assured, as was appropriate for the founder of Harvard's Hasty Pudding Club, Timothy Fuller was also an uncompromising nonconformist. Active in various branches of Massachusetts government, he served as a congressman from 1817–1825, although his political allegiances made him, once again, an exceptional case. Fuller was a zealous democrat, a thoroughgoing Jeffersonian, in the midst of Federalist territory. While in Congress he chaired the House committee on naval affairs, supported John Quincy Adams for President, argued for an enlightened policy toward the Seminole Indians, and opposed the Missouri Compromise. He was much admired as an orator in his home state, and many of his speeches were published. When he died in 1835 he was just beginning what he conceived of as his life's work—a history of the United States.

Timothy Fuller had no private virtues distinct from those of his public life. In both he was the virtuous citizen, the spokesman—even the "tyrant"—of rationalism.[15] In 1809 he married Margaret Crane, also of distinguished Puritan stock. She was the daughter of Major Peter Crane, of Canton, Massachusetts, who had served in the Revolutionary War. Higginson described her as "one of the sweetest and most self-effacing wives ever ruled by a strong-willed spouse." [16] During the second year of their marriage, on May 23, 1810, Sarah Margaret was born in Cambridgeport—the first of eight children. Margaret remembered her mother as a perfect flower of womanhood, a symbol of ideal femininity:

> We cannot be sufficiently grateful for our mother—so fair a blossom of the white amaranth—truly to us a mother in this, that we can venerate her piety. Our relations to her have known no jar. Nothing vulgar has sullied them; and in this respect life has been truly domesticated.[17]

In all other respects Timothy Fuller dominated Margaret's childhood; her mother was literally only a symbol. Her father managed every detail of Margaret's intellectual and social life; he chose her books and her clothes, and decided which invitations she should accept. When the Fullers entertained, Margaret and her father greeted the guests and conducted the evening. Her mother was but a shadowy presence, a timid figure who did not flourish in company.

Determined to give Margaret a classical education, Timothy Fuller began his college of one for Margaret early in his daughter's life. She began to study Latin at the age of six, and the following year found her absorbed in the works of Virgil, Ovid, and Horace. Forced to recite her lessons to her father each evening, she lived in a state of anxiety and overstimulation. The hours of her performance had to conform to her father's erratic business schedule; Margaret had to face his questions whenever he returned, and she did not know when she would be called upon to perform. She later said that her childhood had been horrible and "unnatural"—that it had almost destroyed her. Nightmares and hallucinations "induced continual headache, weakness and nervous affections, of all kinds." [18] Her life formed a ludicrous contrast to the works her father forced her to master—the noble and serene ideas of Roman historians or those of the sage of Monticello. But Timothy Fuller felt that his pupil, like his ancestor, the "glorious Buckminster," should exhaust herself in her zealous pursuit of knowledge. This famous minister had been a precocious and avid student, and Timothy's children were obviously told of his greatest feat of concentration, for Margaret's brother Richard wrote of it with awe. Forgetting everything except his book, young Buckminster stood reading, propped against a mantle: "He remained in this posture, entirely absorbed, for several hours, till he fainted from exhaustion; and the family hearing him fall, rushed in to find him on the floor in a swoon." [19]

Surprisingly, Margaret did not collapse—nor close her books forever—during her painful engagement with her father's world of ideas. But she was a Fuller after all. Determined to match wits with her father, to live up to his expectations, to assert (or create) an identity of her own, she turned her intellect to its first test. Having absorbed her father's favorite lesson—that the intellect ought to be a powerful social force—Margaret decided to examine the Unitarian doctrine and Enlightenment social thought that propelled her father. Finding these theories mere abstractions that lacked vitality and failed to explain experience, she made her first independent decision of consequence—to reject them.

Timothy Fuller had unwittingly prepared his daughter for romanticism. By emphasizing through his own example that life was more important than thought, her father developed Margaret's sense of selfhood. Guarding this private personality, Margaret prepared her mind and heart for romanticism. As she acted out her part in her father's world, she felt that the most important part of herself still lay dormant, veiled from his eyes.[20] Nurturing this secret self, Margaret created a public mask, perhaps in compensation for her physical plainness. To be "bright and ugly"[21] was the best way of having character equal to her father's. Conventional beauty and traditional feminine traits were liabilities in the contest with her father over her own identity. She had seen how he could crush a white amaranth.

When she was thirteen, Margaret met a woman, according to several of her biographers, who seemed to symbolize feminine strength instead of weakness. This visiting British artist, unfortunately unnamed, represented the great world of culture and sensitivity, vitality and style. Margaret's distant yet loving relationship with her own mother had taught her to view femininity in symbolic terms and to realize that she must strive to create a more vital femininity for herself. Both her intellect and her femininity required intense cultivation if Margaret were to become a successful woman, one who could act out her nature. Worshipping the Englishwoman and hoping to learn her secrets, she found her first ideal woman and formed the first of many intense friendships with women. Margaret felt that she and her friend lived in a brilliant world of their own, amid the duller mortals of Cambridge.

Margaret retained this sense of superiority and uniqueness when separated from her idol and sent to the Misses Prescott's

School in Groton. Students there, as she later portrayed them, did not appreciate her and conspired against her. Throughout her life, in fact, Margaret held to the position that society would not tolerate a brilliant deviant whose very existence demonstrated society's inferiority.[22] At age thirteen she already felt "chosen among women"—if only to be destroyed. She was irrevocably different and proud of it.

In 1825 a typical day for Margaret Fuller was certainly atypical for any other fifteen-year-old, even in Cambridge. Returning from the Misses Prescott in Groton in 1824, she had been enrolled in the Cambridgeport Private Grammar School to study Greek, like her male classmates, who were, however, preparing for Harvard. Attending class at noon, she devoted her entire day to self-cultivation. In summer she rose before five, took an hour's walk, practiced the piano, and breakfasted at seven. Literature, philosophy, and literary criticism (often in French) occupied her until she left for school. In the afternoons she read Italian and practiced the piano. After an early dinner she played and sang, and returned at eleven to write in her diary.

Her peers, both male and female, found her most unusual and were impressed. Her life easily lent itself to mythmaking, and she happily affirmed a legend, circulated by the young ladies of Cambridge, that she could do everything at once. Like one of Dr. Johnson's ideal "bluestockings," she had been known to "rock the cradle, read a book, eat an apple and knit a stocking, all at the same time." [23] Girls who attended school with her wondered whether her regal bearing and the casual way she carried her books in her cloak, with such flair, were responsible for her mastery of Greek grammar. Renowned at school for her huge vocabulary in English and Greek and for her recitative skill, Margaret introduced young Oliver Wendell Holmes to a strange new word—"trite." [24] That word sprang to her lips naturally, especially when she thought about women's conventional roles and ideals.

Margaret Fuller continued to search for examples of feminine greatness, for models worthy of imitation, throughout her adolescence. In Mme de Staël's *Corinne* she found a fictional heroine whose life matched her own in terms of great expectations. Like Margaret in New England, the French Corinne seemed totally out of place in England. Her supreme values—beauty, art, and sensitivity—were opposed to those of English society. A glamorous and muselike figure, an *improvisatrice* who drew out the genius of others, Corinne was an oracle and a prophet, not a creative artist. In the novel, her stepmother, Lady Edgarmond, the voice of conventional wisdom, "wished all the faculties she did not share to be looked on as diseases." Like British society, she judged a woman to be "insane, or of doubtful virtue, if she ventured in any way to assert herself." [25] To her, Corinne's sublime ideal of a life of the mind was at best preposterous and totally impractical. At last Corinne found in Italy an atmosphere congenial to her spirit and her development.

In 1827 Margaret and a new friend, Lydia Maria Francis, discussed the novel and the political and social thought of Mme de Staël, contrasting her work with that of John Locke, and with Greek and Roman philosophers. To Margaret, her new acquaintance, eight years her senior, was an ideal friend because she was an intellectual equal. Noting in her diary that Miss Francis was not a superficial, conventional "lady," Margaret described her as "a most interesting woman, natural, free from cant and pretension . . . possessing a peculiar purity of mind." [26] Even if all New England conspired against them, as Britain had frustrated the progress of Corinne, it seemed as if they could form a society of their own—what Edith Wharton later would call a "republic of the spirit." [27]

Drawn together by a mutual disdain for frivolity and insincerity, they, and many other New England women, believed that an artistic sensibility marked the authentic individual. They worshipped the new religion of romanticism. Both Margaret Fuller and her ideal friend, soon to become Lydia Maria Child, agreed that individual growth was life's paramount objective. And both of them believed that other women could be redeemed, raised to a higher life, by a program of self-cultivation similar to their own.

On a less intellectual level many other women in New England had, in fact, also begun to pursue a life of the mind. For these enthusiasts, however, a knowledge of literature served other purposes than the individual and intellectual growth sought by Fuller and Francis. Rather, it certified their credentials as devotees of the romantic quest for sublimity and sincerity. In the worship of art, they not only found a new form of order and value but they found each other.[28] This cult of female friendship was a response to forces that had cast many New England women adrift upon the shifting surfaces of society.

Unlike their ancestors, many New Englanders no longer reserved their intellectual energy for theology, no longer tortured themselves with doubts about their own salvation. The Unitarian faith, embracing rationalism and destroying the power of Calvin's dark vision, had liberated these women from fear, from theology—often from the church itself. Even for many who still sought refuge there, the church could no longer provide the old sense of community.

In addition, the structure and stability of the extended family were also subject to fragmentation and dislocation. Increasing numbers of women were the victims of that disruption caused by the "remorseless process of settlement, migration and dispersal," from Europe to America, from seacoast to interior; and they were victims of the processes of industrialization and urbanization.[29] Without the church and the extended family, the concept of ideal femininity had only the "nuclear family" as a sustaining context.[30] The "true woman" seemed to be more the dream of man and of woman than the reality.

Margaret Fuller and Lydia Maria Francis were as harshly critical of women as they were of American society. They viewed women as symbols of the culture's materialism and artificiality, lamented that the ideal of true womanhood did not produce ideal women, and used this ideal as a yardstick with which to measure their own superiority and create their own ideal of a true woman.

If Fuller and Francis had not continued to grow intellectually, they might have lived out their days writing letters to

each other, worshipping their own sensitivity, and condemning the rest of mankind as boorish inferiors. Both were destined, however, for a wider experience in life and thought that
would make this sentimental and simplistic judgment impossible—however comforting it might have been, since, as one
member of the cult of friendship wrote, "life is short and
kindred spirits are few." [31]

### 3. "I am little better than an aspiration."

In her early twenties Margaret Fuller enjoyed the intellectual
companionship of many kindred spirits in Cambridge, including several young men in Harvard's famous Class of 1829.
Among them, James Freeman Clarke, her Cambridge school-
mate at grammar school, proved himself to be an ideal friend
as Margaret's companion in an intense study of German language and literature. Prompted by Carlyle's enthusiasm for
German romanticism, Margaret completely mastered the language in three months and read Goethe, Schiller, Tieck, Kor-
ner, Richter, and Novalis. In all their works she found that
vitality and life triumphed over pale abstractions. The poetic
imagination, the power and the glory of symbolic perception,
made the artist a heroic and unique figure, godlike in his ability to confront and dominate the vast and sometimes chaotic
universe by enshrining life in a work of art.

Margaret's intellectual appetite, her thirst for individuality
and self-cultivation, grew with her readings, which seemed to
promise her a glorious future. As she had emotionally rejected
the Enlightenment orientation of her father, so too could she
now reject it intellectually. The German masters suggested that
she did not have to unlearn anything; she had merely to keep
growing, and she too could become a vivid symbol of what
she called the "Great German Oak." [32]

Scarcely a year later, Margaret was literally brought to earth.
In 1833, Timothy Fuller, clearly a persuaded Jacksonian, decided to move his family to rural Groton, where they might
pursue a natural life of simple rusticity, close to the soil. There

he hoped his sons would become yeomen, as sturdy and self-reliant as the mythical Jeffersonians he idolized. But Margaret saw nature through the lens of romantic organicism; her interpretation was symbolic, her father's strictly literal. Nature in Groton was not picturesque or suggestive. To Margaret it seemed almost unnatural—static not organic—and stunting to individual growth.

Banished from Cambridge, an intellectual paradise in comparison, she complained of Groton's "genteel but sterile intellectual pattern." [33] She kept in contact with Cambridge society, however, and met Emerson during her tour of duty at Groton. And she admitted that the village had a redeeming grace: solitude. For the first and almost last time in her life, Margaret Fuller had time for uninterrupted thought and for the cultivation of critical skills necessary for a future interpreter of romanticism: "There, too, in solitude, the mind acquired more power of concentration, and discerned the beauty of a stricter method." [34]

Timothy Fuller plunged wholeheartedly into his new life—his was, of course, an even stricter method. He supervised his fifty acres and his children, worked on his history of the United States, and made several public speeches. Every morning he took a walk with his children, illustrating from nature's text the virtues of economy, industry and, conversely, the evils of financial speculation. Fuller's intense involvement with farm life was killing him. His family noticed how exhausted he was after a typical day of earnest competition with his hired hands. As his son Richard described these contests, Timothy Fuller, attempting to prove his strength, would not give up: "We remember him, in the violent heat of summer, loading grain, with the perspiration flowing over his brow, while the hired man was endeavoring to pitch on the load faster than it could be arranged on the cart." [35] Constantly improving his land, Fuller drained a marshy area for later cultivation. Many thought his act was responsible for Margaret's nearly fatal case of brain fever and for his own death. Soon after her difficult recovery, her father came down with Asiatic cholera—the only known case in New England at the time. Timothy Fuller died in 1835, at age fifty-seven.

His $20,000 estate, consisting mostly of real estate, would hardly cover his large family's expenses, including his sons' future educations. Since her mother was ill and her brothers were busy farming, Margaret had to postpone her great dream of going to Europe, and help support the family. While her brothers ran the farm, she supervised their educations and in 1836 was hired to teach German, Italian, Latin, and English history and literature at Bronson Alcott's School in Boston. As Fuller family tradition seemed to will, this venture proved to be both ill-fated and unprofitable.

Bronson Alcott, the father of Louisa May Alcott, was a transcendentalist and, appropriately for a member of that band of New England admirers of romanticism, Alcott had a reputation for being the most impractical man in the United States. By 1830 he had decided that education was his calling. Finding traditional teaching methods uninspiring, he discovered the works of pioneers in progressive education and attempted to put their theories into practice at the Masonic Temple on Boston's Tremont Street. There forty pupils from advanced and cultured Boston society were to grow as individuals; unfettered by routine, freed from the mechanics of rote learning, they would learn to observe and analyze the expansion of their own natures and creative powers.

Each student had his own desk and blackboard and progressed at his own speed amid pleasant and opulent furnishings: ". . . carpets, pictures, busts, a bas-relief of Jesus, and a symbolic figure, Silence." [36] Rich in subject matter as well, the school's curriculum was designed to develop what Alcott called the "Spiritual," the "Imaginative," and the "Rational" divisions of a child's mind. Margaret Fuller felt that Alcott's ideas were simplistic; he seemed "too much possessed with the idea of the unity of knowledge, too little aware of the complexities of instruction." [37]

Alcott was also blithely unaware of the danger of outraging public opinion. Offering a course under the "spiritual faculty" called "Conversations on the Gospels," taught according to Socratic method, he began with an unmentionable topic: sex, as it related—or did not relate—to the mystery of the Virgin Birth. Although his discussion was totally abstract and, of course, spiritual, scandalized parents soon withdrew thirty of his forty pupils. The school did not close completely until 1839, when he admitted a black child and lost all his remaining pupils except one brave soul. Long before that sad occasion in April 1837, Alcott's dwindling finances forced him to let Margaret Fuller go.

In June she accepted a position as assistant instructor at the Green Street School in Providence, Rhode Island. For the princely sum of $1,000 a year she was to teach older girls for four hours daily, conduct independent study courses, and instruct younger girls and boys as well. The director, Hiram Fuller (not related to Margaret), had educational and aesthetic tastes similar to Alcott's. His school occupied a Greek Revival temple, furnished with "velvet-covered desks, a library, piano and busts." [38]

The older girls at the Green Street School found Margaret Fuller fascinating and stimulating. Far from being inaccessible or totally engaged in her own work, she was judged an excellent, demanding, and absorbingly relevant teacher who was not even averse to discussing current events. Sensitive to their problems, she could relate to students and sympathize, from her own continuing experience, with their quest for identity. A course with Margaret Fuller was a living experience, according to her pupils; an outstanding classroom performer, she held them spellbound—which made them look forward to attending class. For one student, Margaret was a more interesting source of study, speculation, and delight than the assigned material:

I think she is *less satirical* than she was last term, & I love her more than words can tell. She is so funny—she makes me laugh half the time—we had such a glorious time Wednesday . . . when we did not recite half the lesson—not more than three pages—I enjoyed that day finely. [39]

On more typical days her exacting standards demanded the best from her pupils. If the class was unprepared, the members could expect to be treated as cloddish and stupid inferiors.

Although her students considered her to be a demanding teacher, they described her as fair and nonauthoritarian. She always presented conflicting interpretations of material and urged students to make up their own minds as she revealed her own point of view. Like Goethe, Alcott, and Emerson, she emphasized the importance of originality, creativity, and individuality and stressed the value of an independent intellectual stance. Her own uncompromising intellectualism served as a model for her students.

Both the teacher and her methods symbolized intellectual dynamism, engagement, and struggle. Often Fuller would not be "satisfied upon a point" until it was investigated more thoroughly. She led her students deeper and deeper into their assigned material. Nothing could be accepted at face value: the secrets of the universe lay hidden, far below surface meanings. Every book, including the Bible, demanded close scrutiny. She used all texts as springboards to independent thought; otherwise, the student would be surfeited with useless knowledge. As one student wrote, mere acquisition of ideas was to Fuller a sterile exercise:

> . . . thoughts would lay upon our minds, like a dry husk, unless they take root sufficiently deep to produce one little thought of our own, something entirely original; then we shall derive advantage from this study.[40]

Several students hoped to model their lives after Margaret Fuller's, although they felt they could not live up to her example or repay her for the valuable instruction she had given them. Those who knew the details of her personal life admired, even idolized, her for her sensitivity, sincerity—and for her sacrifices. Her well-known views upon the subject of women also encouraged her pupils into that life of the mind she represented. Students readily absorbed her scorn for effusive—sometimes deliberately unintelligent—"lady" poets. Margaret Fuller had only ironic contempt for such "female scribblers."

Through these evaluations, both students and instructor judged themselves superior, destined for greater things. Living on a higher plane, they were liberated intellectually from the foolish concerns of the works they mocked. Everyone in her class accordingly seemed "chosen among women," but Margaret herself was their most brilliant example of intellectual superiority.

While in Providence, Margaret Fuller played a prominent role in literary circles and published several articles and her first book, a translation of Eckermann's *Conversations with Goethe.* Her contemporaries began to call her a "transcendentalist," to view her as an intellectual. Admitting in a letter that she did not want to be an intellectual if that meant giving up her femininity, she assured herself that she was a "true woman" and a transcendentalist—according to her own definition of that intellectual stance:

> For myself I should say that if it is meant that I have an active mind, frequently busy with large topics I hope it is so—If it is meant that I am honored by the friendships of such men as Mr. Emerson, Mr. Ripley, or Mr. Alcott, I hope it is so . . . . *But* if it is meant that I cherish any opinions which interfere with domestic duties, cheerful courage and judgment in the practical affairs of life, I challenge any or all in this or the little world which knows me to remove such deficiency from any acts of mine since I came to woman's estate.[41]

Although she felt that teaching restricted her intellectual development, Margaret Fuller was impressed with her influence upon the young women at the Green Street School: "I cannot but feel with a happy glow, that many minds are wakened to know the beauty of the life of thought." With her ideas "flowing clear and bright as amber," she planned to teach a German class to her adult friends in Providence. But the intellectual milieu there was often "flat, stale and unprofitable," and she felt increasingly depressed, "incompetent to do anything."

Literary women of Providence seemed too conservative, "a co-terie of Hannah Mores," to whom Margaret deliberately read the "most daring passages" in *Faust*. She wrote a friend that such an atmosphere made her "impatient and domineering," that "my liberty here will spoil my tact." [42]

Her talent as teacher and conversationalist might save her—allow her to escape the confines of Providence, to find a more creative freedom, and to support herself and live in the Boston area without institutional affiliations. In 1839 she put this talent to use. She began her "Conversations" and became an institution in her own right. Once a week Boston's educated women could receive, for a fee, inspired guidance in expanding their intellectual horizons. That city's most intellectually distinguished women, many the wives of intellectuals, enrolled and made Margaret's idea a stunning success.

Describing the function of her program, Fuller explained why education had failed to develop woman's potential. She emphasized that although women were often encouraged to pursue knowledge and that many were the intellectual equals of men, most women had no opportunity to put their intellects to work—to sharpen talents and extend capabilities. What she called the mythical deficiencies of the female mind were thus realized, for women had no way to keep their minds from growing soft and flabby. She hoped that the "Conversations" would create a sense of order and community, both intellectual and social—"a place of stimulus and cheer," and "a point of union for well-educated and thinking women." They might even make Boston, "a city which, with great pretensions to mental refinement, boasts at present nothing of the kind," into a real intellectual center. [43]

In the "Conversations," Margaret and her class might pursue and master that "stricter method" she had always sought and now defined in encyclopedic and dynamic terms as an ideal intellectual life, a combination of thought and action. Each weekly session was designed to illustrate her strategy. After briefly outlining that day's subject and suggesting how to approach it, Margaret asked for questions or criticisms from the class. Participation was usually very lively; she could count on at least ten regulars to contribute and rarely had to resort to lecturing.[44] Margaret chose subjects she thought would allow her students to transcend controversy and prejudice and examine what she called the great subjects—those subjects treating universal questions of humanity that would provoke her students to lead a *life* of thought and expand their intellectual range. Ancient mythology, the fine arts, ethics, education, and the influence of women were the major topics covered during the five winters of the "Conversations." Fuller made this material come to life and obviously raised the consciousness of many in the process.

Sarah Freeman Clarke, a painter and a sister of Margaret's friend James, gave a most striking description of Fuller's charismatic leadership. Directness and sincerity were the sources of Fuller's power; a confrontation with her might be initially painful—Sarah Clarke described the encounter as a battle or a rape—but it led to intellectual discovery and communication, to friendships distinguished by their vitality:

> She not only did not speak lies after our foolish social customs, but she met you fairly. She broke her lance upon your shield. Encountering her glance, something like an electric shock was felt. Your outworks fell before her first assault, and you were at her mercy. And then began the delight of true intercourse. Though she spoke rudely searching words, and told you startling truths, though she broke down your little shams and defenses, you felt exhilarated by the compliment of being found out, and even that she had cared to find you out.[45]

Another pupil, having no idea how much Margaret would affect her, discovered, through this teacher, a luminous "new world of thought." "A flood of light irradiated all that I had seen in nature, observed in life, or read in books." [46] Fuller's pedagogical techniques were obviously successful in meeting her major objectives: to search for truth and to develop courage, without which all was lost. The women of Boston evidently lived up to her great expectations, transcending that superficial universe of discourse, "the shelter of vague generalities, the art of coterie criticism, and the delicate disdains of good society" where she thought women, insulated from truth, usually lived.[47] For her own development Margaret knew that she must move into a larger intellectual arena; the "Conversations" did not challenge her intellectual superiority—she would always be queen of that kingdom of the mind. In 1840, with her eye on the best "main chance" New England could offer, she accepted the editorship of a new journal planned to be the major voice of New England romanticism. Continuing the "Conversations," she led a double life—in the comforting feminine circle and in the more perplexing intellectual communities of Concord, Cambridge, and Boston.

## 4. The "New Design" of The Dial

As a writer and editor on *The Dial* she had to organize on paper others' thoughts as well as her own. In essays she wrote for *The Dial*, her definition of romanticism and its social and personal significance grew clearer and more profound. Although Emerson and Fuller disagreed from the start on the purpose and scope of the magazine—Emerson wrote most of its introductory message—evidence of the more thoroughgoing romanticism of Fuller was presented in *The Dial*'s preliminary address to its readers.[48]

A new sensibility had emerged in New England—a "new design" and a "new spirit," Fuller wrote in that first address.[49] An increasing number of converts, of "acolytes," from all classes were participants in this "revolution," although nothing distinguished or united them except "a common love of truth, and love of its work." Each individual felt the impact of this revolution in a different manner, each applied it to a different area of social or intellectual life; but under its diverse manifestations the new spirit was "a protest against usage," and "a search for principles."

For many New Englanders—especially young Unitarians—the rational religion of their fathers had generated this rebel-lion. Fuller did not hesitate to imply that rationalism was a lie, that institutions based upon this principle lacked foundation.

As a matter of course, converts to this new way of seeing protested against what she and Emerson called "that rigor of our conventions of religion and education which is turning us to stone." For Fuller, the final test of a transcendentalist was one's attitude toward literature, the "new demands" one made upon it. She insisted that literature re-establish a vital relationship with life and reflect the diversity, uniqueness, and organicism that characterized nature and the cosmos, culture and the individual.

This comprehensive vision and relentless pursuit of the essence of life and art was the core of romanticism. As Arthur O. Lovejoy said, "One thing alone is necessary for the romantic: everything." [50] And, for most romantics, "everything" always meant something else; nothing in the world, in the self, or in society was a merely empirical phenomenon. Margaret Fuller realized that her New England contemporaries, like Emerson and Thoreau, placed ultimate value in this mode of symbolic perception and made analogies between man, nature, and the cosmos without reference to society. Like the British romantics they admired, especially Coleridge and Wordsworth, they were visionaries engaged in a symbolic interpretation of experience loosely based upon Kantian metaphysics. Their synthesis of man and nature rested upon a basic assumption shared by all romantics that was foreign to the Enlightenment mind: diversity, not uniformity, characterized the universe. A dualistic, often multiple, mode of thought and perception must be employed to capture the "process of increasing diversification" in a universe newly alive—a world in which man contained multitudes and stones contained sermons.[51] Emerson's *Nature* (1836), an exercise in symbolic behavior, had taught Margaret and her contemporaries that this method of perception conferred ultimate value on the self and on the role of the artist. An initial confrontation with nature led man to the doorway of an ideal world, the realm of Spirit, which the artist, as master of language and symbol, was most qualified to enter. Through language he interpreted nature and began his rise to the world of spirit. There, far from nature, the artist still symbolized nature: he was a vehicle for a synthesis of the real and ideal realms of experience. He was the best perceiver, the one who had climbed the spires of form and had become a "transparent eyeball"—a new symbol of unity.

Fuller hoped that readers of *The Dial* could, like Emerson's artist-figure, discover and symbolize the essence of nature in their climb to that ideal world. For her this activity distinguished transcendentalists from other people: "Under the fictions and customs which occupied others, these have explored the Necessary, the Plain, the True, and the Human—and so gained a vantage ground, which commands the history of the past and the present." The journal existed to portray this journey—to "report life" optimistically and cheerfully. Even the quarterly's emblem, a sun dial, symbolized the romantic world view and its rejection of Enlightenment images of order and symmetry. For Fuller and Emerson that favorite Newtonian metaphor, the clock, was "a dead face." To them this choice of symbol and syntax reflected instead a world of growth and change: ". . . a Dial as is the Garden itself, in whose leaves and flowers and fruits the suddenly awakened sleeper is instantly apprised not what part of dead time, but what state of life and growth is now arrived and arriving." [52]

Margaret Fuller soon found that her friends on *The Dial* did not demand as much of literature or of life as she did. The crucial difference between Fuller and Emerson, in particular, and the source of her dissatisfaction with his point of view, was that their interpretations of romanticism were irreconcilable. In terms of Morse Peckham's categories of romanticism, Emerson was an analogist, content with experiencing the value of self through symbolic perception, while Fuller had entered the transcendental stage of romanticism.[53] Armed with a knowledge of the authority of the self and symbolic behavior, Fuller, like Carlyle, Schopenhauer—and later Marx— felt compelled to act out her nature, to engage in heroic feats of world redemption.

Although "transcendentalism" is a convenient term to use in defining New England romantics as a social phenomenon, according to Peckham's convincing analysis of European stances, Margaret Fuller was perhaps New England's greatest—certainly its most intellectual—transcendentalist. And her life, her entire intellectual journey, was to resemble that of Carlyle's hero Teufelsdröeckh in *Sartor Resartus* who finally found a way to act, to make a difference in the universe and attempt to save it; passing through the test of "the everlasting no," he accepted the universe as an arena for moral action and went off to join a revolution—never to be seen again. Margaret Fuller, before she followed in his steps, found that her best way to redeem the world—or at least America—was to act as an interpreter of romanticism. To teach others to make demands upon literature was an act of social redemption that required her to maintain a public intellectual stance. Her previous roles as teacher, conversationalist, and leader of women had satisfied the same transcendental impulses on a smaller scale.

Although she agreed that the creative artist was the most sublime symbol of self-hood, Margaret Fuller thought that criticism had a vital, if secondary, function, especially in America. If America could not produce divinely romantic art, it had already produced critics—Fuller herself was proof of that—who could use romantic methods to interpret the works of European masters. She emphasized that translation into English and the consequent refraction through a British lens had distorted German romanticism in America. Readers, and especially critics, should read the originals and learn the native language in order to judge a culture's literature. Only a critic who "perceives the analogies of the universe" could, in her opinion, make a true response to a work of art and analyze it for others. This task required a comprehensive and empathetic vision: the great critic entered into the spirit of a work, then stepped back, circling it and assessing its worth. Like everything else, critics had a dual nature. They possessed the "poetical temperament to apprehend" and the "philosophical tendency to investigate." [54]

In her self-appointed role as romantic critic—"a historian who records the order of creation"—Fuller approached Goethe and attempted to analyze his significance for *The Dial*'s readers. For most literary Americans, Goethe was an untouchable, a fiend whose depravity was matched only by Byron's. Given this consensus, her essay was, as Perry Miller recently affirmed, "a basic document in the history of intellectual freedom in the United States." [55] The fact that a woman defended Goethe was so shocking to the public that the critic seemed as immoral as her subject. Her courageous treatment of such a controversial figure revealed her intellectual audacity. Knowing the risks involved—that she invited outrage and threatened her own sense of identity—she confronted Goethe, his heroines, and his ideas on women. Once more she found herself facing the puzzle of femininity versus her own nature as an intellectual. Could she, as a woman, approach Goethe's intellectual stature?

Prefacing her discussion of his work with a biographical sketch, Fuller conceded most of the arguments of Goethe's detractors. Too cynical and worldly—of "a deep mind and a shallow heart"—too impressed with the trappings of royalty and social status, he had rejected an artist's most divine mission, the search for truth. He had chosen the great world instead of the realm of Spirit, implicitly leaving to others those higher flights into the ideal realm that Fuller most valued:

> The Parting of the Ways! The way he took led to court favor, wealth, celebrity, and an independence of celebrity. It led to large performance, and a wonderful economical management of intellect. It led Faust, the Seeker, from the heights of his own mind to the trodden ways of the world. There, indeed, he did not lose sight of the mountains, but he never breathed their keen air again. [56]

In all his works, Margaret Fuller found that "woman was the Minerva, man the Mars." In *Faust*, Gretchen, like Richardson's Clarissa, redeemed herself and her seducer through her innocence and purity. But that act was not enough for Fuller. *Wilhelm Meister* contained more diverse feminine types and an image of woman as thinker that she found most attractive. Unlike the "graceful though contemptible" Philina, representative of the degradation of a strictly "poetic life," the "celestial Macaria" was "a ruling power": "She was the last hope in

cases of difficulty and though an invalid, and living in absolute retirement, is consulted by her connection . . . as an un-
erring judge in all their affairs." [57]

Margaret Fuller found in Goethe's life many parallels with
her own that made him a less formidable "kindred spirit." She
could easily identify with his temperament; she took as her
own his complaint that he was "either *too volatile or too in-
fatuated,*" always vacillating between extremes, never finding
serenity.[58] Noting that he "was deficient both in outward self-
possession and mental self-trust" she might also have described herself as she was without the mask of assurance she
wore in public. Perplexed by human relationships, Goethe
had found that love and friendship did not live up to his
ideals, and Fuller's extravagant expectations and disappoint-
ments in love and in friendship resembled his—perhaps because of his influence. *The Sorrows of Young Werther,* with its
pessimistic analysis of love, had deeply appealed to Margaret
and her generation.

As unhappy as children as they were later in adult relationships, Fuller and Goethe had had abnormal childhoods
"filled with conflict" and "severe study." "Fettered in false
relations" since youth, Goethe had not tried to transcend
them. To Margaret's disappointment, he finally restricted his
vision to that plane: ". . . ceasing to be a prophet poet, he was
still a poetic artist." [59] For Margaret, as a woman, the intellectual role of prophetic critic, rather like that of Macaria, representative of the Ideal, was a most attractive destiny. Man had
not already occupied that territory: it seemed as if Goethe had
left it to her.

An exploration of Goethe's nonfictional relationships with
women also helped Margaret Fuller define herself. In a long article for *The Dial* in January, 1842, she examined the nature of
woman, and the woman as intellectual, using, of course, a
dualistic method. "Bettine Brentano and Her Friend
Günderode," contained excerpts from Fuller's translation of
these women's letters and of Brentano's strange book on her
friendship with Goethe. Bettina Brentano von Arnim, German
author and admirer of the master, had written a glowing—and

largely fictional—account of their relationship, *Goethe's Conversations With a Child*. Obviously, Bettina played the child most willingly, and Margaret Fuller found this deeply disappointing. What had promised to be a meeting of equal spirits soon degenerated into a "master-pupil" relationship. "Nymph" and "Apollo" were transformed into "the elderly prime minister and the sentimental maiden." Hopelessly unbalanced, the friendship was a total failure; to Fuller it resembled a "giddy ward's" communion with a "Father Confessor." Fuller thought it all rather disgusting—even grotesque. The hysterical Bettina, forced into a horribly self-conscious and unnatural role by Goethe's condescension, was not the woman Margaret Fuller wished to be: she represented, in her relationship with the master, what Margaret Fuller feared she might become. Bettina had tried, however, to realize her nature. The fault seemed to lie in her friendship with Goethe, not in herself. In comparison, Margaret's friendship with the "Sage of Concord" seemed almost ideal. And Margaret, like her many female contemporaries who also made a fetish of friendship, was never optimistic about finding a true friend: "Sad are the catastrophes of friendships, for they are mostly unequal, and it is rare that more than one party keeps true to the original covenant." [60]

Bettina von Arnim was one of the lucky few who would find an ideal friend, a friend who would bring out her nature more successfully than had Goethe. Margaret Fuller devoted most of her article to an exploration of this "ideal relation realized." [61] The shy nun Günderode and the dynamic Bettina represented the realms of spirit and nature, respectively, and Margaret analyzed their friendship as a dialectic between "Nature and Ideal" and a fruitful synthesis of these realms of experience. They formed a romantic universe in microcosm. Margaret was appparently fascinated by them, not merely interested in material for an article she was writing, for she filled her commonplace book with references to these two women and the worlds they symbolized.[62] In *The Dial* Margaret emphasized that Germany, unlike America, nourished such friendships; intellectual discussion flowered there and came as naturally to

German women as "picking a new dress" came to British and American girls. Fuller found it miraculous and a tribute to German culture that the intellectual "energies" of Goethe, Kant, and Schelling became a part of "these private lives" so effortlessly and naturally.[63]

Like Goethe's Macaria, Günderode was a prophetess, an ethereal creature who told the impetuous and impatient Bettina of the serene joys of the spirit—of the life of the mind. Bettina wrote that theirs was a "secret paradise" where "all was new," and far from that "real world" they never discussed. Günderode foretold that the future would be kinder to a woman of action like Bettina, who would have been a hero if she had been a man. For the present, Bettina should recognize her alienation from the world and begin her journey into a country of the mind as lush and gorgeous as Xanadu, where intellectual pleasures would amply compensate her for a life of action. Here the secrets of the universe lay, ripe for discovery; here was a woman's only source of pleasure. If she learned to "labor in thought" she might "unlock deep-hid kingdoms" and find the only happiness available to her:

> Thou wilt have no other way of enjoyment in thy life, than that, which children promise themselves from magic-caverns and deep fountains, through which one comes to blooming gardens, wonderful fruits and crystal palaces, where yet unimagined music sounds, and the sun builds bridges of its rays, upon the centre of which one may walk with a firm foot.

Günderode insisted that this was the world of supreme truth, not a world of fantasy.[64]

Margaret Fuller loved the delicate balance Bettina and Günderode had achieved in friendship. Neither woman was complete without the other. Günderode seemed worthy of imitation, but she was content with abstractions and analogies. (Her mysterious suicide suggests that she found these wanting, after all.) Margaret's heritage and her more active version of romanticism demanded that she, as Timothy Fuller's daughter and an American transcendentalist, play a more active role to affect the world. Wishing to symbolize the best that both women represented, Margaret Fuller sought to combine the life of thought with the life of action as she always had. Intellectual ability and achievement, energy, duty, and conscience must all play a part and make a difference. In contrast to her view of Goethe's character, she wanted her heart to be as deep as her mind.

### 5. "I Stand in No False Relations. . . ."

New England continually thwarted Fuller's self-imposed imperative to act out one's nature. There ideal relations were never realized. *The Dial* did not nurture a sense of intellectual community, and its contributors often seemed dull and uninspiring. Emerson was exasperating: he was frequently distant, evasive, and reluctant to engage in that kind of intense intellectual discussion and passionate friendship Margaret Fuller loved. Thoreau, who despised her, had arranged his whole life as a protest against any form of intellectual or social community. For her, intellectual life and friendship, like nature, art, and literature should be "ever various, ever new."

In "A Short Essay on Critics," *The Dial,* July 1840, she had described the kind of intellectual stimulation she most wanted and would never find in Boston: "Thinking men, not schoolmasters or pleaders" would ideally present their own positions, "be frank with us, and, if now our superiors, treat us as if we might sometime rise to be their equals." [65] Instead, Margaret Fuller suffered what she later called "a gentle excommunication" from the life of the mind.[66] Women friends in Boston, participants in the "Conversations," were not ideal friends either, for they played pupil to Margaret's master. After George and Sarah Ripley began their communitarian experiment at Brook Farm, any hopes Fuller might have had for an intellectual community were soon crushed. Living close to nature, those earnest toilers were too tired after their day's labors to indulge in strenuous intellectual activity. Too alienated from Brook Farm ideals to participate in the experiment wholeheartedly, Fuller maintained only tangential connections with it—a relationship that Nathaniel Hawthorne explored in his satirical novel about Brook Farm and all reformist visions, *The Blithedale Romance.*

Like Margaret Fuller, Hawthorne's Zenobia lived in town. Bedecked with jewels and talismans symbolic of her mysterious powers, this champion of women's rights visited the rural reformers, attempting to convert them to her cause. A symbol of artificiality, she could have no natural relation to their community. Like the reformers, she was easily duped by a ruthless demagogue, but her failure had a dual significance for Hawthorne: in her surrender she betrayed the feminist cause and relinquished her identity as an independent woman. As Hawthorne later said of Margaret Fuller, Zenobia "fell as the weakest of her sisters did." [67]

Fuller, struggling with a dialectic of femininity and masculinity, of individuality and society, and questioning her own identity and intellectual ability, saw herself during her years with *The Dial* in terms similar to Hawthorne's posthumous estimates of her character and significance. Afraid that she lacked identity, ability, and the strength to act, Fuller analyzed herself as a mélange of masculine and feminine attributes in opposition. Her "feminine" nature longed for security and stability; the "masculine rush[ed] out, only to be baffled." [68] She was too alienated—by nature and by choice—from the passivity of "true womanhood" and the frivolity of the "female scribbler's" role to conform to those models; she could only rely upon them as gauges of her own superiority. Building up a new sense of self, creating her own synthesis of real and ideal in contrast to traditional feminine ideals and outside feminine milieus—as she had done in the "Conversations" and in the classroom—was a difficult and self-conscious process. Being editor of *The Dial* was equally difficult and frustrating. Overworked and underpaid, Margaret resigned in 1842, yet continued to write for the journal until its demise in 1844. Because of the difficulty of her work and of her ambiguous position as an intellectual woman, Margaret Fuller searched for a way, as editor and as contributor to *The Dial*, to symbolize her own identity more intensely than she had ever done before. Fellow intellectuals at *The Dial*, Emerson in particular, did accept her as an intellectual, with reservations, but refused to recognize her as a woman. Hawthorne, who also complained of the transcendentalist circle's aversion to reality's more concrete forms, knew exactly what Fuller was doing, and how the obliviousness of her friends forced her to assert herself in protest. After her death he cruelly described her method of constructing herself as an attempt to make what he called a crude and common nature into something superior and spectacular.[69]

An outline of her new synthesis appeared in the July 1843, issue of *The Dial* in a curious article, "The Great Lawsuit. Man versus Men. Woman versus Women." She had found a way to make her private sense of conflict and frustration into a universal symbol of woman's dilemma. Cosmopolitan and eclectic in the extreme, she selected what most appealed to her about woman's nature and social role from the history and literature of various cultures. After ransacking the past in search of romantic symbols of femininity, she made a plea for woman's rights to individuality and development and asserted her own identity as a most individual, and most intellectual, woman.

Temporarily satisfied with this contribution to the "woman question," Margaret Fuller began a new exploration—of America, real and ideal. During the summer of 1843 she traveled to the Far West, sailed on Lake Michigan, and visited Wisconsin, Michigan, and Illinois. Rapid settlement threatened to destroy the natural beauties of this region, although nature there was not always sublime. Fuller thought that this spectacle of man and nature in obvious opposition demanded a sensitive observer with an attitude of wonder, or its significance would remain obscure. The record of her journey, *Summer on the Lakes* (1844), was, like Emerson's *Nature*, a guidebook to romantic perception. The meaning of Fuller's book was not lost on Thoreau, who used it as a model for his *Journey on the Concord and Merrimack Rivers*. Fuller wrote that a good explorer of life and of art must observe every "new form of life . . . by its own standard" and approach even the most unpleasant scenes with the spirit of empathy. Using a romantic lens to record new experience kept one from missing its concrete details and larger significance. She criticized fellow New England voyagers for engaging in stale theological disputes, ignoring the spectacle before them. Acquisitive and abstract, these new settlers saw no significance in their journey, and they had carried too much of New England with them— "their habits of calculation, their cautious manners, their love of polemics." In contrast, Margaret's goal was to "woo the mighty meaning of the scene, perhaps to foresee the law by which a new order, a new poetry, is to be evoked from this chaos." [70]

Although Fuller came to no conclusions about the ultimate significance of the scene, her descriptive and analytical talents in *Summer on the Lakes* impressed Horace Greeley, and he invited her to join his staff on the *New York Tribune*. New England disapproved of anyone—especially a single woman—going to New York City, that barbarous center of corruption and commercialism. To Emerson's horror, Margaret accepted Greeley's offer. Before reporting for duty, she took a holiday with her friend Caroline Sturgis in the fall of 1844. During seven weeks at Fishkill Landing on the Hudson, she expanded "The Great Lawsuit" into a book, entitled more simply, *Woman in the Nineteenth Century*. Living like a Günderode—what Fuller called the "pleasant life of a free nun"—she described the grandeur of the scene that had brought her serenity, where "the days come to an end solid and unbroken by frivolity or conflict." Writing swiftly upon the subject of woman, she seemed part of the great scene she surveyed and described with a lyrical power that matched nature's:

> Happy and blessed have been the weeks of seclusion, the society of the mountains, so bold and calm . . . the river so grand and fair with its two thousand sail, each moving softly as an angel's thought, and looking, in the distance, as spotless and glittering; and its great boats advancing now and then with a triumphant stride, like some noble discovery breaking in upon the habitual course of human events to inform and extend it . . . .[71]

Sailing through history like the boats on the Hudson, she finished the book, refreshed, and prepared to start her new life

in New York City.[72] With Greeley's extensive promotion of
the work, including a front-page review in the *Tribune, Woman
in the Nineteenth Century* made her a celebrity. The new journalist was the talk of New York. And *Woman in the Nineteenth
Century* was commensurate with America's capacity to wonder. It was perhaps the most romantic nonfictional document
America produced in that century. The book was designed to
give a symbolic version of the plight and power of women,
and of Fuller herself as an intellectual woman and American
romantic—just as Emerson's *Nature* had attempted to provide
a philosophical framework for an American interpretation of
romanticism. Both Fuller and Emerson, using women and nature respectively, tried to create a sense of order and a structure that would contain and combine the diversity of romanticism with that of American experience.

According to Margaret Fuller there were few real women in
the nineteenth century. Most seemed to remain children
throughout their lives. Defining the relationship between the
sexes according to romantic principles, Fuller used "man" as a
generic term that included men and women. Man was related
both to the natural and to the ideal realms of experience, and
"life and thought were his means of interpreting nature, and
aspiring to God." Also a dual process, the development of
man would ideally permit the growth of both sexes, since they
were the "two halves" of that organic synthesis—"the great
radical dualism." [73] Nature, always in the process of transformation, never created a purely masculine or feminine type;
both sexes continually took on each other's attributes, and
every individual was a unique synthesis and symbol of nature's diversity.

Men had hindered the development of women by keeping
them in a subservient position. Women should be allowed to
realize their destiny as men had done: ". . . woman, the other
half of the same thought, the other chamber of the heart of life,
needs now to take her turn in the full pulsation." Men must
remove all "artificial barriers" to women's progress and allow
them to enter traditionally masculine strongholds if they
wished—"let them be sea-captains if they will." Fuller argued
that women needed self-cultivation most of all; social and pro-

fessional roles should be enlarged to meet their demands, but individual growth was more important. The romantic mode of perception would hasten this development: "Gather from every growth of life its seed of thought; look behind every symbol for its law; if thou can'st see clearly, the rest will follow." [74] Feminism was accordingly a romantic imperative: for Margaret Fuller feminism *was* romanticism—and vice-versa. To argue for the emancipation of women was also a way to assert her own identity and to make a splendid, almost gratuitous, gesture of principle—the kind of action her father had found most attractive.

Femininity, like feminism, flourished in *Woman in the Nineteenth Century*. Even if most women in her time seemed to be overgrown children, she found in the past records of women evidence to match her own high aspirations. Given this cosmic vision of women's possibilities, she could not argue that women had been mere ciphers in the world history. Greece, Sparta, Rome, modern Europe—even America—had recognized woman's power. From Eve, the Virgin Mary, and Joan of Arc to Fuller's famous contemporaries, women had symbolized diversity, achievement, and strength. In the nineteenth century the diffusion—and religious recognition—of the idea of equality had already transformed relationships between the sexes and had promoted woman's cultural development. A transcendental hierarchy of marriage patterns told this story, and Fuller traced the forms of marriage, from the lowest stage to the "highest communion," exactly as Emerson had outlined the ascending order of romantic perception in *Nature*.

A "household partnership" was the first and lowest order of marriage; it was a matter-of-fact and sensible relationship between a "good provider" and a "capable, sweet wife." [75] For Fuller this antiromantic union, although limited, was "good so far as it goes." A second stage, "mutual idolatry," formed a "closer tie," but ultimately narrowed both partners; in their exclusive devotion to each other they arrested that romantic process of growth that symbolized the higher forms of human life. Of greater value was a third union, a marriage of friendship, of intellectual companionship. For her the increasing number of these relationships in the nineteenth century constituted a new social phenomenon from which she drew optimistic implications for the future. Marriage's most sublime form was analogous to the highest perceptual unity between man and the universe, that moment when Emerson had become a "transparent eyeball." This romantic union of two souls was "a pilgrimage to a common shrine"—highest Truth—and a synthesis of the best qualities present in all lower forms of marriage.

The growing number of women authors in the nineteenth century further symbolized women's progress. Fuller acknowledged in her book what had always sustained her own intellectual life—that the spirit of romanticism, with its emphasis on the spiritual, was responsible for the elevation and achievements of women in her century. The "cold," rational intellect of the eighteenth century had not nurtured or noticed what Fuller called "the especial genius" of women, which was "electrical in movement, intuitive in function, spiritual in tendency"—the very essence of romanticism. Even Mme de Staël had not realized her full potential, had not transcended her eighteenth-century heritage. Her mind, developed in the artificial atmosphere of the salon, "fed on flattery" and was accordingly "tainted and flawed." "While she was instructing you as a mind, she wished to be admired as a Woman; sentimental tears often dimmed the eagle glance." [76] In her romantic synthesis of woman and mind Fuller sought to erase this problem; the truly romantic woman, in her earnest search for highest Truth, would reject all artifice, all false relations, and sentimentality—that most perverted form of emotion.

Romanticism's redefinition of intellectual life encouraged Margaret Fuller to create her synthesis of intellectualism and femininity. Relegating the rational intellect to a secondary role, romanticism had placed intuition, a quality formerly reserved for women, at the pinnacle of perceptual categories. According to this conception, a woman romantic was certainly not a contradiction in terms; the use of both terms might even be redundant. Romanticism's social definition of the most sublime thinker, the alienated artist, also had close parallels with woman's social role in the nineteenth century. Both assumed or were forced to play anti-roles: romantics and women were supposed to lead a life far from the world's rude commerce, and to repudiate materialistic values. Like their male counterparts, women romantics were aliens, scorned and sometimes victimized by society, and their alienation identified them as romantics. For Fuller, women romantics were, however, more victimized and misunderstood than their spiritual brothers because their intellectual progress was always threatened by men.

As prophet and symbol of the female thinker as romantic, Fuller defined an intellectual woman's nature as a combination of those peculiarly feminine traits—"electrical" and intuitive qualities, and "creative genius." As a social type an intellectual woman was an outcast who automatically suffered oppression. She would be considered mad and "unnatural" by society; her "electrical" nature would "repel" and "frighten" the majority of humanity. Under such conditions, to be "bright and ugly" was, as Fuller had always insisted, a blessing—an aid to the development of self-reliance and intellectual potential. Describing woman as a duality of Muse and Minerva, Fuller thought that the latter's more active, aggressive, and independent nature should be cultivated by women, especially women intellectuals, in the nineteenth century. In order to grow they should strengthen their independence by "remaining austerely set apart from all that did not belong to them whether as Woman or as mind." [77]

Margaret's apostrophes to her countrywomen made clear what did not belong to the thinking woman—vanity and feminine conquests, and all "false pleasure." As woman and as intellectual, she should relinquish these for the "love of truth, the love of excellence." Noting that American life seemed most congenial to women's intellectual development, Fuller stated that creating more and more opportunities for mental cultivation was more important than speculating about the ultimate intellectual contribution women would make. Nature would, in its continual transformations, disprove all static hypotheses. Fuller, however, as prophetic critic, had to commit what she recognized as the prophetic fallacy: most women with intellectual potential would naturally assume the role of muse; they would play "Corinne" to male artists and not make cultural contributions themselves. Intellectual women of the future would, like Margaret, be better critics than creators. Intellectual work accomplished by women would be identical to Margaret's conception of her own work: it would be unfinished, representative of the renewing and purifying aspects of nature. Woman's soul, and her thought, was "modified by her femininity" and "it flows, rather than deposits soil or finishes work." [78] Fuller's was a self-fulfilling prophecy—in all senses—and the representative woman of the nineteenth century turned out to be Margaret Fuller.

At the end of the book Fuller turned to her New England heritage to keep her synthesis of romanticism, femininity, and intellectualism from falling apart. But it was too late. To sum up her argument she wrote that she would use the form of a sermon, but this Puritan structure broke down under the weight of her data. Since, unlike many romantics, she was not trying to create a dysfunctional style, this formal strategy revealed her intellectual dilemma—her inability to transcend her past, no matter how desperately she tried, or to find a stricter method to order the data of romanticism and relate it to femininity. [79] The sermon was, however, an appropriate form for a world redeemer to use, and the book was a guide to conduct and to salvation for others and for herself. And, in characteristic romantic fashion, she had found in femininity and in feminism the sermons she had hidden there.

*Woman in the Nineteenth Century*, a *Moby Dick* of feminine lore, contained as many contradictions as did Melville's novel. Feminism and romanticism seemed to cancel each other out, like those two whales—the ghosts of Locke and Kant—poised on opposite sides of Melville's whaling ship. Romanticism's emphasis on unique self-hood had led Margaret Fuller straight back to that old "woman of genius"—to the ideal of "true womanhood" she had attempted to replace with her more vibrant, active, and romantic model of femininity. Although Fuller, like Ishmael, survived this shipwreck, her book raised the question of the value of romanticism to the cause of feminism—a problem glimpsed by only a few feminists in the nineteenth century. By combining femininity, feminism, and romanticism, Fuller had forged an identity as unstable as nature's—a synthesis subject to continual transformation, tenuously held together by sincerity, energy, and passion—by woman's "electrical" nature. And she had made herself a symbol of woman's future role as world redeemer—an ultimate transcendental gesture of self-assertion and justification for her future acts. Armed with this faith, she approached the meaning of America in its literature and in her confrontation with its largest city.

## 6. "A time of wild and exuberant life. . . ."

The *Tribune* appointment made Margaret Fuller America's first professional book reviewer, but her work on that paper, with the largest circulation in the city, covered not only literature but the entire cultural life of New York. She reviewed art exhibitions, musical performances, and public lectures, as well as popular and often bizarre enthusiasms, such as the faddish water cure. In addition to cultural criticism, she wrote reform journalism. Like Niagra Falls, New York City was a torrential experience that "filled the whole of life and superseded thought," but it was not sublime.[80] From the Greeleys' window Margaret could see the prison, Blackwell's Island. After visiting prisons and institutions for the poor and insane, Margaret wrote graphic descriptions for her readers, hoping to awaken them to the necessity for reform. To be a good critic she felt she could not ignore either the facts or the implications of the city as a chaotic urban experience. It required the same perceptual talent she had brought to the West. For a "comprehensive" critic, art *and* life demanded the same perspective and treatment.

In the midst of New York's literary wars, of the "tomahawk school" of literary criticism, Fuller worked according to higher principles and raised literary criticism from a form of personal slander, and of superficial literary coverage, to a serious intellectual activity.[81] In the 1840s, she and Edgar Allan Poe—although he made an art of vindictiveness—were America's most serious and analytical literary critics; and their work generated a new standard of excellence and a new respect for literature. To Fuller most New York critics were not critics at all. No one seemed willing to judge a book on its own terms, or even to investigate what these might be. The *Knickerbocker* journal ridiculed most foreign literary contributions from outside the British Isles—especially those from Germany. Its editor, Lewis Gaylord Clark, saw his magazine and himself as the incarnation of New York sophistication—worldly, elegant, and slightly Rabelaisian. Clark's column, "The Table," recounted the brilliant conversation of his set, transmitting their social and intellectual values and tastes to the eager provinces. The *Knickerbocker* set and their admirers—especially those originally from New England—prided themselves on their inability to understand the New England mind of Emerson or the German brand of romanticism that appealed to him. They thought the "Sage of Concord" was full of metaphysical nonsense, and did not miss an opportunity to make fun of *The Dial*. Politically, "old Knick" was Whig to a man, and its literary taste was equally conservative. Before discovering Dickens as the way of the future, Clark's clan had worshipped the American trinity of Bryant, Cooper, and Irving, and had insisted that Sir Walter Scott was the model most appropriate for American imitation and expression.[82]

The Young America movement, led by Evart Duyckinck, with broader literary tastes and democratic political affiliations, attempted to establish more flexible critical standards. In the short-lived *Arcturus* and in the *Democratic Review*, Young America searched for an original, totally American genius, and was soon committed to producing one immediately—from its own ranks. Horace Greeley's loyalties were split between the nativists and the Knickerbockers. He had political ties, although strained ones, with the Whigs, and he sympathized with the reformist and romanticist leanings of Young America. An enthusiastic supporter of *The Dial* and of the spirit of New England romanticism, he considered Fuller's appointment a great coup for the *Tribune*. Overcoming what he called his "vulgar prejudices against professional women" [83] was not very difficult in her case, for by hiring her he could demonstrate his faith in the feminist cause and have a truly romantic intellectual, authenticated by New England, and not involved in the bitter literary feuds of New York.

Margaret Fuller's work lived up to Greeley's fondest expectations. All her writings stressed her independence from that "spirit of partisanship" she thought was ruining both literature and criticism. [84] Promoting European literature spurned by the *Knickerbocker* and discounting Young America's hopes for an instant American literature and genius, she was a symbol of intellectual self-reliance. She was, however, often sympathetic with Duyckinck's circle and wrote complimentary reviews of several of that group's most bizarre literary productions. Their courage alone—a trait she found lacking in most New York literati—made Margaret admire the Young America critics. Her own courage, integrity, and intellectual honesty amazed even Horace Greeley.

In her *Tribune* articles on literature she explicitly defined her critical methodology and standards and used them to evaluate European and American literature, to analyze the relationship between them and the problematic nature of American artistic exploration and achievement. Fuller announced that the major problem confronting both American artists and critics was that there was no American literature. Like woman in the nineteenth century, it was an adolescent at best. And critics were as childish as artists and women. For her new public, and for the critics of New York, Margaret Fuller defined art as "a medium for viewing all humanity, a core around which all knowledge, all experience, all science, all the ideal as well as the practical in our nature . . . arrange themselves into one harmonious whole." [85] This cosmic and comprehensive vision of the nature and possibilities of literature required that her criticism complement and evoke the spiritual essence of a work, and place it in an organic relationship with life.

As a romantic critic, Fuller never merely described a book; the act of interpretation was paramount. A cosmopolitan orientation reinforced her sense of organicism and heightened her appreciation of diversity. As Mme de Staël and Goethe had, Fuller argued that each culture made a unique contribution to a total synthesis of world cultures, that each nation must be comprehended on its own terms. As Goethe had said, a cosmopolitan spirit made it possible to grasp the essence of each culture from within its own "center."

Modern England, conventional and predictable, seemed to lack a center, and Fuller found it recalcitrant to analysis or organic synthesis. She admired British artists like Coleridge and Wordsworth and was the first American critic to discover Browning, but, as she had privately confessed in her commonplace book, Sir Philip Sidney was the last Briton to achieve a perfect balance between real and ideal, thought and action. The genius of France, its "talent for communicating observations with ease, vivacity and conciseness," was reflected in novelists like George Sand, Eugène Sue, and Balzac, whom Americans often dismissed as immoral.[86] Fuller, on the contrary, insisted that Americans had much to learn from them, and from what was to her the deeper, more spiritual German mind, the essence of philosophical idealism. She thought that the literature of France and Germany in particular would play important roles in that synthesis of the future—the American mind. A knowledge of European literature would give order, structure, and depth to the restless, energetic, and often superficial spirit of Americans—would help give them a character. In her vision of America, an intellectual version of Tom Paine's melting pot—of minds and books—Fuller foresaw the development of America as symbolic of that total synthesis of world cultures that was a favorite romantic dream:

> As men of all countries come hither to find a home and become parts of a new life, so do the books of all countries gravitate towards the new center. Copious infusions from all quarters mingle daily with the new thought which is to grow into American mind and develop American literature.[87]

Fuller insisted that this transfusion would save America from becoming totally materialistic. To raise its spirit to a plane even remotely ideal would be a splendid feat in a country she found increasingly "stupid with the lust for gain." Although still a "European Babe," America already needed to be reborn, cleansed of corruption and avarice.[88] The only distinct quality that she discovered in the "puzzle" of America was "energy." Before America and its literature could come of age, she wrote, the settlement of the continent must be completed, Americans must have leisure to create a civilization, and must cultivate and prize "moral and intellectual values" as well as "political freedom." [89] That "riper time" would witness the birth of American literature. Until then, since one "cannot have expression until there is something to be expressed," she thought that "all attempts to construct a national literature must end in abortions like the monster of Frankenstein." [90]

As she surveyed the field of American letters, Fuller found many monsters whose inflated reputations seemed to invite her intrepid criticism. Confronting that darling of American verse, Henry Wadsworth Longfellow, she called his work artificial and derivative; the poet of nature was unnatural and a mere celebrity.[91] American magazine verse and fiction, especially the works of "female scribblers," were "the paltriest offspring of the human brain." [92] Of that popular triumvirate—Irving, Cooper, and Bryant—she had little to say. In agreement with critics and the public, she said Bryant was America's foremost poet; although to her that meant very little since she found American poetry in a pitiful state. Cooper's greatest contribution was his evocation of nature, of a world irrevocably destroyed by the rapid settlement of the American continent. Irving's descriptive talents and his "genial" prose would have graced any epoch; his reputation was secure because, as she ambiguously noted, no one else wished to imitate or replace him. Wishing to encourage new talent instead of merely praising past accomplishments, Fuller admired Poe's work and wished that he would conduct deeper explorations of the mind and write a truly "metaphysical novel." [93] For her, even her favorite American writers were not romantic enough.

She found that this same basic criticism applied to history and philosophy as well as to imaginative literature. Few had achieved a synthesis of real and ideal. In history the work of Bancroft was superior to Prescott's, but neither man was truly a romantic historian, according to Fuller's criteria. Both failed to capture the essence, the inner life, of the cultures they described. She named Emerson and William E. Channing as her period's giants in philosophy and ethics. She found Channing, with his emphasis on human dignity and spirituality, so admirable that she called him a "godfather at the baptism of this country." Although the "Sage of Concord" had the same purity and dignity, his was a "very different mind." [94] He was a truly "profound thinker"—always an ambiguous compliment in her critical and personal lexicon of values.

From the perspective of New York and of her new audience, Emerson's popularity required explanation. She wrote that his subtle and pleasant style charmed even those who stood "stupefied before the thoughts themselves," admitting that most of his admirers belonged in the latter category. Finally, his work was too abstract. He "was the man of ideas, but not an ideal man." [95] His work lacked the sense of life that was crucial to her romantic sensibility, and she blamed his failure on New England. Intellectuals and women, and especially women intellectuals, were blighted by that region's conventional and restrictive social codes—by the "starch of convention" and the "ice of prejudice." [96] She testified, from personal experience, that no passionate temperaments could thrive there. All were stunted by a society that had reached "a perfection of minute scrutiny beyond what it ever was before in any age or place." [97] She found that New York, in contrast, was America's vital center. With its insistence on the concrete, its mistrust of purely speculative activity, New York had reinforced her old suspicions about New England, altered her perspective, and even simplified her prose, giving it a new directness and clarity.

New York, containing multitudes, even promised Fuller an ideal man. James Nathan seemed to be a man of culture, sensitivity, *and* passion—a Sir Philip Sidney in the flesh. Her friends, especially the Greeleys, did not share Margaret's enthusiasm for this ideal lover and friend. After meeting the famous Miss Fuller at a literary evening, Nathan escorted her to an exhibition of a plaster re-creation of the city of Jerusalem. They were soon involved in a clandestine affair, complete with trysts and ardent letters, that raged from February, 1845, until Nathan fled to Europe in June. More interested in what Fuller could do for his reputation than in her devotion, Nathan was a headhunter, not the kindred spirit whose sincerity, integrity, and passion Fuller thought matched her own. Envisioning theirs as that highest form of union, a quest for truth, Fuller was disappointed when Nathan failed to measure up to her personal and cultural ideal, her insistence that both people and nations should always "take the narrow, thorny path where Integrity leads." [98] Before she realized that he had strayed from this objective, and from her, she wrote to him beseeching him to be careful with the potentially destructive power he held over her, for she had a destiny as a woman: she was one of those "few in whose lot the meaning of the age is concentrated." [99] Demonstrating that she was chosen among women—or men—she continued with her work during the hectic months of their relationship. The next summer she too went to Europe, not in search of Nathan (who had married), but in search of the soul of that Old World she had long dreamed of visiting. Sailing with her benefactors, Marcus and Rebecca Spring, Margaret left America to begin another new life.

Greeley arranged for her to cover Europe for the readers of the *Tribune,* and she sent thirty-three dispatches back to her paper. After making the expected pilgrimages to rural England (Wordsworth country), London, Paris, and Rome, she wrote an assessment of Europe and its impact on an American. Illustrating her own thesis that "the American in Europe, if a thinking mind, can only become more American," she pronounced the Old World soulless, corrupt, and decadent and cast her allegiances and her principles with the Italian revolutionary movement—and, by implication, with all European and British democratic partisans.[100] Only when caste, class, and privileges were eliminated could England's cruel contrast between wealth and poverty be abolished. France, so full of talent yet so "shallow and glossy still" might then be regenerated; and Italy, fettered by a tyrannical Austria with "its royalty that represents nothing," was most symbolic of the "amazing" and "monstrous" failure that was modern Europe.[101]

From this European perspective she judged her countrymen in equally harsh terms. Americans were of three types— "servile," "conceited," and "thinking." Only the first type was utterly beyond redemption. Unlike the European aristocrats they wished to emulate, these "thick-skinned dandies" lacked the only virtue of breeding—"refinement." Traveling abroad merely to spend lavishly and indulge themselves, the "servile" Americans were "parasites," utterly despicable and thoroughly "shallow." "Conceited Americans," in their total rejection of European civilization, at least had an independent spirit. With a proper development—with "culture and thought"—they might come to represent that most superior American type—the romantic, "thinking" American, a skilled eclectic and cosmopolitan who, like Margaret Fuller, wished to transplant the best—and uncorrupted—fruits of the European experience to American soil.[102]

Margaret declared that she flourished upon Italian soil as she never had in America. She was sympathetic to Italian revolutionaries and they, in turn, seemed to appreciate her as a woman and as an intellectual. With Mazzini and his supporters, she felt herself become part of a vast drama of revolution and transcendence. At last she thought she had found a true community of thinkers engaged in a great cause. There, all hearts did beat to that iron string as they had not in Concord. Although she feared that she had come too late, that her life might be a failure, she looked forward to the years ahead to redeem her from that American intellectual life, which, she said, had forced her to "waste" her energy totally upon "abstractions."  [103]

She had not arrived too late, however, to find the right man—a man not given to abstractions, a zealous partisan of the revolution—the gentle Marchese Angelo Ossoli, ten years her junior. Margaret Fuller became his mistress, had his child, and finally consented to marry him shortly before they sailed for America. [104] Although she wrote paeans to the quiet joys of motherhood, Fuller's life as a mother was unusual. She lived dangerously, hiding her child in the mountain village of Reiti, nursing the wounded during the siege of Rome, and writing letters home—literally from the barricades—urging American support for Italy. She had begun what she considered her finest work—a history of the Italian revolution. This work, unfinished like her father's history of America, was lost at sea.

After their hopes for an independent Italy were destroyed, Margaret and her husband planned to take their son to America to seek a new life and to face what she called the "social inquisition" that awaited them. [105] Dreading both the voyage and their American arrival, she feared that the trip would end disastrously either way. Foundering in a storm on the reefs off Fire Island, New York, the ship *Elizabeth* broke up after twenty-four hours, on July 19, 1850. Refusing to be separated, Margaret and her husband stayed aboard and perished with the ship. Their son also drowned in the heavy seas when a steward made a vain attempt to carry him ashore.

Margaret Fuller had ardently wished to be remembered as a *woman* intellectual and, as if in deference to her wishes, the American press, the public, and her friends indulged in an often grotesque orgy of mythmaking after her death. Although many saw her as a strange and exotic feminine mutant, or as a two-headed calf, no one forgot that she was a woman. Margaret had criticized Mme de Staël for not being able to "forget the woman in the thought"; Margaret's public now forgot the thought in the woman, destroying her deliberate synthesis of intellect and femininity. Making her a celebrity, friends and foes alike ignored the terms by which she had constructed herself and her contribution to American critical thought. It was easier for everyone to think of her image instead of her ideas.

Covering every detail of the drowning, several papers described the scene as the literary gathering of the century. Everyone was there: Emerson and Thoreau reportedly mourned on the shore. New England issued many statements about the "American Corinne," forgetting that Fuller had rejected that heroine long ago. No one remembered that she had found most of the famous women of her time very disappointing and judged them harshly in the *Tribune*. Even her dramatic and somewhat awkward meeting in Paris with George Sand had not altered Fuller's opinion.[106] However admirable Sand was, in person and in prose, she was not self-reliant. She was a symbol of failure like Bettina von Arnim, whom Fuller had rejected in prose as severe as her judgment: "I did not value Bettina so much. She had not pride enough for me . . . I knew she would end in nothing." [107]

All foreign models had failed her, except one. Fuller had mentioned in *Woman in the Nineteenth Century* the Countess Emily Platter, an obscure heroine in "the last revolution in Poland," whose "dignity," "purity," and power were never compromised. Fuller had compared her to Joan of Arc: in their brief careers, both women "only did enough to verify their credentials" and then died.[108]

Margaret Fuller, too, left a brilliant and inconclusive record. Her life was a symbol of intellectual growth and energy, uncertainty, instability, and diversity. The life of the mind that she led illustrated all the romantic criteria she cherished; it symbolized a process of growth, forever unfinished, as diverse as nature's. She wanted to be a woman of ideas and an ideal woman, and she had worked all her life to construct herself as a work of romantic art. She knew that she contained multitudes of selves that would always confound her interpreters, and that she defied analogy.[109] That was her purpose. Seeing herself as a homeless "pilgrim and sojourner on earth," she realized that serenity and security were not for her.[110] Since she was a woman and a romantic she was drawn into that forest of contradictions from which only the greatest virtuoso might wrest a sense of unity—the debate on femininity and intellect. This was her tragedy. The controversy over the mind of woman, and the compromises worked out in it, reflected a cultural anxiety that she absorbed, being a woman in the nineteenth century. Since she was also working outside accepted syntheses of intellect and femininity, she always doubted both her femininity and her intellectual worth—she was forced to confirm them afresh every day. Her courage always kept pace with this sense of inferiority; they were the components of her dual nature. No wonder she found women who proved themselves and then disappeared so appealing. That was the best way to go down in history.

# (3)

# Women's
# History and Feminist Thought
## Romantic Discoveries and Transformations

*You ask me if I have not sanguine hopes of success. My dear friend, I have no sanguine hopes, about anything.*

—Lydia Maria Child

*Books are needed because of our defects and limitations. . . . We are fast exhausting old ideas, and a new revelation must come. Old thought has been discussed and rendered frivolous, near to triteness. God will give us the new.*

—Elizabeth Oakes Smith

*The fear that a woman may deviate the slightest from conventionalism in any way, has become a nervous disease with the public. Indeed, so little is she trusted as a creation, that one would think she were made marvelously beautiful, and endowed with gifts of thought and emotion only for the purpose of endangering her safety–a sort of spiritual locomotive with no check-wheel, a rare piece of porcelain, to be handled gingerly–in fact, a creature with no conservative elements within herself, but left expressly thus, that man might supply them, and lead and guide, and coerce and cajole her, as it please him best.*

—Elizabeth Oakes Smith

Elizabeth Oakes Smith
*The Schlesinger Library, Radcliffe College*

Elizabeth Ellet (below left)
*The Schlesinger Library, Radcliffe College*

Lydia Maria Child (below right)
*The Schlesinger Library, Radcliffe College*

## 1. Intellectual and Social Origins

In eighteenth-century America, Abigail Adams urged her husband to "remember the ladies": [1] neither John Adams nor any other contemporary male statesman or historian, however, heeded her warning. They shared neither her concern with the legal rights of women nor her awareness of women's role in history. For that matter, much the same criticism may be made of eighteenth-century female historians. Adams' contemporary, Mercy Otis Warren, did not mention women in her *History of the American Revolution* and, in fact, paid her homage to the male establishment with a demeaning explanation of her own conduct in assuming the role of historian, arguing that while those more qualified to write (men) were caught up in war and later in constructing the new Republic, a woman might interpret events for posterity, lest they be lost to history. Historian Hannah Adams even further restricted her proper concern, insisting that she was merely a "modest compiler, as befits a true woman." [2] She left the contributions of women out of her histories of religion, New England, and the Jewish people. Clearly, both Warren and Hannah Adams were self-conscious about their own roles as female historians, and their defensiveness reveals somewhat why each lacked either, or both, a feminist consciousness and an awareness of women as serious subjects for historical work.

For these women, "true woman" still existed outside that "Great Chain of Being" where men made history, just as they properly belonged on the sidelines of the intellectual fray—observing and recording masculine deeds from the safety of the "woman's sphere" for future masculine historical analysis and synthesis.

Beginning in the 1830s, American intellectual women, as if in belated response to Abigail Adams, began to resurrect and place in a historical sequence the memory and deeds of great women. No doubt their data, like Margaret Fuller's, were sometimes consciously arranged to provide a theoretical framework that extended and intensified the feminist consciousness emerging during this decade; yet women's history and feminist thought were by no means synonymous in the minds and works of the major contributors to each subject. More often, a complex and sometimes incompatible relationship existed between the two in the period before the Civil War—a consequence of their diverse origins and contrasting attitudes.

Both women's history and feminist thought, whether synthesized or carefully separated, began to attract the attention of women intellectuals in the pre-Civil War period because of these subjects' seeming inoffensiveness. They answered the question: What kinds of intellectual activities could women engage in without being overcome by self-consciousness and the need to rationalize their work so elaborately that thinking itself was impossibly encumbered? Both women's history and feminism seemed, almost by definition, part of "woman's sphere." No masculine traditions or conventions stood in the way of women who wished to enter these fields of thought and action. Indeed, who else but women could possibly be interested in either subject? Beneath the dignity of men's attention lay these unexplored regions—countries of the mind that women could cultivate on their own terms.

The romantic revolution was crucially important in directing women to these two particular areas and in determining their approach. The historicist impulse generated by romanticism [3]—that passion to investigate and unveil the unique spirit of each and every culture, ancient and modern—encouraged women historians to unearth the essence of that mysterious and invisible essence, woman herself, and to collect all possible data, no matter how obscure, and to wrest from that material the essence of the female experience. Without the influence of romanticism, women might not have discovered or explored the female past, present, or future; or, if they had, both the nature of their historical quest and their accomplishments might have been very different. The unmistakable debt Margaret Fuller owed to romantic thought was owed as well by other major contributors to women's history before the Civil War.

The romantic vocabulary also suggested new ways to think

about women—as unique individuals whose lives were also to be interpreted as expressions of the cultures they represented. The favored concept of diversity was the key to woman's record, as it was to the study of nature and nations, and it also suggested that women, regardless of individual and cultural differences, could still be unique as a class. Because each nation—and each individual—had an essence all its own, all women could be grouped together on the basis of their exclusively female characteristics. Defining these qualities was a source of difficulty and disagreement, and a pretext for discussion for all Americans who thought about women. This was especially so for both historians of women and feminists who, while reflecting this cultural concern, attempted to add new symbols and arguments to the American debate on the "woman question."

This search for female uniqueness tempted others besides Margaret Fuller to construct a "feminine mystique." [4] "Woman thought," wrote the feminist Elizabeth Oakes Smith in 1851, was a power never recognized nor correctly analyzed, for men had always defined woman's nature. [5] And no wonder women had accepted their findings, since the "lions have written all the books." Women must reject all such masculine creations, Smith urged; only then could they begin to search for the "laws" of their own being and discover "their own individuality—their own singleness of thought." When investigated and analyzed by women, the power and the glory of "woman thought" would be revealed to all the world as a basis not only for female intellectual and social action but for the larger task of world redemption.

To invoke this abstraction was a favorite technique employed by feminists and historians in search of a new female ideal. Historical perspective and comparison could then be used to give "woman power" a sense of particularity and concreteness. History served all these thinkers well, for, without the contexts and parallels it offered, their symbolic descriptions of women's nature would have sounded very familiar— like Mme de Staël describing Corinne's essentially feminine genius or Margaret Fuller discoursing upon woman's intuitive, "electrical" mind. History was indeed indispensable; without it the romantic vocabulary was often indistinguishable from the language and values of the "cult of true womanhood." Even with history, unfortunately, many of these feminist constructs often resembled only too closely those older feminine ideals that women thinkers were attempting to reject or refashion into more vital symbols of womanhood.

Regardless of the difficulties involved in creating new ideals of womanhood and the often contrasting attitudes of feminists and historians of women, both groups invoked similar symbols in their works, and even those who bitterly opposed the feminist movement implicitly accepted feminist portraits of a "new woman." The ideal woman drawn by Elizabeth Oakes Smith was a symbol of vitality, a symbol equally attractive to both feminists and "separatist" historians of women:

> Now the true full woman must be more enlarged, more reflective, contemplative, and more loving even. Her tenderness has a broader field, even as her thoughts have; she is capable of more; she feels the stirring of more within herself, and feels a stirring to action too—for all power is vital, and wherever it may be lodged, it will out at some time.[6]

Thus, echoing Mme de Staël's reflections on the nature of power, Smith had limned her new ideal: she called it "the woman of intellect."[7]

Apart from these shared assumptions, symbols, and strategies derived from romantic thought, women's history and feminism had distinct social origins. After American women held the world's first women's rights convention in 1848, their subsequent meetings and strategies, successes and failures, were noted by British and European observers throughout the nineteenth century. Several aspects of the female experience in mid-century America help explain why a small band of educated, middle-class women thought group action would instill a feminist consciousness in ever larger numbers of American women and effect reforms necessary to improve women's condition.

The rhetoric of intellectual and social equality—and all other aspects of the Jacksonian Persuasion—seemed to include women, even to invite their active participation in the rejuvenation of American society. But if one looked closely at the changing patterns of family life and female roles, the ideology of equality contained a bitter paradox: while male opportunities were expanding, female opportunities were shrinking. American women were losing rights they had once enjoyed in that simpler, agrarian world idealized in Jacksonian rhetoric. In the eighteenth century, American women had played a great variety of social roles, both within and without the home, that in the nineteenth century were no longer considered part of woman's domain.[8] The wife of that culture hero, the "yeoman farmer," had worked hard, yet her role could confer dignity and a sense of both equality and community. Although many of her tasks might be classified by sex, they were not devalued as "woman's work," for her duties were necessary to the well-being of her family and its future. Outside the family circle, women had once acted as lawyers ("attorneys-in-fact"), midwives, and small businesswomen selling almost everything, not just feminine articles. By mid-century these female types had become extinct.[9]

Urbanization, industrialization, and the professionalization of activities once performed by women were responsible for the altered pattern of family life and female duties. Many traditionally feminine duties were, by mid-century, being performed in factories. These industries created a new class of female laborers and a distinct "working class" woman whose life and status bore little resemblance to those of more fortunate women. While social status prohibited the latter from doing wage work in the new cottage industries and sealed her off from that female world of mill and factory, the professional training and certification becoming essential for work in medicine, law, and higher education denied her access to these fields. Below the formidable heights of the professions were the territories still open to her—nursing and teaching. Thus, the "middle-class" American woman was caught in the midst of a status revolution: in direct and ironic contrast to tenets of equality and increased opportunity voiced by Jacksonian America, her opportunities were dwindling.

As female opportunities for wider social action shrank, the rhetoric of domesticity expanded, as if in compensation, to enhance the importance of "woman's sphere." The domestic idea, and the family structure it reflected, however, were relatively new historical phenomena just attaining their full strength in the mid-nineteenth century. Consequently, although the domestic ideal emphasized community and harmony between the sexes within the family, it, in fact, fostered a sense of isolation and sexual segregation, which encouraged women to think of themselves as a class apart.[10] These women, faced with increased demands to assert "true femininity," now as sublime guardians of a "child-centered universe," instead formed a depressed class, often experiencing a sense of disorientation, if not deprivation. These new psychic stresses within the family are now recognized as the tensions associated with the birth of the modern "nuclear family." [11]

The emergence of American feminism has been attributed, in part, to the pressures brought about by this structural transformation of family life.[12] But although this change created a class of potential converts to the feminist persuasion, in order for that conversion to actually occur, these women had to be made explicitly aware of their own paradoxical position and then exposed to the feminist alternative. The specific experiences of American women in the reformist activities that occupied Jacksonian America served as the needed catalyst. While organizing female antislavery societies and exercising their sole political right, the right to petition, as a protest against slavery; while listening to foreigners like Frances Wright give lectures on scandalous subjects—feminism and free love (!) and the Grimké sisters' eloquent denunciations of slavery and fervid support of feminism—at a time when a woman speaking on a public platform was shocking in itself; while hearing of, and sometimes visiting, strange communities devoted to exploring alternatives to traditional social structures and to the creation of ideal societies, American women simultaneously exposed themselves to feminist alternatives and fortified themselves for the battles that were subsequently to support an indigenous American feminist movement.

From these experiences the women who would later organize the American feminist movement learned the techniques of organizing for reform, activities that fostered a sense of solidarity with other women united for a common purpose and convinced that their goals could be achieved. The first female public speakers served as models for American feminists, encouraging them to assume public, and unpopular, stances. Both utopian communitarian experiments and the Jacksonian emphasis upon equal opportunity influenced American feminists to develop a plastic social vision, to view America as a malleable culture that might turn out in innumerable ways—a country of the future, where woman might yet blossom, once all artificial restrictions upon her growth were removed. These presently existing disabilities and discriminatory practices became for American feminists what the "Monster Bank" symbolized to Andrew Jackson—evidence of the corruption of America by aristocratic practices of exclusion and domination.

The emergence of a distinct feminist consciousness and of organizations designed to spread it throughout America was accelerated in particular by the lessons women learned in abolitionist circles. In speaking against slavery the Grimké sisters soon saw parallels between the condition of slaves and that of women. The clerical denunciation of Sarah Grimké—the famous "Pastoral Letter" issued by a group of Protestant ministers who denied that Christian women could act as public lecturers—merely deepened her commitment to feminism, for she had already been delivering women's rights lectures and preparing a book based upon them before the ministers' attack. Although she wrote the first detailed feminist argument published by an American, *Letters on the Equality of the Sexes and the Condition of Women* (1838), and despite the discrimination she had suffered as a woman abolitionist, Sarah Grimké did not direct herself toward organizing women around the issue.[13] In 1841 a plan for affirmative and widespread social action was originated by Lucretia Mott and Elizabeth Cady

Stanton. After experiencing their own great awakening at the World's Anti-Slavery Conference in London, they concluded that the time had come for women to organize and to act upon their own behalf.

Stanton became the chief intellectual architect of American feminism; and hers remains the most vividly rendered account of the London experience, for it was essentially her story—and a very American tale. In one of her many contributions to the gargantuan project she helped initiate and execute—the five-volume *History of Woman Suffrage*—Stanton wrote of the origins of American feminism. Even twenty years later, the London incident had not lost its flavor or sense of immediacy; to write of it in the 1880s was to relive it and, by presenting that experience ironically, to invite her readers to share it.

After considerable debate in America, Garrisonian abolitionists had decided to send female delegates to the World's Anti-Slavery Conference. When they arrived, the convention-at-large immediately rejected their credentials, and for the next five days the women delegates sat in silence in the gallery, listening to endless orations upon the essential humanity of the Negro and the inhumanity of slavery. Although William Lloyd Garrison joined the women to protest their treatment, thus forfeiting his right to speak to the convention, Stanton's husband of only two weeks kept his seat down below. Watching and listening to the proceedings, his bride concluded that none of the participants was even remotely aware that women were part of the human race.[14]

The British women in attendance seemed somewhat dismayed at the proceedings too; but Stanton thought that they, being British, would just ruminate endlessly upon the problem without doing anything about it. As an American, she planned to act immediately; American men sorely needed "educating" upon the subject of women, and American women should call a convention to consider all aspects of woman's inferior condition and possible solutions to her plight.[15]

Seven years later she found time away from her considerable domestic responsibilities to plan that first meeting in Seneca Falls—her home since shortly after marriage. There her experiences as a wife and mother had intensified her commitment to feminism; in that small rural community, isolated from all forms of the social and intellectual stimulation and companionship she had known and relished, Stanton realized that total domesticity was a form of slavery which had no relation to the sublime rhetoric of "true womanhood." [16]

Although she could personally equate domesticity with slavery, her London experience had influenced her to regard the interests of slaves and women and the securing of rights for both groups as necessarily separate enterprises. Sitting in the balcony in London so surprised even one already acutely aware of injustice to women that, in a shock of recognition, Stanton had severed all ties between women and slaves, between reforms in their behalf, just as her connections had been severed from that august body of reformers assembled to protest against slavery who had denied her the right to participate in their protest. When a collection of what she described as the world's most educated humanitarians were incapable of granting human rights to women, the time had come for women to work for themselves. Indeed, who else was left to speak out against their own "oppression" except women?

In contrast to the almost linear progression of American feminism's social origins, those of women's history were as diverse as the interests, temperaments, and talents of individual women who wrote about it. Like many feminists, Lydia Maria Child, the first American intellectual to record women's history, was deeply committed to abolitionism, her intellectual contributions to that cause rank her with the most important Americans engaged in antislavery work. However, just as Stanton came to view feminism and abolitionism as separate concerns, Child kept her work in women's history and in abolitionism carefully distinct; moreover, she remained aloof from the feminist movement until the 1870s and never equated women's history with women's rights in her own writings.

Neither did the period's most industrious historian of the American woman, Elizabeth Ellet—a rabid antifeminist who viewed the movement as a crime against nature. Yet apart from several asides to her readers condemning the feminists, Ellet's work often read like a feminist interpretation of history.

As a historian she never wavered in her commitment to re-create the past without distortion; when women's record demonstrated what she characterized as oppression and discrimination, Ellet did not spare her readers these "facts." Like her, Child officially condemned the women's rights movement, although in a much milder fashion; yet her work reveals a developing feminist consciousness and her letters illustrate her covert alliance with those whom she sometimes termed foolish extremists.

Regardless of their ambiguous and overtly hostile relationship to feminism, these two historians compiled data most useful to feminist thought. The data they amassed and interpreted also made the female past accessible to general audiences, perplexed and concerned with the nature and social role of women and eager to read interpretations of each. Ellet and Child showed their readers that women did have a history, a complex and serious story worthy of attention and respect. A closer look at their lives and works reveals how and why these two women, whose temperaments were so vastly different, began to collect—to construct and reconstruct—a usable past for women.

Following in the tradition of Margaret Fuller, Elizabeth Oakes Smith, on the other hand, took women's past and transformed it into a theoretical framework for the feminist persuasion—a step neither Ellet nor Child could take. The work of these three intellectuals represents the unique contributions American women made to intellectual history before the Civil War: In the process of thinking about women they made it a more sophisticated and problematic undertaking, and generated a dialectic between the subjects of women's history and women's rights from which both feminists and antifeminists drew insights and inspiration.

## 2. Lydia Maria Child:
*The Many Worlds of Women and an Intellectual's Dilemma*

As a child in Medford, Massachusetts, during the first decade of the nineteenth century, Lydia Maria Francis often saw her neighbors gawking at the aging scholar, Hannah Adams—pointing her out as the village eccentric. The citizens of Medford were fond of citing Adams as a most graphic example of how learning could ruin a woman, and the young Maria, wanting above all to become a "true woman," did not wish to emulate Hannah Adams in any fashion. If that harmless old woman could not take a walk around town without being ridiculed as a "learned woman," it was obvious that women must be very cautious about the kind of knowledge they acquired and the way they chose to display it.[17]

Yet, in her own intellectual career, Lydia Maria Child was drawn to the same subjects Hannah Adams had chosen—the history of religions and the nature of New England's past—and as a historian she too insisted that she was, in Hannah Adams's words, merely a "modest compiler, as befits a true woman." Child's first work was a historical romance concerning the relationship between Puritan and Indian culture in early New England. Predating James Fenimore Cooper's works on these themes, *Hobomok*, finished in six weeks and signed "by an American," was an immediate success; its nineteen-year-old author became a celebrity—the toast of Boston and Cambridge literati. Her fears allayed—everyone admired her work, no one branded her a female pedant—she soon gained a large audience for each successive work. She also acquired a husband.

David Lee Child, a young lawyer and ardent abolitionist, was not what the Francis family considered an ideal husband. Ignoring their objections, Lydia Maria accepted his proposal and entered domestic life with enthusiasm, determined to show her family that even without money their marriage would be an ideal union. In 1829 she offered her experience to the public in the best-selling *Frugal Housewife*, from which one could learn how to live simply, wholesomely, and rather elegantly on practically no income. The author soon discovered that this was to be a lifelong task for her—that she would have to be continually frugal with the money she earned to forestall bankruptcy. Her precarious financial status made it impossible to live up to that ideal of domesticity she cherished: she could never be sure that any house she so carefully

made a home would be hers for long.[18] She relied upon her
wedding gifts to transform even the rudest dwelling into a
place of genteel charm—until David sold them without con-
sulting her.[19] Regardless of such lapses, he was revered by his
wife as a delightful husband and intellectual companion.

Marriage also brought out the basic conflict of her intellectual life. As a member of her brother's household in Cambridge, she had been within the inner circle of New England
transcendentalism. Nourished on romanticism's basic texts in
her brother's extensive library, in conversations with his
friends, and in her close relationship with Margaret Fuller,
Child had delighted in purely abstract intellectual pursuits;
her philosophical and literary investigations had made her
value an aesthetic life above all intellectual stances. Marriage
drew her into the thick of abolitionist agitation. David Child
was a contributor to William Lloyd Garrison's *Liberator* and
later editor of the *National Anti-Slavery Standard*—a post that
his wife would also occupy. To this abolitionist circle her original commitment to a contemplative life was immoral: intellectuals must be activists when confronted with pressing issues
and social evils like slavery.

Unlike Fuller, who experienced and attempted to resolve
similar conflicts between a life of action and one of contemplation, yet remained aloof from abolitionist circles, Child found
that she had literally married that cause. Perplexed by the
arguments she heard and read every day—the compelling and
eloquent logic of Garrison and her husband—caught between
conflicting intellectual and social orientations and values,
Child attempted to ignore the question her dilemma raised:
What kind of intellectual life would be virtuous for anyone
confronted with current social problems and appropriate for a
"true woman" as well? Thinking about women was temporarily more comforting and certainly more profitable; *A Mother's
Book* (1831), another domestic manual, and *The Little Girl's
Own Book* (1831), a book of games for girls, testified to her
growing popularity as a foremost arbiter of traditional femininity. It seemed as if the young woman who had studied Kant
and Mme de Staël with Margaret Fuller had turned her back

upon them and had also declined to follow her husband into abolitionist agitation.

Two years later Lydia Maria Child wrote not another domestic guide but the first antislavery volume to be published in America. Her *Appeal in Behalf of that Class of Americans Called Africans* (1833) was a cogently reasoned and carefully documented attack on slavery, so convincing that it was responsible for drawing many Americans—among them, Wendell Phillips, William Ellery Channing, Charles Sumner, and Thomas Wentworth Higginson—into abolitionist ranks. It was, in addition, an early work in black history for it contained sections on African customs and a history of slavery and its impact on American culture.

Literary Boston was stunned by the *Appeal*. The only woman allowed to enter the Boston Athenaeum had researched and written this shocking book there, and Child's passport to culture and respectability was soon revoked. Although David Child's editorials protesting Andrew Jackson's treatment of the Cherokee Indians had, in the late 1820s, influenced his wife to research and publish a brief history of the Indians in New England—*The First Settlers of New England*—it was Garrison who finally converted her to the antislavery position. Like Stanton's experience in London, Child's meeting with Garrison left an indelible memory; it was the event that transformed her life. "Old dreams vanished, old associations departed, and all things became new," she wrote, when he "got hold of the strings of my conscience and pulled me into reforms . . . . " [20]

The same year in which the *Appeal* was published, Child began to write women's history, publishing the first of a projected five-volume series to be entitled *The Ladies' Family Library*. Innocently enough, the first title was *Good Wives*, a compendium of "true women" behind men great and small. Such a reaffirmation of feminine domesticity, coming in the same year as the *Appeal*, did nothing to protect Child from the opprobrium of old friends and her large reading public. The sales of her books dropped as quickly as did her social prestige. Although she probably knew that *Good Wives* could not save her

from criticism, her venture into women's history comple-
mented her decision to become a public and publishing abolitionist. Writing and thinking about women's history began to
serve as a kind of mental compass that kept Child from losing
her balance as she moved into the dangerous world of reform.

As an uncompromising abolitionist, Child always gave that
cause priority over all other needed reforms, including wom-
en's rights. For her it was impossible to equate the plight of
slaves with that of women; thinking perhaps only of women
in her own situation, she considered "woman's sphere," regardless of how narrow and restrictive it might be, a paradise
compared to the world of slavery. Child's conception of women's history and its function in her own intellectual life further clarify why she refused to make parallels between slaves
and women or to assume an active feminist role. In search of a
haven from calamity and change, Child hoped to find in the
history of women a refuge from the abolitionist controversy in
which she had become so thoroughly embroiled.

At first her motives and her ideals resembled Sarah Hale's:
both wished to find in history irrefutable evidence of "true
womanhood." If life afforded so few examples, surely history
contained multitudes that she could re-create, giving life to
that favorite abstraction—ideal femininity. In its entirety,
Child foresaw *The Ladies' Family Library* as a private academy
for the training of "true women," as both symbol and elabora-
tion of that world elsewhere—"woman's sphere." The series of
books would always be there, on the shelf, no matter how unstable and uncertain life itself might be.

As Child became more deeply engaged with her material,
the nature of the series began to change. Her romantic orientation, her intellectual curiosity and vitality, and her admiration
for courageous and gallant spirits, regardless of their "true
femininity," led her far afield from *Good Wives* to the panoramic *History of Women in All Ages and Nations* and onward to
a composite biography of Mme de Staël and Pauline Roland.
At this significant point the publishers' dwindling capital
forced them to cancel the rest of the series. Its shifting empha-

sis, from woman playing her traditional role to woman as individual, reflects the author's changing conception of women and their history. Ransacking history for female symbols of uniformity she had, in a characteristically romantic fashion, found diversity instead.

The *History of Women in All Ages and Nations* was a celebration of that diversity, and was a personal and cultural voyage of self-discovery for Lydia Maria Child. Determined to include all women everywhere, she presented Romans and Russians, Athenians and Austrians, Spartans, Swedes, and Swiss—even Walachians and South Sea Islanders. Her summaries of the roles women had assumed in each culture demonstrated a tolerance for alien customs, an ability to understand the mores of different cultures without judging them harshly—a broad intellectual perspective that is entirely absent in the 950 pages of Sarah Hale's *Woman's Record,* published sixteen years later. Although Hale did include some women of whom she strongly disapproved, her general tactic was to leave out those—her American contemporaries in particular—who did not conform to her standard of ideal femininity. Child, with a romantic intellectual's panoramic vision, wished to include everything about the female experience. Hoping that some pattern of unity might emerge no matter how much data she collected, Child turned to the American woman and placed her within a cross-cultural perspective.

The future of the American woman and the outcome of the American experiment each seemed as uncertain for Lydia Maria Child as they had for Margaret Fuller. Child concluded that only if virtue triumphed would America form a distinctive and distinguished culture, and her interpretations of the changing nature of American society made the fate of virtue, of the American woman, and of the Republic, seem highly problematic. Fearing that wealth and luxury were transforming America, she astutely described an emerging class structure in which highest prestige was conferred upon the woman of leisure. For one who considered work beneficial to all, and especially to women, the declining value of "active industry"—increasingly considered a "bar to gentility"—implied a loss of virtue and the potential failure of the American experiment.[21]

Urbanization merely deepened her pessimism: America's rapidly growing cities, especially New York City, were nurturers of vice and corruption. They contained decadent women of wealth and leisure as sexually corrupt as European courtesans, but Child assured her readers—and herself—that they would never outnumber their foreign counterparts. After all, she noted, American women were often characterized, even defined, by their prudery, and she gladly accepted that criticism as a virtue—within the limits of decorum. To protest *too* much was in her opinion both vulgar and boring.

Child was acutely aware of the female status-revolution around her and its implications for the American woman. No matter how bleak the future of woman's work might seem, however, most people were still engaged in honest toil—a fact that gave her some comfort and the hope that the trends she saw might yet be reversed. Finally, in summing up the American woman, Child described her as without direct political influence; even so, American women had more "influence and freedom" than women anywhere else.[22]

The history of intellectual women, their past and potential roles and contributions, was a different story—much more ambiguous and depressing than that of American women in general. The only hope for an intellectual woman lay in the future, and the march of democracy would determine her fate. For Child, as for Margaret Fuller, even the greatest female intellect of all, Mme de Staël, was tainted by her "artificial" nature, and Child despised artifice in any form. Paris was, according to a popular saying, where Bostonians went when they died, she once wrote a friend; what a perfect place for the Boston "aristocracy," where even the flowers were "artificial!"[23] That Parisian milieu had ruined Mme de Staël; regardless of her democratic principles, she had been corrupted by the aristocracy she rejected.

In contrast to such an age of "artifice," Child saw the nineteenth century as an age of transformation in which the image of the intellectual woman might be altered and enhanced. For Child, the diffusion of knowledge and spirit of practicality that accompanied it were the distinguishing characteristics of her own era.[24] Now that knowledge was no longer the property of the elite, women might be learned without pedantry—a trait exclusive to aristocrats and "bluestockings," both of whom she regarded with equal loathing and contempt. Even if they symbolized this new age, men still regarded learned women with disdain and suspicion, she observed, yet at least one could hope that a spirit of tolerance might increase as men witnessed the lives, practical and true, of contemporary women thinkers. In any case, Lord Byron had, in Child's opinion, said it all, and she quoted him with enthusiasm: "I care not how blue a woman's stockings are if her skirts are long enough to cover them." [25] Living out that motto, however, did not entail wearing a mask of feminine passivity, for Lydia Maria Child sealed her letters with the words, "While I live I'll crow." [26]

Child regretted that lives of "true women," distinguished by a total allegiance to that ideal of womanhood supposedly so valued by society, never seemed quite worthy of the historian's attention. The long garments of that role had made women invisible: the quiet "domestic virtues" were always eclipsed by violence, discord, and the deeds of male heroes. Even when women had acted bravely according to masculine standards—Child was surprised how courageous they had been in all epochs—their deeds were seldom recorded.

Frustrated by the scarcity of material on women's social history, and romantically attracted to exotic and unusual personalities, she returned to the fascinating Mme de Staël, publishing her portrait together with a short life of another prominent figure in the French Revolution, Pauline Roland. Her interpretations of these extraordinary women and the social upheaval Child found so terrifying were carefully addressed to her audience. Framed as she wished American women to view them, her portraits of Mme de Staël and Roland reveal, in addition, her view of her own role as a historian of women. She would play Virgil to the Dantes of her generation—women lost in the maze of the female past and confused by the present who wished to understand their relation to the more complex and corrupt civilization of the Old World. In this book Child would lead them without harm through the inferno of revolutionary France. There, American women could meet two spirits from whom they might learn much, including the meaning of being an American and a woman—and the dangers of being an intellectual woman.

"Abandon hope all ye who enter the halls of genius, especially if you are female" was the clearest message the departed had given the historian to bring to women in the nineteenth century. Child called the life of Mme de Staël "a long continued and brilliant triumph" so far removed from "the ordinary lot of mortals" that any sense of identification with such a personality—with the "vividness of her fame"—was impossible for other women.[27] That was just as well, Child concluded, for Mme de Staël had warned other women, even her own daughter, not to follow her example. Her life was an agony of suffering, from the "envy and evil feelings which always darken the bright path of genius"—especially of a female genius, who would pay a greater price than a man if she refused to "submit to the opinions of the world." Speaking to all American women, Child emphasized that "none of us would wish such a destiny for a sister, or a child."[28]

Pauline Roland, the subject of Child's second biography, also felt it futile for women to assume autonomous and public intellectual stances. Child reargued Roland's position on the subject: the very choice of an intellectual life would alienate the intellectual woman from both men and women, yet her works and her life would always be judged by sexual criteria. Excellence, above all, would not be tolerated. If critics found it impossible to discredit the quality of her work they would try to pronounce it derivative; if these tactics failed, defects of character, real or imagined, could be exposed. Then, a woman thinker would find herself in a curious state of equilibrium: her intellectual excellence would be "fully counterbalanced by the publicity given to her defects."[29]

Child found Pauline Roland a more accessible and congenial

subject than Mme de Staël, for she had been a "good wife," one who had defined her own intellectual identity in relation to her *philosophe* husband's, who had worked with him on the infamous *Encyclopedie*—who had even followed him to the guillotine. In contrast, Mme de Staël's autonomy and her brilliance were frightening; she had been, Child concluded, a woman of "extremes" whose life was marred by "excesses." [30] Unlike Sarah Hale, however, Child still found her admirable for her "expansive freedom," her "mighty energy of soul, which never found room enough in this small world of ours." And, most important, she was not an evil woman: even her faults sprang, like a Greek hero's, from "the excess of something good."

These judgments provided Child with a certain distance from her subject, essential not only to being, as she put it, an "impartial biographer," but to fulfilling a psychological imperative as well. By implicitly convincing herself and her countrywomen not to be intimidated, not to feel inferior to the splendid Mme de Staël, Child could not only avert her eyes from this blinding image but she could avoid comparing her own work with Mme de Staël's—and thus competing with the woman she had called the greatest female mind in history.

Lydia Maria Child also needed to insulate herself and her work from the most brilliant women of her own generation in order to continue her intellectual career. Reading Elizabeth Barrett Browning's *Aurora Leigh* had made her feel so intellectually inadequate that she feared she might never be able to write again; although she insisted that such unquestionable proof of female genius raised her spirits and the world's opinion of women, it lowered her own self-esteem as an intellectual. [31]

Comparing herself to Margaret Fuller was equally unnerving and debilitating. Freely admitting her own shortcomings in a letter to Margaret, Child praised and criticized the newly published *Woman in the Nineteenth Century*, revealing her own strategy of intellectual survival among the giants. Blaming her own shortcomings—"I have no critical skill, and you have much"—upon what she always considered a scanty and superficial education, she thought Margaret's book was flawed by too much learning: "It may be the mere habit of elaborateness; but it has the appearance of effort. The stream is abundant and beautiful; but it always seems to be *pumped,* rather than to *flow.*" To Fuller, who wanted above all for her thought to "flow" and knew how rarely she succeeded, such criticism probably hurt; it seemed aimed with deadly accuracy at her weakest point. Child admitted that she had often envied such thorough learning as Margaret's, but it was too late now to woo those muses they had once courted together. Her letter implied that her limitation was a virtue after all: she would write effortlessly, unencumbered by that great weight of knowledge under which Margaret—and her prose—always strained. And she did. Child also found it amusing to disguise her own intellectuality: while Margaret read on and on through the seasons, she had been merely "listening to the grass grow." [32]

In her letter Child mentioned rather whimsically that a change in intellectual style would also entail a loss of identity: "If I were now to attempt to be something other than I am, I should be neither one thing nor the other." [33] This was Child's greatest fear. Only a will to believe could stave off the depression and sense of intellectual and social disorientation that constantly threatened to overwhelm her. At any moment she might plunge into the "dark and comfortless regions of utter skepticism," as Mme Roland had when she embraced what Child called the "wild and wicked systems, which the French dignified with the title of Philosophy." [34]

As a Unitarian, Child had absorbed those deistic principles in a form so mild and diluted that when she discovered romantic thought the Unitarian church could not hold her. And, like so many of her contemporaries who shared this experience, she had great difficulty in maintaining affiliations with any religious institution. Always in search of a church she could join with conviction, Child never found one. Attempting to retain some semblance of religious faith, she refused to read works such as Harriet Martineau's or to meet the visiting Englishwoman, who wanted to discuss American abolitionists with her and was most disappointed at Child's "disinclination" to be introduced.[35] Such confrontations were too dangerous for one already in a state of almost cosmic uncertainty: "To put the soul on *such* a track is like sending a bird out into the long cold storm. Who can be sure that it will come back to the Ark with an olive-branch in its mouth?"[36]

Her lack of religious conviction, she reasoned, only increased her "horror of [religious] infidelity" and proved that her faith had never been strong if it could vanish so easily.[37] Determined that no one except her most intimate friends would know of her ambivalent and "peculiarly isolated" spiritual stance, she wore a public mask and called it a "crystal heart" where no confusion reigned.[38] She also reserved her sufferings as a woman for her friends' ears only.

Although life, especially life in America, was "fragmentary" and "disjointed," being female had increased her sense of dislocation; her sex made it extremely difficult to find a "position in life" as men could.[39] Child placed her own life within a historical context, recognizing that her personal dilemmas as a woman and an intellectual were cultural dilemmas as well. She saw herself as a small figure lost in a vast intellectual and social transformation—"everywhere, the old lines of thought seem to be undergoing a process of decomposition, and entering into new combinations."[40]

Woman's history was a ballast against chaos and skepticism, a refuge from the ominous signs she continually reported in other work and in correspondence; it provided the sense of continuity lacking in American culture and in the life of the female intellectual, haunted by uncertainty and ambivalent about everything—especially herself. For these reasons she could not endorse a life of the mind as a viable option for women. Neither past nor future warranted optimism—"I have no sanguine hopes about anything"[41]—and women's history and her own life demonstrated that a "stoical endurance" was the best stance, especially for a woman thinker.[42]

Unlike Margaret Fuller or other flamboyant intellectuals she analyzed, Child found any form of publicity more and more distasteful as she grew older. Caught between conflicting im-

pulses like so many intellectuals of her generation, she loved
solitude, yet felt guilty if she did not participate in the reform
whose morality she could not deny. Drawn into the abolitionist struggle, she hated political strife and narrow-mindedness
of both reformers and politicians.[43] Distrusting both abstract
thought and social activism—poised between these intellectual
stances—she lacked the conviction to present herself or the
women she found in history as vivid symbols of what Smith
had called the "new woman," the "woman of intellect." One
who was, in her own words, "afloat on an endless sea, without rudder or compass" could hardly encourage others to follow her example.[44]

Instead of offering herself as a symbol of female achievement or endorsing an intellectual life for women, Lydia Maria
Child gave her readers *The Ladies' Family Library*, as unfinished and fragmented as her own life, in which they could
read about the great varieties of female experience. Such data
gave women a usable past; it provided evidence of their existence and a means of identification with their history. A tragic
sense of loss permeated that past, for life meant change and
deprivation to Child, and women's record was no exception.
There were no heroes, no women singled out for approval, no
activities endorsed as superior to any others, for all women
were heroes, confronting the same inscrutable universe from
whatever vantage point their many worlds afforded. These interpretations of women's history were offered in a spirit of
friendship and a sense of community with other women by
one whose greatest skill was to state her lack of conviction
with such authority and vitality that hers was one of the nineteenth century's most interesting American minds.

### 3. Elizabeth Ellet and the American Woman:
*The Past Recaptured*

Elizabeth Fries Lummis Ellet, whose mind, temperament, and
historical method differed greatly from Child's, was the first
scholar to reconstruct the past of the American woman from

primary sources. She is the mother of modern women's history in America. Beginning her intellectual career as a romantic critic and Italian literary scholar, she wrote numerous articles and a book on Schiller before she began to investigate woman's record. Before the Civil War she published *The Women of the American Revolution* (two volumes, 1848), *Pioneer Women of the West* (1852), and *Women Artists in All Ages and Countries* (1859). Reaching a large audience—*The Women of the American Revolution* was in its fourth edition by 1850—her work undoubtedly made many Americans newly aware of the roles women had played, both in American culture and in other nations and epochs.

The greatest problem Ellet encountered as a historian is one that still perplexes students of women's history, and one of her major achievements was to make this problem explicit to her contemporaries. In the preface to *The Women of the American Revolution* she describes this difficulty. During the seventy-five years since the Revolution, Americans had, to Ellet's horror, destroyed almost all evidence about women of that era. Moreover, extant data was often of dubious value and authenticity—"liable to the suspicion of being distorted or discolored by the imperfect knowledge, the prejudices, or the fancy of its narrators." [45] Skepticism was thus indispensable to the historian of women, who must separate fact from fiction and try to keep the latter out of the historical record.

This commitment to accuracy made Ellet equally wary of secondary sources, and most of these did not mention women at all. She reserved her greatest contempt, however, for "political history," those accounts of the American Revolution that treated women's role in that struggle only "vaguely and incidentally." Given this sad state of scholarship, Ellet had to rely primarily on private papers—the record most liable to be destroyed by descendants of women of the American Revolution. Decrying what she contemptuously styled "this manuscript-destroying generation," she urged her contemporaries to preserve all documents relating to the American woman, lest she be lost to history. [46]

From private papers and the collections in the New York

Historical Society, Ellet pieced together the story of American women during the Revolution. Above all, she insisted, that record was factual: if she had failed to establish a document's authenticity, she had discarded it. Accordingly, her portrait of the American woman was, she felt, a bare outline that awaited the strokes of "more fortunate limners." All data did, however, point to an indisputable conclusion: women had played prominent roles as nurturers and guardians of the spirit of liberty Ellet cherished. Women instilled this consciousness into sons who later fought for that concept, and women's unflagging support and democratic zeal helped sustain men through many a long battle.

In addition to strengthening democratic ideals through their domestic roles, women had played a variety of social roles, had undertaken work usually accomplished by men, and had sacrificed for the common goal of liberty. Women were not "unsexed" by assuming roles outside the home, for the future of America hung in the balance.[47] For Ellet, democracy and domesticity were natural allies, and woman's role in the family was most important of all. The spirit of liberty began at home and was generated by women; without them, Ellet's work suggests, the American Revolution might not have occurred.

*Pioneer Women of the West* shows the American woman proving her versatility and excellence once again in the domestication of the continent. As if to confirm Catharine Beecher's ideal in history, Ellet collected documents relating to the lives of women—unknown, uncelebrated, and obscure— whose revolutionary spirit, strength, and capability had made westward migration and settlement possible. Across generations and across the country these "sisters of America" with their shared ideals and actions supplied Ellet with the basis for a definition of the American female character: zealous guardian and promoter of the democratic faith, a symbol of strength, endurance, and vitality. And all her research demonstrated that the American woman was not a passive creature in any sense. Her activity, more than her piety and purity, distinguished her; by playing a variety of social roles she was a force in history even beyond that domestic realm where her power and strength flourished. Everywhere the historian looked, woman's record buzzed with activity—and with a great deal of autonomy and strength that made clinging vines seem hopelessly outdated.

Like Lydia Maria Child, Elizabeth Ellet viewed women's history through a romantic lens. Although she wrote that the essence of any historical moment, of any culture or individual, could not be totally recaptured by historians, she urged them to approach the past with empathy and attempt to discover and duplicate to the best of their ability a period's "life-giving principle, too subtle to be retained by the grave historian." [48] Like her equally romantic contemporary, George Bancroft, and Mercy Otis Warren before him, she defined the essence of America as the spirit of a great people whose collective dream and heroic actions continually ensured the success of the American experiment. Everyone, great and small—and especially women, no matter how obscure—belonged in the American story; a study of "representative" men and great individuals would give only a partial view of the American experience.

Although they were not "ordinary" women, female artists deserved to have their story recorded and revivified for the nineteenth century. As a romantic, Ellet was attracted to artistic personalities and was amazed that, as Child had pointed out, no one had studied women who had distinguished themselves in the visual arts. Taking her cue from Child, perhaps, and her remark upon the invisible female artist, Ellet traced the work of female artists from ancient Greece to nineteenth-century America and found hundreds of obscure and long-forgotten examples. Carefully placing each artist within her particular culture and relating her art to the prevailing condition of women, Ellet saw a direct correlation between female roles and artistic excellence: "The more enlarged is the sphere of her activity among any people, the greater is the number of female artists who have done and are doing well, by their sustained and productive cultivation of art." [49]

History also demonstrated to Ellet that woman's artistic impulse was too powerful to be suppressed regardless of how "degraded" her status was; even when, as in the ancient East, she was the "mere slave and toy of her master," her response to this condition was artistic, and she viewed herself as an art object, creating elaborate ornaments to complement her beauty. The ancient feminine tasks of weaving and spinning were also outlets for artistic expression, and in these artifacts the "undying germs of art were hidden." Like Ellet's conception of the American experience, her chronicle of the female artist symbolized a triumphant march from bondage to freedom; the flame of art, like the spirit of liberty, burned brightly throughout women's history, even in the most unlikely places and circumstances.

Given Ellet's correlation between women's art and social role, the future of the female artist looked bright indeed. The unprecedented extent of freedom granted women in the nineteenth century was for Ellet sufficient cause for optimism; the past fifty years had witnessed a remarkable outpouring of "female talent and skill," which she partially credited to the growing popularity of art collecting among the wealthy and to the growth of art appreciation among the general public. But, Ellet added, the historian must also relate the rapid progress and increasing number of women artists to their social "liberation" from "the thraldom of old-fashioned prejudices and unworthy restraints which, in former times, fettered her energies, rendered her acquisition of scientific and artistic knowledge extremely difficult, and threw obstacles in the way of her devotion to study and the exercise of her talents." It was woman's increasing educational opportunities that spelled freedom to Ellet; the "so called 'emancipation' " advocated by feminists would only retard women's progress, for theirs was an unnatural course, "contrary to the gentleness and modesty" that distinguished their sex.[50]

Ellet urged her readers to ignore feminist arguments, as she had, and even to use women's history to disprove feminist claims. Her enthusiastic reading of the past would, she hoped, offer encouragement not despair. History, that "great teacher of the Present," illustrated the rapid progress and triumphs of women artists, just as it chronicled the deeds and strengths of

American women.[51] The American woman as artist had now come of age and she seemed to Ellet the most splendid creature of all.

Devoting the last section of her book to a lengthy sketch of Harriet Hosmer, Ellet saw a lesson for all women in the American sculptor's brilliant success. A young woman from Watertown, Massachusetts, Hosmer relentlessly pursued her career, overcame all obstacles, and won fame and glory in the great world of art. Now, her ambitions realized, Harriet Hosmer worked in her Roman studio and received admirers from near and far. Ellet interpreted her life as a romantic dream come true; Hosmer was a vivid symbol of the artist as hero, whose picturesque life contained an equally romantic message. Hosmer's "industry" and "perseverance" had made her "genius" flower,[52] but Ellet wished above all to remember and revere her sublime aspiration:

> Better to aspire and fail than not aspire at all; better to know the dream, and the fever, and the awakening, if it must be, than to pass from the cradle to the grave on the level plane of content with things as they are.[53]

Elizabeth Ellet identified strongly with such a symbol of artistic excellence and fought bitterly and ruthlessly for a literary reputation of her own. Unlike Lydia Maria Child, Ellet was ambition incarnate, and she proved to be a formidable enemy to anyone who seemed to stand in her way. The poet Frances Osgood, Edgar Allan Poe, and Rufus Griswold were the most prominent victims of her wrath. Ellet could be kind to women artists in her book, but not to a contemporary like Frances Osgood, whose poetry both Poe and Griswold considered far superior to Ellet's. In retaliation, she succeeded in making the trio miserable, but not in vindicating her own reputation as an artist.[54] Perhaps that was the reason Ellet turned to women's history, where she would have few competitors, in contrast to the number of would-be literati vying for distinction in that vicious literary world Margaret Fuller had criticized so vehemently.

If Ellet had failed as an artist she could still go down in history as a pathfinder and pioneer historian of women. She found the American woman a particularly congenial subject, for she pictured herself squarely within the tradition of those revolutionary women whose lives she recorded. Ellet, too, like her mother before her, was a daughter of the American Revolution; and she closely identified herself with another historian, Mercy Otis Warren.[55] As her spiritual descendant, Ellet would take up where Warren had left off, placing women within the narrative of revolutionary America. Thus, unlike most intellectual women in mid-century America, Ellet had easily found a female model on her own soil to emulate and admire without ambivalence.

Elizabeth Ellet had a supreme confidence in the significance of women's history that is still refreshing to the reader. She saw absolutely no reason to apologize for her work or justify its importance; women were, by definition, worthy objects of study. Her work generated images of woman as hero, as symbols of diversity and individualism; and it encouraged her readers to think of women as "types," whose social roles and achievements had varied from nation to nation, epoch to epoch. The American woman, in particular, was to Ellet a kind of superwoman. Although her powerful female types were potentially subversive to the unvarying vision of ideal femininity, Ellet was able to maintain her pluralistic conception of women's history as well as a total allegiance to the "cult of true womanhood," which all her work implicitly repudiated. History itself had shown her that woman's power was not a passive force. Who could say what glorious triumphs the future held for her?

## 4. Elizabeth Oaks Smith:
*Feminism and History Synthesized*

The concepts of female diversity and individuality present in Elizabeth Ellet's work were the main themes of Elizabeth Oakes Smith's *Woman and Her Needs*. Written in 1851 for the

*New York Tribune* and published in book form three years later, these articles brilliantly demonstrated the validity of those affinities between feminism and women's history that Child and Ellet refused to recognize. Following Margaret Fuller on the *Tribune*, Smith skillfully manipulated and merged the vocabularies of romanticism and feminism in a direct, colloquial style without the difficulty Fuller often experienced:

> Our right to individuality is what I would most assert. Men seem resolved to have but one type in our sex. They recognize the prerogative of the matter-of-fact Biddy to raise a great clamor, quite to the annoyance of a neighborhood, but where's the use of the Nightingale? The laws of stubborn utilitarianism must govern us, while they may be as fantastic as they please.[56]

History presented so great a variety of female "types" to Smith that she found it ridiculous for all women to be "squared" to the domestic standard, to one definition of "woman's sphere." How could anyone use uniform criteria to confront such women as Mme de Staël, Cleopatra, or Héloïse? "Where is their world? Can it be narrowed down to the four walls of the salon or the nursery?" History revealed, too, that great male heroes were not "born of your tame women"; on the contrary, mothers of such men as Wesley, Washington, and Napoleon had been "brilliant, individualized, strongly marked characters," and their fathers had been undistinguished at best—"orderly, sensible, dull people." American history, in particular, illustrated the power and influence of women; like Ellet, Smith emphasized their role as "Mothers of the Republic" and warned that to degrade women—and the women's movement—in thought or deed was to dishonor the memory of those stalwart defenders of liberty: he who "casts contempt upon them, endorses his own shame." [57]

The emergence of American feminism must also be analyzed historically, Smith argued, urging critics of the women's movement to remember their American heritage. Feminism was not, as its detractors so often insisted, a foreign import. To Smith it was a natural outgrowth of the American experience and a reflection of those ideals and principles cherished by all Americans. Stanton's use of the hallowed Declaration of Independence as a model for her "Declaration of Sentiments" regarding women's rights, had caused many contemporaries to gape at that feminist document, aghast at such audacity. The Founding Fathers, Smith wrote, would not have been surprised; standing "upon the firm base of human freedom" they might have suspected that "some day their daughters would sift thoroughly their opinions and their consequences, and daringly challenge the same rights." [58]

In addition to its essentially American nature, the feminist movement also developed and strengthened the American character of its female supporters. They exhibited, according to Smith, the most desirable American traits—resolution, intellectual capability, versatility, and vitality. Most important, feminists were not content to "fret and dawdle," to "be miserable themselves and make all within their sphere miserable"; they proposed to act upon their principles without delay. [59]

Smith also related the emergence of American feminism to what she called the new spirit of energy at work in the nineteenth century and the vast changes in female roles that had occurred since the Middle Ages. "Modern mechanism" had removed much of women's traditional work from home to factory; consequently, women in advanced societies were no longer "condemned solely to the productive and laborious part of the domestic arrangement," which had defined life for their female ancestors. Rapid technological and social change in America had severed many connections between generations of women; yet, such differences seemed insignificant when modern women were compared to their sisters in the Middle Ages. This female type, whom Smith termed "the woman of the Chivalrous Ages," had wiled away the hours doing elaborate embroidery, "distributing alms," and supervising many servants. History had thankfully made such activities obsolete, for no modern woman, Smith emphasized, would be content with such a life. Most unbearable of all, however, were the long vigils such women kept; no contemporary woman could possibly find the patience to "lean from her balcony watching for the first gleam of her lover's plume returning from his seven years' warfare." [60]

Smith's new female type, in contrast, reflected the energy of her era. Her new ideal, the "woman of intellect," which so many found attractive, was a veritable dynamo in comparison to her historical predecessors. As she had already arrived on the world stage, Smith argued that to talk of restraining her "new woman" was to indulge in folly and self-delusion. *Woman and Her Needs* stressed that women who symbolized the "woman of thought" knew who they were and where their advantages lay.

Realizing that if her energies and talents were suppressed her fate would be even worse than that of her medieval sister, Smith's "new woman" faced the future; having already experienced "that stirring to action" characteristic of her type and unknown to most women in history she would not easily forget the taste of that new knowledge. Feminism was her greatest ally. When the goals of that movement had been achieved, "the woman of intellect" would be tolerated—even welcomed—in all her diversity. The pluralistic conception of female roles was, for Smith, basic to a feminist consciousness, and it would benefit men as well as "new women." When marriage for all and domesticity for women were no longer the only options, free choice would breathe fresh air into the close world of "woman's sphere." [61]

Although both men and women might be pressured into marriage, regardless of how unfit either partner might be for the conjugal tie, for Smith it was the distinct social roles that men and women assumed in American society, and the dual standard of behavior determining those roles, that perpetuated women's degradation and inferiority. Feminist principles should be implemented immediately, for she declared that the American woman was in a pitiful state—marriage was a disease from which she rarely recovered. Consequently, Smith admitted that the most rabid antifeminist rhetoric was a correct description of woman's nature. But antifeminist interpretations were unacceptable because society, not nature, had created and ensured woman's stupidity and feebleness. Most

American women unfortunately were still in this almost primordial phase; only a lucky few had managed to evolve into Smith's new female type. A mere glance at the latter should convince even the greatest skeptic that feminists were on the side of civilization, not merely discontent:

> It is because woman is compressed that she is mawkish, and treacherous, and petulant, and meager . . . . Look at the pale faces, the feeble step, the uncertain and disaffected faces of half the married women that you see, and contrast them with the firm, upward, joyous look of the few, whether married or single, whose whole being has been recognized, and then say which realizes best the intents of the Creator.[62]

Elizabeth Oakes Smith also viewed herself as a distinct historical type—the Puritan girl who had been miraculously transformed into the new "woman of intellect." The "Puritan maiden" represented to Smith a "repression" so total that she occupied one of the lowest rungs on the ladder of female evolution and was destined to remain there.[63] In contrast to "the woman of intellect," the Puritan girl lived in an almost medieval world of fear and superstition.

Smith's autobiography described her childhood as typical for all dutiful daughters in New England. At age six Elizabeth was already intimately familiar with spiritual torment. Puritan theology made her tremble for the salvation she feared would not be hers, and encouraged her to test her faith by what she called her "system of self-inflicted torture." But burning her fingers and conducting similar experiments merely increased her doubts of ever joining the elect who were worthy of salvation. Trying to live up to the deeds recorded in Foxe's *Book of Martyrs* was, she concluded, impossible for one who could not stand pain, one who "knew from the first that I was of a flimsy make."[64]

Elizabeth Smith's mother reinforced her daughter's sense of inferiority at every opportunity, reserving her greatest contempt for Elizabeth's intellectual potential. Noting that her mother would "never endorse my mental capacity," Smith wryly added that her mother had proved her own by memorizing the entire Old Testament. Internalizing her mother's low opinion, Elizabeth soon lived up to it; she began to reveal such "hesitancy" in her lessons that she suffered a mental breakdown at age six.[65]

This distant relationship between mother and daughter and the destructive competition it generated colored Smith's future relationships with women. Although she believed in female solidarity it always remained an abstract concept, and she always preferred to keep her distance from even those female admirers who flocked to her lectures. Rather, just as her mother had criticized her intellect, Smith now criticized the intellectual inability of most women to reason effectively, confiding to her diary that their inability to "generalize"—the way they took everything as "a personal affront"—made her "prefer the Lecture Room" where she could maintain her distance.[66]

Parents of Puritan girls demanded as much obedience, Smith wrote, as did the God they worshipped, for "a parent was in the place of God, and an implied wish had the force of a command." Her mother's first commandment was marriage—as soon as possible. Elizabeth had wanted to become a schoolteacher, but soon gave up that ambition, knowing that submission was inevitable. She, like so many others, she wrote, was but the passive instrument of her mother's will. It was impossible to establish any sense of identity or autonomy, for whatever self and whatever passion the "Puritan maiden" had was "buried under a vast substratum of Duty." [67] Propelled toward a fate for which she was totally unprepared, she abandoned hope and, like a rudderless boat, drifted toward that great unknown—marriage:

> And thus the dreams of the Puritan child came to a close, and thus down the rapids inclined my little barque. It was no sudden, irresistible descent. With a weird feeling of "what's the use," I felt myself impelled, and yet cast longing eyes toward idealisms, vast and undefined, which I was not permitted to grasp. I was Puritan, blood, bone and soul; by long descent trained to obedience . . . . I, a cautious little elephant, felt the platform

shake beneath me, and there was nothing for me to do but to take to the water.[68]

In her autobiography, Smith described the fateful day of her own marriage as she thought it had appeared to those in attendance—"a melancholy spectacle and a sad wedding," held on such a bleak, rainy day that she remembered overhearing servants whisper, "A lowery day and a lowery bride." Smith described herself as "a mere baby, no more fit to be a wife than a child of ten years," given in marriage to a man "almost twice my age," who "wore spectacles and was very bald." Seba Smith, editor and part owner of a paper in Portland, Maine, had graduated first in his class at Bowdoin College; he was, Elizabeth wrote, well respected by many friends and an able scholar, a modest man with "an unblemished moral character" from the day of their marriage to his death. To her mother's disappointment—who was, Smith slyly pointed out, an "ultra conventional woman"—the groom's "contempt for fashionable and conventional usages" included wedding rings, and he refused to provide one, deeming it "a foolish appendage to a bride." [69] Never forgetting her wedding day, Elizabeth continually returned to the theme of early marriage in her feminist writings. Regardless of how such matches might turn out, young girls who knew nothing of sex or homemaking were plunged overnight into a new world for which they were totally unprepared; there was no continuity between their girlhoods and married lives—except more obedience.

Famous as "Major Jack Downing," that untutored yet astute political satirist, Seba Smith had little interest in his wife's intellectual potential and was not amused by the feminist arguments she later advanced.[70] Failing fortunes, however, led him to encourage her to utilize and develop her talents; the editor's wife soon turned serious author, writing historical sketches of famous women, essays, fiction, and poetry for newspapers, women's magazines, *Graham's*, and the *Southern Literary Messenger*. A long poem, *The Sinless Child*, published in 1842 in the *Southern Literary Messenger* brought her fame and Poe's admiration and approval, and reflected her growing sense of individuality and the emergence of her feminist consciousness. *The Sinless Child* was truly her story, a romantic narrative of Smith's progression from childhood to self-hood. Admirers easily identified her as the heroine of the poem, reinforcing her new image of herself.[71] She was fast becoming a public symbol of the "woman of intellect" she would later call "the new woman of the nineteenth century." The poem's signature also announced her new identity—Elizabeth Oakes Smith. All her previous work had been signed "Mrs. Seba Smith," a designation she now found inappropriate for a woman who had achieved distinction in her own right. Discovering a distinguished male ancestor—an Oakes who had been President of Harvard in 1675—she added that surname, changed her children's surname to Oaksmith and attempted without success to have her husband change his name too. Now a distinct individual, she explored in a poem entitled "Wife" that narrow world she had left behind.[72]

Throughout the 1840s Elizabeth Oakes Smith was part of the inner circle of New York literati. When the statesman Henry Clay met her in this milieu he described her as an incredibly charming "new woman" of intellect: "Seldom has a woman in any age acquired such ascendancy by the mere force of a powerful intellect. Her smile is the play of a sunlit fountain." [73] Smith herself saw the American literary world in harsher terms. Reviewing *Aurora Leigh* for the *U. S. Magazine,* she wrote that Elizabeth Barrett Browning was fortunate to live in a culture that supported and sustained female talent; if she had been an American her poetic genius might not have flowered. "Had she appeared in America, where the competition is greater, and the prestige of rank and genius less, where new opinions are so severely handled, Elizabeth Barrett Browning would have been hunted down by press and pulpit, even worse than the gifted Margaret Fuller was." [74]

In 1851 Smith found the intellectual stance most congenial to her own temperament and skill and left the literary life for the lecture platform as one of the first women invited to join the lyceum circuit. Touring the West, the South, and the Atlantic States, she lectured on feminism, famous women in history, religion and abolitionism. Charging fifty cents for three of her most popular lectures, "Manhood," "Womanhood," and "Our Humanity," she seemed to many listeners as impressive as her words—a vivid symbol of an intellectual woman.

She recognized and understood the significance of her new role by explicitly rejecting those rationalizations commonly used by women to justify their intellectual activities. Admitting that she did need the money her lectures brought, she emphasized that asserting her own intellectual authority was her primary motive and "insisted upon standing entirely upon mental capabilities." As she noted in her journal, "If I had abilities I preferred to be accepted on the ground of capacity alone as men claimed to be accepted." [75] If women assumed any other posture, they were traitors to their sex, and Smith reserved her harshest criticism for those who had joined the enemy's ranks.

"Literary women" in particular, Smith wrote in *Woman and Her Needs,* deserved contempt for perpetuating assumptions of women's inferiority. Their work held female character and potential in such low esteem it seemed obvious to Smith they had accepted male definitions of femininity. This was, of course, not surprising; for it insured their popularity precisely because their books offered no new interpretations of woman and her sphere. Consequently, their work, like the "twaddle written by the other sex," was totally inaccurate—they were totally unaware of that concept of female diversity central to Smith's reading of women's history. In addition, Smith noted, "literary women" often heaped contempt upon men as well as women; domestic guides often characterized husbands not as mature individuals, but as babies or "beasts" to be manipulated. [76] That neither sex could even recognize the other's humanity was for Smith the best argument for feminist reforms.

Worst of all the "literary woman's" crimes, however, was her total insincerity about her role and her accomplishments. Smith asked in *Woman and Her Needs:* How could any self-respecting woman who had achieved success outside of the home deem all such careers unsuitable for other women? [77] Her answer underscored the necessity of feminist reforms:

Having internalized society's contempt for their sex, "literary women" lacked respect for themselves and for other women and, consequently, the courage to assert their individuality and to admit that success was most enjoyable and fulfilling. Instead, such women dissembled, insisting that a life of total domesticity would have been preferable to the course they had pursued. To Smith, any woman who used this tactic had totally discredited herself, her sex, and even the God who had given her the talents she abused:

> If any woman of genius is so untrue to herself as to say she should have been happier as an in-door, painstaking, fireside woman, careful for the small savings of a household, holding the rod *in terrorem* over unruly urchins, and up in the morning early, to scold the servants . . . she is from some cause disqualified for the holding of God's beautiful and abundant gifts in reverent stewardship . . . .[78]

Such devious and evasive behavior pointed to the basic question implicit in all of Smith's feminist writings: If the "cult of true womanhood" made women lie to gain admittance, something was terribly wrong with the standards of ideal femininity. Moreover, a "true woman" must not only lie to the world but be untrue to herself as well. Thus, Smith had turned the "true woman" upside down: She was a false, dishonest creature unworthy of the name of woman or of the culture that created her, for all her traits were those most abhorrent to Americans.

Smith cast her lot instead with all "true women" whose lives and ideals merited that adjective and offered herself, with no apologies, as a public model of the "new woman" whose emergence and impact she had traced in her writings—the "woman of intellect." She wished to be remembered as a "new woman" in the tradition of Fanny Wright and the American feminists she admired. Although she attended several women's rights conventions in the 1850s, she never felt quite comfortable in a group enterprise. Like Lydia Maria Child, she was a solitary figure at heart, an intellectual loner who could not identify herself completely with any milieu:

> For myself, I may not sympathize with a Convention—I may not
> feel *that* the best mode of arriving at truth to my own mind—I
> may feel that its singleness of import would be lost to me while
> standing in the solid phalanx of associated inquiry; but these ob-
> jections do not apply to the majority of minds, and I reverence
> their search in their own way, the many converging lights of
> many minds all bent upon the same point, even although I my-
> self peer about with my solitary lantern.[79]

Speaking to one of these conventions she described the
major dilemma feminists faced: "The idea of a true noble
womanhood is yet to be created. It does not live in the public
mind." [80] Elizabeth Oakes Smith devoted all her skills to establishing that concept in prose and in person. She made her
ideal and her feminist arguments come to life for her lyceum
audiences and her readers, lending the feminist cause the
credibility and dignity its opponents sought to deny and attracting new supporters to the feminist persuasion. She
brought news of that movement to a larger audience than feminists could draw—to sometimes uneasy and often hostile listeners who were most curious about what really went on in
those strange conventions they generally did not attend. Her
lectures stressed that women were generating in those meetings "a better and nobler sympathy for each other" and the
"growth of a loyalty full of promise," [81] and Smith urged her
public not to laugh at them—that feminists and their activities, like other aspects of women's history, should be seen and
interpreted with accuracy, with a tolerance for diversity, and a
respect for human excellence, regardless of sex. She hoped that
in her work all women might share in her own transformation
from "Puritan maiden" to "woman of intellect" and that the
time would come when every woman could, like Smith, be
"recognized as an intelligence, and not be compelled to dwarf
herself lest she should be thought unfeminine." [82]

Intellectuals working more closely within the feminist movement drew upon Smith's talents as a writer and a speaker and
benefited in their own interpretations of women's history from
the data compiled by Child and Ellet. Their story reflects how

they put the stamp of romanticism upon feminist thought and the institution they created—the women's rights convention—an arena uncongenial to Elizabeth Oakes Smith, off limits to Lydia Maria Child, and positively unthinkable to Elizabeth Ellet.

# (4)

# Within the
# "Phalanx of Associated Inquiry"
## Intellectual Women and the
## Institutions of American Feminism

*A woman is nobody. A wife is everything. A pretty girl is equal to ten thousand men, and a mother is, next to God, all powerful . . . . The ladies of Philadelphia, therefore, under the influence of the most serious, "sober second thoughts," are resolved to maintain their rights as Wives, Belles, Virgins, and Mothers, and not as Women.*

—*Philadelphia Public Ledger
and Daily Transcript*

*The American woman has a sort of* post mortem *post-mistress notoriety; but with the exception of handling letters of administration and letters mailed, she is the submissive creature of the old common law.*

—Judge Hurlibut

*Feminism, like Boston, is a state of mind.*
—Rheta Childe Dorr, *A Woman of Fifty*

## 1. Elizabeth Cady Stanton and the "Declaration of Sentiments"

Preparing for the first women's rights convention at Seneca Falls, New York, Elizabeth Cady Stanton felt as well equipped to lead a movement as she was to "construct a steam engine." [1]

Elizabeth Cady Stanton
*The Schlesinger Library, Radcliffe College*

Antoinette Brown Blackwell (below left)
*The Schlesinger Library, Radcliffe College*

Paulina Wright Davis (below right)
*The Schlesinger Library, Radcliffe College*

But Lucretia Mott and her sister, visiting Seneca Falls for the day, and Stanton's neighbors, Jane Hune and Mary Ann Mc-Clintock, agreed with her that the time had finally arrived to announce a convention. Their unsigned call was published in the *Seneca Falls Courier* on July 14, 1848—only five days before the meeting.

With little time to devise policy and formulate strategies of argumentation, Stanton and her friends gathered in the Mc-Clintocks' home on the Sunday before the convention, still perplexed by what Stanton called their major dilemma: How could a small group of women not visibly "oppressed" make a convincing case for female degradation? [2] Temperance and abolitionist speeches offered little help; there seemed to be no models that would support their case. Then, one of America's major documents came to their aid.

Spying a copy of the Declaration of Independence, Stanton proposed that it be revised to include women under its aegis and adopted as their model; surely this unimpeachable source would add weight and credibility to the feminist persuasion and, hence, be the perfect text from which to develop their arguments. Chosen as the group's best writer, Stanton composed a series of twelve resolutions—including number nine, that women be given the right to vote—entitled the "Declaration of Rights and Resolutions" and later the "Declaration of Sentiments."

For one who had known since childhood that the Jacksonian Persuasion, in the process of revivifying and re-creating the spirit of the Declaration of Independence, did not apply to women, the decision to use the Declaration of Independence to advocate a series of radical reforms—she insisted until her death that nothing more radical had ever been conceived [3]— was quite appropriate, if not brilliant. It was itself an illustration of the logic of the Jacksonian Persuasion, a characteristic intellectual response of the venturous conservative. Stanton's strategy offered, she thought, maximum respectability and the clearest possible formulation of the issues delineating the woman's dilemma.

To her astonishment, the public was aghast; many thought her resolutions a joke, a parody—in all senses—of the original.[4] The convention itself generated a storm of protest and ridicule that Stanton had not anticipated:

> No words could express our astonishment on finding, a few days afterward, that what seemed to us so timely, so rational, and so sacred, should be a subject for sarcasm and ridicule to the entire press of the nation. With our Declaration of Rights and Resolutions for a text, it seemed as if every man who could wield a pen prepared a homily on "woman's sphere." All the journals from Maine to Texas seemed to strive with each other to see which could make our movement appear the most ridiculous.[5]

To counterattack, Stanton needed much more than the indispensable legal knowledge she had gained from her father, his library, and his apprentices. Now launched as a public defender of feminism, she wrote that she and her friends had to survey and master many fields of knowledge: "In answering all the attacks, we were compelled to study canon and civil law, constitutions, Bibles, science, philosophy, and history, sacred and profane." To share their new knowledge, Stanton and her allies in the local community found another model most appropriate. "In imitation of Margaret Fuller's Conversationals," they formed The Seneca Falls Conversation Club, which gave to that community what Fuller would have called an "intellectual center." There was, according to Stanton, a spirit of true intellectual community and camaraderie among the men and women who attended the weekly meetings. The club was an egalitarian society in many ways: it was a debating club where all members presided and participated in turn, each learning the rules of procedure, knowledge that would subsequently prove to be indispensable at feminist conventions; and it was a social gathering that included women and men from outside the local "aristocracy," the "small clique" that Stanton thought existed in every village and hamlet in America, dominating its intellectual and social life. Hindsight now makes clear that the club was also a dress rehearsal for the many feminist conventions that would be called throughout the 1850s and a microcosm of what would occur at many of those conventions.[6]

After the business of each meeting was concluded, The Seneca Falls Conversation Club was transformed, rather paradoxically, into an American salon where men and women danced and had a "general chat."[7] According to Stanton, everyone felt intellectually congenial and socially at ease, enjoying themselves immensely. There is no reason to discount her testimony as that of a biased observer, for her boredom threshold was extremely low and she loved wit, laughter, and interesting conversation. Her love of fun and her refusal to feel guilty about enoying herself—even her insistence upon her right to be amused—formed a refreshing contrast to the moral earnestness that so often surrounded her and marked her epoch.[8] Due in large measure to Stanton's presence, The Seneca Falls Conversation Club seems, among the many American salons in mid-century, the one most closely resembling Mme de Staël's. Only in Rome, for example, did Margaret Fuller enjoy herself in a similar setting, for in Concord it seems that no hearts beat to the sounds of laughter.[9] Wit flourished in rural New York—ironically, perhaps, since it often withered in more "civilized" America.

Stanton, of course, did not picture herself as an American Mme de Staël, but she thoroughly enjoyed Lydia Maria Child's biography, admiring its subject as she did all unusual and outstanding individuals (the more bizarre, the more attractive she found them). Without any of Child's ambivalence to Mme de Staël, Stanton exclaimed upon finishing the book, "How I do love that woman!"[10]

Elizabeth Cady Stanton and her friends had truly "lit out for the territories." Expanding their knowledge of women's status and history and refining their intellectual strategy as they traveled, they skillfully borrowed from tradition and experience whatever else might add strength and validity to American feminism and to the institution they had created—the women's rights convention.

## 2. Feminist Conventions and Concepts

As an institution, the feminist convention during the 1850s was a movable feast—a college and a long conversation. And, just as feminist thought continually expanded and retained its flexibility, the social institution of feminism, the convention, remained receptive to intellectual innovations and contributions. In neither thought nor deed did pre-Civil War American feminism coerce or "oppress" its adherents; that favorite irony of James and Hawthorne did not apply until after the Civil War, when feminism faced a new set of problems and, attempting to gain a larger constituency, found itself on a collision course with other reforms. Before such transformations occurred, however, the entire institutional framework of American feminism seems to have been a large-scale version of Stanton's Conversation Club for intellectuals of both sexes. For a few shining hours during the 1850s the "women had all the logic," as Thomas Wentworth Higginson said; [11] and leading male intellectuals joined them with conviction, a spirit of camaraderie, and without acute self-consciousness at the thought of being a *male* feminist. Stanton was extremely proud of them all. She insisted that the nation's best minds were in feminist ranks; regardless of how often newspapers characterized them "as illiterate, ill-mannered, poverty stricken," or a "crazy set of *long*-haired abolitionists," feminists were to her "splendid specimens of manhood and womanhood." [12]

To attend a typical convention of the 1850s as observer or participant was to confront all facets of the female experience simultaneously. At each convention letters were read from the "heroines" of the movement who could not attend, and the proceedings and resolutions of previous conventions were also presented. Representatives from different regions reported changes in state laws—for better or worse—regarding women's political and legal status across the nation. [13] These speeches on the condition of American women indirectly introduced Americans to one another: a New Englander could listen to a woman from a remote world like Kansas, perhaps surprised that she too spoke English and the language of feminism. Surprisingly, (especially in comparison with feminism in the 1970s) there seems to have been little condescension toward "backwoods" feminists by the representatives of "civilization." Conversely, feminists from the East often traveled to states they would not have dreamed previously of visiting; and their "errands into the wilderness" in behalf of feminist agitation led them to discover and explore their expanding culture.

Cosmopolitan, both intellectually and socially, the feminist convention introduced its audience to the many worlds of women from documents and from the personal examples of its diverse participants. Women in history and the present lived side by side at each meeting. A treatise on Bolognese women in the fifteenth century might be followed by a report of a recent invention by an American woman. Such a juxtaposition of historical periods made it seem as if women from ancient Athens and medieval Italy were present in the convention hall, brushing elbows with contemporary Americans. The juxtaposition of female past and present was both a basic experience for those who attended and a basic strategy for those who constructed feminist theory.

As if to offset such disorienting experiences, the feminist convention had, in addition to its format, one comforting tradition in the person of Dr. Harriot K. Hunt of Boston. Each year, no matter what changed or what might be learned during the convention, one could reasonably expect to hear Dr. Hunt deliver her annual protest against taxation without representation, and learn how the famous physician had fared that year in her bout with the law.[14]

All the foregoing emphases and experiences made the feminist convention a most cosmopolitan institution. Both personally and culturally it was what André Malraux has termed "a museum without walls." It is difficult to imagine, in fact, that anyone who paid close attention to the proceedings could leave a convention without thinking of women and their history in a more plastic sense. Everything that happened in a feminist convention underscored that "woman" was indeed no monolithic figure, unchanged from time immemorial. History and experience pointed out, as had Child, Smith, Fuller, and Ellet, that a pluralistic conception of womanhood was essential and inescapable for anyone who looked closely at woman's record and who wanted to shape her future prospects.

Most important for the female audience at each of these conventions was its exposure to feminist argument. One could learn from attending these meetings how to support the feminist position. Through the vocabulary of romanticism with which intellectual feminists described the past, present, and future possibilities of women, one could learn to wield their favorite concepts—with conviction and authority—and gain in the process a new sense of confidence. As Stanton later wrote in *The History of Woman Suffrage*, this spiraling sense of self-esteem among women was the most exciting aspect of each convention.[15] Listening to the various speakers, hearing women organize material from a variety of sources, was itself an important learning experience. Women and men often developed new respect for female intellectual ability where previously they had been skeptical because of a particular speaker's personal example and cogent text. Thus, in the arena where women presented their case for reform they might also finally put to rest that nagging suspicion that women could not think. Feminists themselves might even end the debate on intellect and femininity that obsessed American culture. By their own intellectual behavior, feminists seemed the best equipped to "settle the question of woman's capacity to reason." [16]

### 3. The Grammar of Romanticism

Since historians of American feminism have paid little if any attention to the romantic orientations of leading intellectual feminists, it is not surprising that feminist arguments and rhetorical styles before the Civil War have been greatly oversimplified, and often rendered lifeless and boring.[17] Far from being a single message dully reiterated, resounding without change throughout the 1850s, feminist thought continually evolved, as intellectuals added new concepts, images, and historical knowledge to their stock of arguments for social change. The dynamic metaphors with which romantics described the cosmos, all cultures and peoples, helped keep feminist rhetoric and argument open-ended and able to absorb and utilize new information.

Writing to the Westchester, Pennsylvania, convention in 1852, Sarah Grimké—no longer an active participant in feminist conventions—set the intellectual tone for this convention. Her letter reveals how the romantic orientations of intellectual feminists permeated a typical convention. She described society and civilization in her letter as organic processes marked by incessant transformations. Within this perspective she saw the present condition of women as a historical watershed; now in a "transition" phase, woman was, like the emergent "chrysalis," about to burst forth from her cocoon, to undergo her metamorphosis from "the baby to the intellectual being." [18]

Like Margaret Fuller, Sarah Grimké thought that most women in the nineteenth century were but children writ large: theirs was to be a country of the future. Yet, as Elizabeth Oakes Smith always emphasized in her writings and speeches, Grimké also recognized that nothing could stop the process of female transformation or divert women from their grand destiny as world redeemers. Although she warned the Westchester convention not to become overly optimistic or to underestimate the powerful opposition feminists still faced, her rousing letter portraying women as emblems of cosmic growth would not support a pessimistic forecast of woman's future possibilities. In addition, Grimké invoked the spirit of Margaret Fuller and advised the participants at Westchester to adopt Fuller's words as their motto and guiding principle: "Give me Truth. Cheat me by no illusion." [19]

The Syracuse National Convention of 1852, held shortly after the Westchester meeting, again reveals the romantic orientations of feminist proceedings. Presiding over this meeting was Paulina Wright Davis of Providence, who chaired and organized many conventions in the 1850s and began to publish a feminist journal, *The Una*, in 1853. Like Grimké, Davis honored the memory of Margaret Fuller and once told a convention over which she presided that it was Fuller who belonged in the chair. Lamenting that death had taken away such a leader, Davis spoke of feeling woefully inadequate in comparison: "[Margaret Fuller] was, and still is, a leader of thought; a position far more desirable than a leader of numbers." [20] However, as her speeches and writings make abundantly clear, Davis was also a "leader of thought."

Paulina Wright Davis gave a virtuoso performance at the Syracuse National Convention in her presidential address—a speech that dramatically contrasted the role of women in ancient mythology and history with her role as a nineteenth-century wife. Modern woman, Davis said, had lost the tremendous power she had once exerted; for Davis, the contemporary woman was not even a child. She was a nonentity.

Speaking of women who had played significant roles as shapers of civilization, Davis turned to the myth of Pandora, revising it to make Pandora stand for good as well as evil. Pandora had, according to Davis, introduced the possibility of hope and choice between these opposing principles. In contrast, the married woman of the present day played only a negative role, and Davis described the stages of female experience after marriage as a living death in a "series of dissolving views." The beautiful and radiant bride barely survived the marriage ceremony, so quickly did she become "the child wife," trapped in the American home—for Davis, the bleakest house of all. There, the young matron began her rapid decline, "pining in the darkness of her home—life, made only the deeper by her inactivity, ignorance and despair." Hardened by these winters of discontent, the American wife became "the heartless votary of fashion, a flirt, or that most to be dreaded, most to be despised, a married coquette; at once seductive, heartless and basely unprincipled." [21] Age would rob her of even these wicked diversions, taking with her looks any remaining hope she might have for a life of significance. Like Gibbon's theory of civilization and Thomas Cole's series of paintings, *The Course of Empire*, Davis's American woman, like nature and all cultures and individuals, passed through the stages of birth, decay, and death—with one crucial difference: the American woman moved from youth to decadence, bypassing civilization or, in personal terms, maturity.

Despite the debilitating lives most women led, they were, Davis wrote, able to respond and to reflect the new energy which she defined as the distinguishing mark of her century. Applying that favorite Carlylean metaphor—old clothes as traditional ideas and social customs—to female experience, Davis described the mission of feminism as the fashioning of new garments, new ideas, ideals, and social institutions, appropriate for woman and her development in an "age of energy": [22]

> We commence life where our fathers left it. We have their mistakes and their achievements. We attempt to walk in the paths they trod, and wear the garments left by them; but they are all too short and narrow for us; they deform and cramp our energies; for they demand the Procrustean process to conform the enlarged natures of the present to the past. While the human soul, like the infinite in wisdom and love, is ever governed by the eternal law of progress, creeds and codes are always changing. [23]

In her Syracuse address, Elizabeth Oakes Smith also emphasized the breakdown of traditional forms and the rise of new institutions. Stressing in particular the revolutionary nature of feminist goals, she encouraged her listeners to think of themselves both organically, as part of nature's dynamism, and historically, as actors in a vast drama of change as they battled against what she called the most ancient of mankind's errors, the subjection and devaluation of women:

> Do we fully understand that we aim at nothing less than an entire subversion of the present order of society, a dissolution of the whole existing social compact? Do we see that it is not an error of today, nor of yesterday, against which we are lifting up the voice of dissent, but that it is against the hoary-headed error of all times—error borne onward from the footprints of the first pair ejected from Paradise, down to our own time? [24]

In a letter read to the Syracuse Convention, Elizabeth Cady Stanton also outlined the far-reaching goals of feminism and noted that the movement was beginning to have a more beneficial effect on public opinion than ever before. Despite its many enemies, feminism was beginning to make a difference in American life. Many who had once jeered, she wrote, now took the matter seriously. Stanton urged feminists to think of political equality and the franchise as only the first step in an ongoing process of a total revolution in social equality and in the emerging consciousness of all women. After securing their political rights, Stanton hoped that women would continue to change all aspects of their lives by investigating and eliminating oppression everywhere—including within the "family circle." [25]

Angelina Grimké also wrote to the Syracuse meeting, emphasizing the power and the importance of both the cause and its allies. Her letter, similar in tone and symbolism to her sister Sarah's letter to the Westchester meeting, generated what Stanton described as a "spirited discussion" and prompted Dr. Harriot Hunt to move that the convention declare "spontaneity" a "law of nature." [26] Like Davis, Stanton, and Smith, Angelina Grimké saw present social institutions as on the verge of total "dissolution." "The wrinkles and totterings of age are on them," she declared. The power of Truth would, Grimké hoped, make all such wicked organizations unnecessary. Above all, she hoped that feminism would not adopt what she might have called the organizational fallacy:

> What organization in the world's history has not encumbered the unfettered action of those who created it? Indeed, has not been used as an engine of oppression. The importance of this question can hardly be duly magnified. How few organizations have ever had the power which this is destined to wield? The prayers and sympathies of the ripest and richest minds will be ours. Vast is the influence which true-hearted women will exert in the coming age. [27]

In these letters and speeches, Smith, Stanton, the Grimkés, and Davis revealed their romantic orientations and those conceptions of the historical process romanticism suggested. From comparative surveys of world cultures they found that women, although often oppressed, had been a force in history, and that female roles articulated the basic concerns and values of particular cultures. The past, as woven by intellectual feminists, was a tapestry that illustrated the significant deeds of women and simultaneously subordinated them to the grand design of masculine culture. In their exclusive preoccupation with the latter, most historians, writers, and artists had accordingly ignored or hopelessly distorted woman's record, further obscuring it in each successive work. In feminist analysis, then, discrimination against women was also marked by the patterns of change and growth with which they described the evolution of feminism. The oppression of women might be the world's oldest error, but it was not a static entity. It too was in the process of multiplication and change, continually bringing more and more data forward that feminists had to confront, and further distorting the reality of the female experience in history and in the present.

These feminists tried to make women a part of history and to ensure their future transformation into self-determining individuals by interpreting cultural change as an organic process. The agent for this inevitable metamorphosis was the feminist revolution. It had already created, according to feminist thought, autonomous women who could serve as examples of female excellence. Like the historical models intellectual feminists discovered and re-created, several of their contemporaries served as heroines, worthy of imitation and esteem as "true women." What most people meant by "true woman" was not even a contradiction in terms for most American theorists of feminism. With few exceptions, "woman" and "woman thought," as Elizabeth Oakes Smith called it, did not yet exist for them—except in history. As romantics, intellectual feminists saw the world as newly alive. Nature, the cosmos, each individual, women as a group, feminism as both institution and idea—all were interpreted as processes generating energy and change that would give birth to "new women" in the nineteenth century. Then, as Margaret Fuller had always wished, they could act out their nature freely.

Narrowing their focus from world civilizations to American culture, intellectual feminists soon developed one of their most striking images and arguments: America as an "aristocracy of sex." In her 1854 "Address to the New York State Legislature," which was printed and read aloud at several conventions, Elizabeth Cady Stanton used this concept to explain the plight of American women and to justify feminist arguments for legal, economic, and psychological equality. Structuring her speech according to the stages of the typical female experience—woman as wife, mother, widow—Stanton found that in each of these roles women suffered discrimination and degradation. She included a very atypical female as well: "woman as woman." This was Stanton's ideal but, she concluded, it was certainly not America's.

By "woman as woman" Stanton meant woman as individual, as a human being who was intellectually "equal to the proud white man himself." Although women had demonstrated historically their capability and versatility—by assuming diverse and significant social roles—American law still refused to give them the basic rights of citizenship and accordingly failed to recognize their humanity. "Classed with idiots, lunatics and negroes," American women had even fewer legal rights, Stanton asserted, for "the negro can be raised to the dignity of a voter if he possess himself of $250; the lunatic can vote in his moments of sanity, and the idiot, too, if he be a male one, and not more than nine-tenths a fool." [28]

The legal disabilities under which American women suffered were, in Stanton's analysis, the logical result of lawmakers' submission to the false authority of custom and their ensuing inability to think about women as human beings. Either as individual or in her relationships with men as wife, mother, or widow, the American woman was controlled by the absolute and arbitrary power granted to men under the law. Stanton then illustrated her thesis with concrete examples of what actually happened to women during the stages of life she had outlined.

Upon marriage, Stanton argued, a wife gave up her legal identity unless she lived in a state such as New York, which allowed her to inherit property from her parents. Even then, she paid taxes on her income without representation at the polls. If a husband died intestate, his widow legally lost half of the estate. If she recovered from this common form of economic disaster, she was once again taxed without representation. Emphasizing that American society's hallowed view of motherhood was not supported by law, Stanton pointed out that mothers had no rights: Children were the "absolute property" of fathers who could do anything with their offspring without gaining a mother's consent. Stating that no authority justified such treatment, Stanton asked rhetorically:

> Can it be that here, where we acknowledge no royal blood, no apostolic descent, that you, who have declared that all men were created equal—that governments derive their just powers from the consent of the governed, would willingly build up an aristocracy that places the ignorant and vulgar above the educated and refined—the alien and the ditch-digger above the authors and poets of the day—an aristocracy that would raise the sons above the mothers that bore them? [29]

Women in real aristocracies fared much better than did the American woman, Stanton declared, for the rights and privileges of rank were never denied them. This bitter paradox was Stanton's main theme. Underlying all her arguments was a message difficult to ignore: Did not America's treatment of women make a mockery of the country and all its ideals? If one granted that point, feminism itself became a very American phenomenon—another American revolution.

Like Elizabeth Oakes Smith, Stanton thought no one should be surprised that the daughters of the American Revolution would confront Jacksonian America as their forebears had faced England and "demand at your hands the redress of our grievances." [30] When women won their independence Stanton pictured them joining men to form a "natural aristocracy" such as the one Thomas Jefferson had envisioned. The "best and the brightest" men and women would almost automatically assume power and authority once all artificial barriers to female participation in American society were removed. Thus, the very structure of Stanton's feminist persuasion reflected the ideals of Jacksonian America. She too revivified the spirit of the American Revolution, sharing the same vision of an ideal society and the dream of restoring and restructuring American society according to those "lost worlds" of Thomas Jefferson and his friends.

In the resolutions of the Albany Convention of 1854, where copies of Stanton's speech were distributed, Antoinette Brown emphasized that "the caste of sex" was a "remnant of despotism and feudal oligarchy" which she called a disgrace to American principles. "For males to govern females, without consent asked or granted," Brown argued, "is to perpetuate an aristocracy, utterly hostile to the principles and spirit of free institutions." [31] Like Stanton, Brown came from upstate New York, and her own experience with that "free institution," the American ministry, gave her words great authority. After completing Oberlin's theology course and being refused ordination, Brown began to devote more and more of her intellectual talents to feminism during the early 1850s. Although in 1853 she was ordained as a Congregationalist minister in Wayne County, New York, her increasing skepticism and liberal views alarmed her congregation, and she voluntarily gave up the post after one year and soon joined the Unitarian faith. Her knowledge of religions and acquaintance with Hebrew was particularly important to American feminism, for Brown could tackle that formidable document, the Bible, and demonstrate that its tenets *supported* rather than *refuted* feminist claims. At the Syracuse Convention in 1852 she reinterpreted Genesis, arguing that in the original Hebrew one could find nothing to support the theory of male domination as God's law:

This rule was no more approved, endorsed, or sanctioned by God, than was the twin-born prophecy, "though [Satan] shall bruise his [Christ's] heel." God could not, from His nature, command Satan to injure Christ, or any other of the seed of woman. What particle of evidence is there then for supposing that in the parallel announcement He commanded man to rule over woman? Both passages should have been translated 'will,' instead of 'shall.' Either auxiliary is used indifferently according to the sense in rendering that form of the Hebrew verb into English.[32]

Antoinette Brown seems to have been attracted to the study of theology in order to reinterpret it so as to give women a wider sphere of thought and action. Her revision of St. Paul's doctrine, "Let your women keep silence in the churches," was published in the *Oberlin Quarterly Review* during her student days. Brown's speeches and lectures—her very presence at a feminist convention—undoubtedly assuaged the nagging fear of transgressing biblical laws that plagued many feminists. Also Brown could, like Stanton, confront and castigate legal tradition and practice as a "wholly masculine" body of precedent and custom, hopelessly biased against women and thus incapable of conceiving of women as citizens.[33]

Although her marriage in 1856 and her growing family (she was to bear seven children) soon removed her from the institutional centers of feminism, she was an important intellectual force in the movement during the decade before her marriage. Her compelling lectures and speeches, such as the one delivered at Albany upon "the aristocracy of sex," underscored the main themes of American feminism. She was particularly adept at discrediting the feminists' female opposition; mimicking the opponents, Brown once exclaimed, in mock horror: "Intellectual Women! Oh, they are monsters!" She stressed that this was the characteristic response of "idle" women, not "true women."[34] In contrast, all "true hearted men and women" supported feminism and, she told her audience at Albany, it was up to them to restore America to the vision of its founders, to "remove the stigma resting on this republic, that while it theoretically proclaims that all men are created equal, deprives one-half of its members of the enjoyment of the rights and privileges possessed by the other."[35]

Antoinette Brown's apostrophe to "true" women and men and Elizabeth Cady Stanton's frequent assertions that "all true women of this generation" were in the movement demonstrate another basic feminist strategy: unsexing the "true woman." [36] Turning the concept of "true womanhood" against their adversaries, feminists could then utilize their female opponents, their very lack of female support, to great advantage. By creating an anti-image of woman whose depraved nature they wished to transform into an authentic woman, feminists established in addition their own "true womanhood." In her "Appeal to the Women of New York" (1854) Stanton coolly appraised her enemies, telling how "humiliating" it was to hear any woman say she had all the rights she needed or wanted. [37] Stanton then used such a statement to illustrate the thesis of female oppression:

If, in view of laws like these, there be women in this stage so lost to self-respect, to all that is virtuous, noble and true, as to refuse to raise their voices in protest against such degrading tyranny, we can only say of that system what the immortal Channing did of slavery, "If," said he, "it be true that the slaves are contented and happy—if there is a system that can blast out all love of freedom from the soul of man . . . I ask for no stronger argument against such a slavery as ours." No! Never believe it; woman falsifies herself and blasphemes her God, when in view of her present social, legal and political position, she declares she has all the rights she wants. [38]

Parallels between women and slaves—both were slaves of men and partners in intellectual and social bondage, according to Stanton's analogy—and the image of the lady as a decadent trifler and slave to fashion pointed up the impossibility of being a "lady" and a "true woman" simultaneously. Like a slave's humanity, a lady's "true womanhood" had been progressively destroyed by the peculiar institutions of male domination. Female abolitionists had left a heritage of this kind of argument from which feminists could draw. One had even gone so far as to suggest that what society called a "true woman" was a dead woman, stifled from earliest childhood "by a process of spiritual suffocation" so total that a "lady" was "that sort of woman who is dead while she lives." [39]

Sarah Grimké's *Letters on the Equality of the Sexes and the Condition of Women* (1838) had also set a precedent for this form of argument. Defining the lady as a creature of artifice and immorality, Grimké had turned the concept of "true womanhood" upside down and subverted that ideal for feminist purposes. Describing American women in terms of a hierarchical class structure, she placed "the butterflies of the fashionable world," a type with which she was most familiar, at the apex of American society and judged them as beyond redemption—dead to virtue, too depraved for salvation.

Below them was a larger class, taught to consider marriage as life's primary aim. Education was subordinated to this major goal; it was far more serious, Grimké noted, to distract a girl from her cooking than from her lessons. Given these social values and expectations, women thought of themselves "as a kind of machinery, necessary to keep the domestic engine in order, but of little value as the *intelligent* companions of men." [40] Having so thoroughly internalized the domestic ideal and its corollary, the concept of female inferiority, women met and absorbed that root assumption in all areas of American life; they could hardly be expected to respect themselves or their abilities, Grimké concluded, and all women, rich and poor, were accordingly united by their oppression. "Slaves," "butterflies," and the class between them faced the same problems in Grimké's analysis. The differences among women were only a matter of degree.

Hoping to frighten her audience, to make them see the interconnected plight of each and every woman Grimké had described, Stanton also conjured up the "butterfly" in her 1854 address to the New York Legislature. Since the lawmaker's daughters belonged to "the small class of fashionable butterflies," it was no wonder that they were incapable of understanding feminist argument; but, warned Stanton, they might not always be in such fortunate circumstances, as her illustrations of women's legal status made only too clear. Even the daughter of a legislator would, like her poorer sisters, need protection when winter came.[41] Thus, for Stanton and other intellectual feminists, their female opposition merely underscored the validity of feminist descriptions of women's degradation and of their arguments for reform. America was a vast storehouse of illustrations for their thesis of female degradation.

Feminists also appropriated another argument from the enemy camp as further proof of women's oppression: Women really were their own worst enemies, as antifeminists were the first to point out. Stanton, Brown, Smith, Davis, and Grimké all agreed: Women had been so thoroughly conditioned to be the "second sex" in a masculine culture that they were unable to grasp any of the basic tenets and themes feminists advanced. Conversely, men—especially in America—were accustomed to thinking of justice, human rights, and social and political equality as abstract concepts that could be translated into their personal and civic lives as Americans. Feminists often noted that even men who opposed them to the death at least understood what they were talking about.

While capitalizing upon the women who were not with them, feminists also insisted, from the basis of their analyses, upon the concept of female solidarity. A sense of strength derived from shared purpose, such as Angelina Grimké had evoked in her letter to the Syracuse convention, was indispensable to feminist thought and action, for it too helped discredit opponents and heighten the legitimacy of feminist claims and of the role of feminist leaders. Many intellectuals signed letters to each other "thine in the bonds of sisterhood," and the feminist convention was designed to create that spirit, regardless of how quickly it might evaporate once each meeting adjourned.

By arguing that feminists were "true women" united by both their virtue and the degraded status that made such virtue subject to the whims of men, feminists hoped to change their image in the press and in the popular mind alike, refuting the common assumption that, as Stanton put it, they were a handful of malcontents, "sour old maids," "childless women," and "divorced wives." [42] To combat this stereotype, feminists were forced into a rather paradoxical position, which made the concept of solidarity much harder to prove—even on paper. Wishing to stress that they were indeed "fortunate" women, that even these "had felt the insults incident to sex . . . as every proud, thinking woman must," [43] Stanton urged feminists to ally themselves with their less fortunate sisters in order to establish the common identity and dilemma shared by all American women.

Like American novelists who attempted to write about America as a whole while sectional strife unraveled the country into warring regions, feminists in a sense closed their eyes and hoped they were speaking for all women. Stanton insisted that she was a mouthpiece for women who worked in factories as well as for the privileged wives and daughters of men of wealth and professional attainments. Invoking the spirit and support of America's most oppressed women, Stanton called them the real "true women" of America and justified her own role as their spokeswoman. [44]

This compromise again reflected the strategy of the Jacksonian Persuasion—the dream that cultural unity and the restoration of old values would be achieved through the fragmenting processes of accelerating economic and technological growth. As other Jacksonians could not see that their idea of a "main chance" might destroy any remaining vestiges of that simpler world they wished to re-create, Stanton could not have realized that the same concept would, after the Civil War, help shatter her dream of unity among American women, making the worlds of American women increasingly difficult to synthesize with her formulation of the feminist persuasion. The intellectual focus and many of the principles Stanton advocated would have to be abandoned, replaced by what Aileen Kraditor has termed the "argument of expediency," [45] and Stanton herself recorded that transformation in *The History of Woman Suffrage*.

Throughout the decade of the 1850s, however, the romantic synthesis that was American feminism and the conventions that reflected that orientation continued to support the idea of female solidarity and to celebrate that ideal as a process as organic and inevitable as all other phenomena in a romantic intellectual's universe. As fond of uniting and hopefully resolving metaphysical opposites as persuaded Jacksonians were of reconciling social conflicts, the romantic intellectual as feminist united these traditions, symbolizing, quite appropriately, the intellectual and social traditions from which she came. Just as a romantic felt compelled intellectually to bring together all possible data and experience, no matter how vast and contradictory, in combinations only an intellectual virtuoso could synthesize, romantic intellectuals involved in both the theory and the institutions of American feminism hoped to bring all women together, no matter how different their experiences might be. Likewise, they saw the concepts of female solidarity and female opposition to the feminist persuasion as opposites that could be resolved by feminism itself. Invoking both in turn, most feminists of the 1850s preferred to place their emphasis on their female enemies.

No matter how ephemeral solidarity might seem and how remote the lives of factory women were, female opposition was highly visible. Its ranks were filled with "fortunate" women like themselves whom intellectuals could accordingly attack without guilt—and with relish. "Scribbling women," in particular, were sitting ducks for the often deadly marksmanship of feminist intellectuals. When caught in the sights of Stanton's wit and intellect, for example, "literary women"—as she contemptuously referred to them—were given no chance.

Where were all the "literary women" of whom America was so proud? Stanton often asked. Why were they so reluctant to speak out on women's rights? The answer was obvious: the literati were as enslaved as all other women—perhaps even more so. As hostages of masculine culture, they served at the public's pleasure; having no power of their own, they stood to lose status—and money—by joining the feminist movement, by deviating however slightly from the ideology of "true womanhood," which all of their productions supported. Stanton wrote that she understood their plight and their position—

even pitied them, for she was sure they would live to regret not having joined the "true women" of that generation in the feminist phalanx.[46]

Among the "dilettante literary women" she used as examples of female degradation, Stanton's favorite target was Sarah J. Hale. Although Stanton was not included in *Woman's Record*, she did not ignore its author—delighting in recognizing and ridiculing her. In that mammoth "woman's record" Stanton helped write and compile in the 1880s, *The History of Woman Suffrage*, she praised Hale for "exhuming nearly seventeen hundred women from oblivion," and thus providing a "valuable book of reference for the girls of today." That was Hale's only accomplishment, however, for Stanton characterized and caricatured her as a "thoroughly politic and time-serving" woman, "whose pen never by any chance slipped outside the prescribed literary line of safety, to cheer the martyrs to truth in her own generation." [47] Since Hale declined to set out for new territories in the feminist caravan, she was, Stanton suggested, nothing more than a moral and intellectual coward—and a bigot as well. The amusing picture she drew of Hale thinking about several women whom Stanton ranked with the greatest of her time suggested that Hale herself would be lost to history, swallowed up in that great gulf that separated her from the "true women" of her generation:

> Sarah J. Hale, shuddering over the graves of such women as Harriet Martineau, Frances Wright, Mary Wollstonecraft, George Sand, George Eliot and Lucretia Mott, might furnish a subject for an artist to represent as "bigotry weeping over the triumphs of time." [48]

Women like Sarah Hale, however, were still powerful opponents, regardless of what might happen to them in historical records of the future. With major cultural arbiters of femininity like Hale ranged against them, feminists were not surprised that their numbers were so small. "Vocal" feminists, whose dual mission was to elevate society's consciousness and the status of women, would always be a minority, Elizabeth

Oakes Smith wrote in 1853: No wonder it was so difficult to "make the idea of a true, noble womanhood . . . live in the public mind." [49] Smith had earlier concluded that feminist conventions and lectures could not accomplish this task alone. Opponents of feminism had access to the American press, and arbiters of "ideal femininity" like Hale had powerful magazines, such as *Godey's Lady's Book*, that served to transmit their conceptions of women's condition and their hostility to feminism to a larger public than feminists could ever draw to a convention or a lecture. Although several newspapers gave them a good press and the *New York Tribune*, in particular, gave them space to present their views, Smith stressed that feminists were extremely vulnerable to friends and foes alike, for they served at the pleasure of the few papers that welcomed their contributions. Accordingly, feminists needed a journal of their own if they were to effect and mold public opinion. In response to this need, Paulina Wright Davis launched *The Una*, the most important journalistic clearinghouse for feminist theory during the years of its publication between 1853 and 1855—the forum for intellectual women engaged in the feminist movement.

### 4. The Una:
*A Journal of Liberation*

In the pages of *The Una* one finds the interplay of history and female ideals within a romantic context characteristic of pre-Civil War feminism's distinctive style. Surrounded by quotations from Goethe, Kant, Schiller, Emerson, and Ruskin are accounts of "lost" women in history and in contemporary America. Forgotten "greats" and oppressed seamstresses face each other in the journal's columns. Analyses of woman's intellectual potential, of women in the American labor force, excerpts from feminist speeches and proceedings of feminist conventions, book reviews, historical essays, fiction and poetry—all testify to the broad range of interests and talents brought to the journal by its editors and contributors.

Margaret Fuller's spirit seems to preside over each issue; the journal's motto, "Out of the Great Heart of Nature Seek We Truth," clearly reveals the presence of that romantic imagination Fuller symbolized for her contemporaries.

In *The Una*'s first number the Reverend A. D. Mayo discussed the significance of the "woman problem" and the importance of the feminist solution: Woman's potential was already evident; having demonstrated their talents and capabilities, women were already on the lookout for outlets for this "new energy." Would it be given constructive outlets, allowed to "refresh society," the Reverend asked, or be repressed, dooming women to lives of bitter resentment, or, worst of all, tempting them "out into the wild and destructive ways of sin"? [50] Since it was too late to deny female energy and ability, the only alternative, the only real question America must ponder was how this energy and ability were to be used.

Having cleverly legitimatized her undertaking by leading off with a male spokesman and churchman, editor Paulina Wright Davis outlined her journal's objectives and established her own credentials as "true woman." Admitting her great misgivings about her role and "a diffidence, amounting almost to maidenly timidity," she wrote that the urgency of the woman problem had forced her to swallow her fears and pursue a virtuous course of action. She proposed to discuss all aspects of the woman question—"Rights, Relations, Duties, Destiny, Sphere"—with "candor and earnestness" and promised "never to be in a hurry, never to get ambitious or avaricious." Glad that her journal would not aim for a "literary reputation," Davis rejected elitism as well. *The Una* was to be an open forum, with room for all thought that was "fresh and new," closed only to celebrities, the "famous" in search of publicity, and all "claptrap measures." *The Una* would depend only upon the good will of its subscribers and "faith in principle." [51] Davis' "prospectus," in the first issue of February 1853, outlined the "aims and objects" of the monthly journal:

> Our purpose is to speak clear, earnest words of truth and soberness in a spirit of kindness . . . to discuss the rights, duties,

sphere, and destiny of woman fully and fearlessly. So far as our voice shall be heard, it will be ever on the side of freedom. We shall not confine ourselves to any locality, sex, sect, class, or caste, for we hold to the solidarity of the race, and believe if one member suffers, all suffer, and the highest made to atone for the lowest. Our mystical name, *The Una*, signifying *Truth*, will be to us a constant suggestion of fidelity to all. [52]

Paulina Wright Davis began publishing *The Una* in Providence, Rhode Island, at her own expense. Residing there with her second husband, she was a popular member of that city's literary coteries. Although her advanced opinions isolated her from other Providence communities, among whom she "dwelt like a sort of foreign princess," she was "too much of a reformer for adoption into the 'society' set of the city, too alien in purpose to suit its great cotton manufacturing families, and too heretical for its college folk." [53]

Davis turned her own alienation, her time, and her money to feminism's advantage. In 1850 she had been the principal organizer and architect of the First National Women's Rights Convention held in Worcester, Massachusetts—the only woman who could devote all her time to that project. This work made Davis indirectly responsible for drawing John Stuart Mill into the feminist fold: It was as a consequence of this convention that his wife, Harriet Taylor, wrote her famous article upon its proceedings for the *Westminster Review*, upon which Mill's subsequent *On the Subjection of Women* drew so heavily.

In addition to her extensive intellectual contributions and her organizational talents, Davis was also important to American feminism as a public symbol of the feminist as "true woman." Stanton, in particular, was fond of using her as a living refutation of that stereotype "sour old maid," which so many automatically applied to feminist women. Davis was proof, Stanton wrote, that

> this typical strong-minded woman of whom we hear so much in England and America, is after all a 'myth'; for the very best specimens of womanhood in both countries are those who thoroughly respect themselves, and maintain their political civil and social rights. [54]

Paulina Wright Davis was, according to all accounts, a woman of great beauty, charm, and elegance; she was, a friend once remarked, especially interesting because of the "graceful audacity" of her manner.[55]

Her life resembles in many ways the story of Cinderella. Like Elizabeth Cady Stanton and Antoinette Brown, Paulina Davis was originally from rural New York State. Born Paulina Kellogg in Bloomfield, New York, in 1813, where her father was a volunteer soldier in the War of 1812, she arrived, to his delight, on the day the Americans recaptured Detroit. In her portrait of Davis, Stanton wrote, her father "would often jocosely refer to those two great events on the 7th of August, 1813." Like Elizabeth Ellet, Davis was a daughter of revolutionary America; her grandfather had served on Lafayette's staff and had fought as a colonel in the revolution. He had purchased land near Niagara Falls, where Paulina's family moved when she was four years old. Her father and mother, Stanton wrote, "possessed great personal beauty, and were devotedly attached to each other." Both died shortly before Paulina's seventh birthday, and her carefree childhood in that frontierlike region she loved came to a close. She was sent to Le Roy, New York, to be "civilized" by a stern Presbyterian aunt.

The frequent revivals that swept this community fed Davis's growing spiritual torment, yet suggested a possible last chance of salvation through a life dedicated to missionary work. Like Elizabeth Cady Stanton, who continually returned in her writings to her conversion from both orthodoxy and evangelicism in tones of awe and delight, as if she were permanently astonished at her escape, Davis, in future years, spoke with great relief of her "great awakening," her escape from the Presbyterian faith and the fire and brimstone awaiting the damned, among whom previously she was certain she belonged. Since Davis's experience so closely paralleled her own, Stanton obviously enjoyed recording it for *The History of Woman Suffrage*. Davis had told her, Stanton wrote, that she was "not a happy child, nor a happy woman, until in mature life, I outgrew my early religious faith, and felt free to think and act from my own convictions." [56]

Her first husband was most instrumental in her intellectual emancipation and subsequent development. He arrived just in time to change her plans of becoming a missionary in the Sandwich Islands, which Stanton called the current "Mecca to which all pious young women desired to go." Francis Wright, a rich, young merchant from Utica, New York, convinced Paulina, according to Stanton, "that there were heathen enough in Utica to call out all the religious zeal she possessed, to say nothing of himself as the chief of sinners, hence in special need of her ministrations." [57] Their marriage in 1833 brought Paulina in contact with the many worlds of American reform. In Utica the couple plunged wholeheartedly into each of them, from abolitionism and feminism to health reform. For the twelve years of their marriage, until Francis Wright's death in 1845, they found it immensely rewarding to attack all the forces of reaction together.

During her first marriage, Paulina Wright devoted her intellectual energies to feminism and to the study of physiology and anatomy, subjects which women, in particular, were totally ignorant of. A knowledge of their own bodies was, for Davis, crucially important for women, both personally and professionally. It was indispensable for any woman trying to achieve her own identity and for those women who wished to prove themselves worthy of entry into professional medical schools—all still closed to women. As she clarified her own intellectual stance and goals, Paulina Wright realized that her interest in feminism had originated in the darkness of her religious torment.

Confused as a girl by religious controversies over woman's role in the church, whether women should be visible or invisible, she found herself, as an adult, perplexed with "conflicting emotions and opinions in regard to all human relations." Once taught a basic lesson of romantic thought—that "happiness did not depend on outward conditions, but on the harmony within, on the tastes, sentiments, affections, and ambitions of the individual soul"—she found that this "philosophy of life" clarified and intensified her commitment to feminism.[58]

As a young widow with a handsome inheritance and no children she lectured on anatomy and physiology to female audiences in the East and Midwest, using a Parisian mannikin of a woman's body—the first to be imported to America—to illustrate her speeches. When she undraped the model, some observers, horrified at such audacity, fainted. Others ran from the lecture hall. Among those who remained, however, were several women who later became part of America's first generation of female physicians. While delivering lectures in Providence in 1849, Paulina met and married Thomas Davis, a recent widower and jewelry manufacturer, and continued to devote herself to the feminist cause by writing articles and addresses and organizing feminist conventions.

In her account of the origins and progress of American feminism, published in 1871 as *A History of the National Woman's Rights Movement, For Twenty Years,* Paulina Wright Davis wrote candidly of the rise and fall of *The Una.* The prospects for this venture had seemed splendid at first, when fifty subscribers signed up at the Syracuse National Convention, but almost immediately an "unexpected difficulty met the editor." Both the journal's circulation and the editor's purse were too small to ensure its success, and Davis could find very few contributors willing to live on principles alone. Few volunteered to write for *The Una* without remuneration. Her predicament was very similar to Margaret Fuller's as editor of *The Dial.* Davis soon found herself putting out whole issues almost singlehandedly, and exhausting herself in the process of producing the magazine and worrying about its future. "The editor's labors were made so arduous in writing over various signatures, in order to give variety," she remembered, "that in two years her health became seriously impaired." Moving *The Una* to Boston in December 1854, and taking on an associate, she was able to keep the magazine alive for ten months before it "expired from inanition," and Davis sadly concluded: "Thus failed a hope and an agency which should have been the *pride* of women." [59]

If anyone could have saved *The Una* by sheer will and energy it was the new co-editor, Caroline Healey Dall of Boston. The daughter of an extremely wealthy Bostonian and an invalid mother of whom little is known, she was supremely self-confident of her intellectual ability, her own courageous spirit, and excellent character. Her life story might be entitled, "the strange career of the merchant's daughter." The historian Barbara Welter has recently described how Dall interpreted and acted out her life in terms of the popular saga of the merchant's daughter who, "faced with her father's ruin, was forced to make her own way in the world." In the process, Welter writes, "she stood up to outrageous fortune with fortitude, convinced that her character as well as that of her parents would be improved by the change in circumstances." [60]

For Caroline Dall, as for so many other Protestant Americans uneasy about the relationship of wealth to virtue, financial failure could be converted to spiritual success, offering its victims the chance to prove themselves worthy of salvation. In addition, Caroline Dall always insisted that her father, Mark Healey, although an "India merchant," was no mere materialist even before he lost his fortune. He did not conform in the slightest to the stereotype of the merchant prince, she wrote in her autobiography, for he was an "eminently intellectual" man, a Unitarian, and a lover of free inquiry. "He desired above all that I should form my opinions independently of his." [61]

Dall's father taught his daughter the alphabet by the time she was eighteen months old, encouraged her intellectual development throughout her early years, and taught her methods of concentrating that formed what she called subsequently her "iron" memory. [62] In addition, Caroline was taught by governesses and in private academies and became fluent in several languages before she reached her teens. Later, as so many of her friends went to Harvard and she remained in close contact with them, moving freely among the various intellectual milieus in Boston and Cambridge, she wrote that she felt like a Harvard alumna herself. Also during this period, Elizabeth Peabody opened her bookshop in Boston, the first to stock contemporary foreign literature, and Caroline became acquainted with romantic thought. A whole new world opened before her eyes, and she always thanked Peabody for this initiation.

Independent of her exposure to and awareness of other influences, male and female, she still regarded her father as the master builder of her own character. He had created her independence and her sense of intellectual authority. Because of his influence she could not remember ever being without an opinion of her own.[63] And for Caroline Dall, opinions, informed and considered, were meant to be shared—even forced upon others—not hoarded in private.

Unable to suppress her thoughts, Dall often uttered them in so candid and didactic a manner that she made many enemies. She was certainly incapable of ever playing disciple, or "Corinne," to anyone. While attending ten of Margaret Fuller's "Conversations" in 1841, she was warned by Elizabeth Peabody that Fuller and Emerson had stared in disapproval at her own outspokenness in those meetings. Dall replied that their opinions were of no consequence to her. Sensing that Fuller disliked her, Dall attributed Fuller's disdain to the fact that with her unwavering "instinct of self-possession" Dall could not be Fuller's disciple, could not become "so enamored of any, as to lose my own centre."[64]

The "Conversations," however, made a lasting impact on her life, Dall insisted; and her distance and "iron memory" benefited both teacher and pupil, for Dall recorded the "Conversations" she attended and published them in book form in 1897. Although her writings usually praise Fuller unequivocally, a note of ambivalence often creeps into the most lavish paeans to the woman Dall called the greatest intellectual woman America had ever produced.

Her ambivalence about Fuller was not merely the result of personal differences and conflicts. During the "Conversation" phase, Fuller represented an intellectual style Dall could not admire. Her early experiences, with Joseph Tuckerman's ministries among Boston's poor—indeed, all her heritage—conspired to make her shun a life that was not a virtuous illustration of duty and usefulness, just as Fuller's own background helped propel her from the "Conversations" to what she called "a life of action." Actively helping Boston's poorest citizens was far more important than pursuing the studies Dall loved. Once again, her steely resolve and self-discipline came in handy to quench her intellectual impulses: "I knew that if I had any danger—it was that of loving the intellectual too well and pursuing it too far." [65]

Although her father had envisioned a purely literary life for Caroline, he undermined his own goals by fostering her independent spirit. He had wished her to continue her studies in Europe, and she had always bridled at the thought. His financial collapse in 1842 (the result of the panic of 1837) changed the course of her life and that of her father's wishes for her future. After several months of intensive job-seeking she found herself in a foreign world on American soil—at a female academy in Georgetown where southern politicians based in Washington, D. C. often boarded their daughters. There the stern moralist taught, appropriately enough, mathematics (in an incongruously lush setting) to young women who must have seemed to their teacher blithely unaware of the moral imperatives that governed her life. In 1844, she returned to more familiar surroundings and renewed her acquaintance with Charles Dall, a young Unitarian minister working in a Tuckerman ministry in Baltimore, and soon married him.

Caroline remembered hearing Dall deliver the Harvard Divinity School Address years before and recalled how impressive she found both his person and his eloquence. [66] Clerical associates, however, recorded in an obituary that he had always exhibited "peculiarities of mind and temperament," [67] qualities that marriage to Caroline soon accentuated. In a curious role reversal for a period in which the invalid wife was a commonplace, Charles's health soon failed; the couple soon moved to Boston, and a son and daughter were born in the five years spent there. In 1850, the family left for Canada where Caroline helped Charles with the duties of his new pastorate. The Canadian sojourn ended in 1854 with Charles's sudden attack of brain fever. The Dalls returned to Boston. The next year Charles took off for India as a missionary, leaving his family behind and returning to America for short intervals during the next and last thirty-one years of what suddenly became a robust and healthy life.

Caroline Dall, by meeting the challenge of being left alone

with two children, once again proved herself in the face of adversity. In addition, she at last discovered an intellectual style congenial to her talents and her temperament within the feminist movement she had previously shunned. Uniting intellectual activity, duty, and usefulness, and highlighting the importance of both women's history and the role of historian, American feminism served as the catalyst for Dall's intellectual development and contributions before the Civil War.

Here was a life of the mind Dall might lead without compromise and without guilt. She had embarked upon this course while still in Canada, contributing several articles to *The Una*. Now, back in America, she became a more active contributor, an active feminist organizer, and a participant in many conventions. Like Elizabeth Oakes Smith, however, Caroline Dall was not truly comfortable within the "phalanx of associated inquiry." She too preferred to work alone, to write and deliver lectures. Like Smith, Dall came to see herself as a symbol of the intellectual woman of the future, and she agreed with Smith that the natural home, the new salon, of the "woman of intellect" was the lyceum, in particular, and the lecture hall in general. As she wrote of Mme de Staël in *The Una*, Dall believed that the spiritual descendants of this inspiring woman—such as Dall herself—could exert a mighty influence if they had a forum.[68]

Although her title on the journal's masthead was co-editor, Dall insisted during her tenure that she was only *The Una*'s historian of women. "Our own duty consists in ransacking the records of the past, and supplying biographical matter to these pages."[69] Dall did not regard this as an insignificant function. Any duty she assumed was a sacred responsibility and that of historian was crucial to feminism's ultimate success:

Without reading the past clearly, it is impossible to go to the root of present evils. Many a reform fails for want of accurate knowledge based on this, of what is needed to be done. Not only a firm purpose, a clear insight, a brave soul, and a true moderation are needed to effect the desired change in the social and political position of woman, but a positive knowledge of all that relates to her past condition. Her history is yet to be written. The materials of it have floated for centuries on the waves of Time, and to gather the far-scattered but significant waifs is the task we propose to ourselves, a much more important aid to the reform than may be at first imagined.[70]

As *The Una*'s house historian she mentally traversed the globe and the centuries, especially delighting in unearthing new examples of female intellectual excellence and in vindicating female reputations that she felt male historians and artists had hopelessly distorted through the ages. "Ancient Athens' " most glorious women intellectuals—Aspasia, the beloved of Pericles, and Hypatia, the learned daughter of the head of Alexandria's Platonist school—were quickly redeemed by the historian. Aspasia was not an immoral courtesan, and her union with Pericles was likewise untainted; theirs was the greatest marriage of true minds in all history.[71] Hypatia, "clothed in wisdom as in a garment, and honored by the flower of the whole civilized world," had been vulgarized beyond recognition in Charles Kingsley's historical novel, *Hypatia; or, New Foes with an Old Face* (1853).[72]

Although Dall objected to historical fiction in general, for its distortion and lack of factual data, it was for her an especially deadly genre for female characters. In this case, Hypatia's aversion to Christianity led to her execution. Thus she had refused to accept what Dall interpreted as but one of many new religions that would, like the older Greek myths, 'degenerat[e]' into weak corrupting myths." A mob had murdered her because she was "influential as a mind," although, Dall wrote, one would never guess from Kingsley's novel that the "martyr" was anything but a "weak, presuming woman, fitly punished for meddling with matters that she did not understand."[73] Readers of *The Una* and listeners at feminist conventions where Dall frequently read excerpts from her articles could, she hoped, form true pictures of women abused by history and historians.

Caroline Dall wrote for *The Una* many detailed narratives of Italian women throughout the centuries. Part of her lengthy series, "The Women of Bologna," was read aloud by the author at a feminist convention. Italy was to Dall what Germany represented to Margaret Fuller before she too discovered Italy: it was the promised land—a veritable paradise for intellectual women. She marveled at how effortlessly intellectual ability seemed to be transferred from one generation of Italian women to another, as Fuller had depicted the flowering of woman's intellect under the "great German oak." Italy seemed all the more glorious to Dall when she thought about the shabby treatment women thinkers received in England and America:

> We are forcibly struck, in the first place, with the pride which the Italians feel in their learned women. In England and America, women are not only obliged to excuse themselves for possessing any unusual amount of learning; but their *friends*, in turn, must apologize for the love they bear such women. "Yes," you will hear them saying, "we love her in spite of her learning. You cannot guess how lovely she is in her family, how kind she is to the poor, in spite of all her acquirements." In spite of! In Bologna, we hear nothing of all that. Fathers, brothers, and lovers do their utmost to encourage and sustain the love of learning in women; and, at the present day, people of the middle class will tell you pleasant traditions of Bassi, Baltiferri, and Agnesi.[74]

Among all the learned Italians, Caroline Dall's favorite was Maria Gaetana Agnesi, whom the historian re-created as an Italian version of herself. Taught by her father, Maria was soon so talented a linguist that she was christened "the walking polyglot." Moving to the field of mathematics, she found her intellectual home in "geometry and speculative philosophy." [75] Although this choice was a parting of the ways between the historian and her subject, Dall evoked the quality and depth of the Italian's mind in words she hoped would apply to her own:

> Her learning was a sound and solid thing; that she was not obliged to batter thin, and spread over a wide surface. It would stand wear, bear questioning, and shine all the more for the friction of a discussion.[76]

When she published her *Una* articles in book form, *Historical Pictures Retouched* (1860), Dall explained in her preface the shortcomings of the portraits she had "prepared in Provincial loneliness, and want of opportunity." Since women in general did such poor work, given their degraded status, she thought it imperative for every woman to make "her best, her slowest, her most faithfully prepared contribution," for "whatever looks slipshod, ill-considered, or undigested, makes the heart sink." Her duty as a historian, however, outweighed this consideration.

There were, for Dall, two kinds of workers in the field of history—"Seekers" and "Observers." She defined the former's function as discoverer, preserver, and guardian of the past: "Seekers" should "collect, collate, test, and simplify material," "decide what is worth saving, and what must be permitted to drift down the dark gulf of the past." Then the "Observer" took over as interpreter. "It is the business of the Observers to make use of this material, and permit philosophic thought, general knowledge, and rare culture, to do their work with the accumulations so brought together." Women had already done yeoman service as "Seekers," Dall emphasized, but their work, almost by definition, lacked "perspective" and required the skilled touch of the "Observer," of whom the world and women's record had as yet known so few.[77] Therefore, Dall had come forward as a pioneer in this great endeavor:

No feminine jury—no *human* jury, I would rather say, constituted equally of men and women—has, thus far, summoned the witnesses of the past. An experimental knowledge of the workings of woman's nature, a wide charity for the positions into which uncommon strength of good or evil kind may force her, is needed to illuminate the doubtful pages of human life. Shadows may yet fall over spotless names; and prodigies of wickedness, illuminated by some devout scholar's labor, may still be drawn into the sunlight of truth, and show some glimpses of their human origin.[78]

The urgency and sublimity of her mission had, Dall concluded, compelled her to write articles for *The Una* in which readers could see women's history from a qualified observer's vantage point. These portraits were the best she could draw at present, she insisted. She only hoped they would be judged truly superior as had her earlier collection, *Woman's Right to Labor*, which also contained many *Una* contributions. That book was, Dall implied, the work of an American Agnesi; the portraits must be judged by the less sublime criterion of social utility.

Paulina Wright Davis and other contributors to *The Una* judged contemporary female literary productions according to the same uncompromising standards Caroline Dall gleaned from romantic thought and applied to art and life. Very few works written by women passed muster in *The Una*, and the journal frequently assailed female literati who castigated the woman's movement. To those searching for Truth from within the "great heart of nature" concerning all aspects of the female experience, any falsifications of that record warranted exposure and denunciation in *The Una*'s pages.

To confront what she considered the greatest of all falsehoods, Davis shrewdly printed many letters to the editor from anonymous or obscure correspondents (she may have written many herself) that attacked the whole range of antifeminist sentiment in America and the institutions of press and pulpit that perpetuated it. Mary F. Love of Randolf, New York, quoting lengthy passages from Lydia Sigourney in her letter, wrote that her "heart sank" when she saw the "sweet singer of Hartford"—America's "boast and pride"—blithely dismiss the subject of women's rights: "Bright visions of flowery fields and singing birds will not satisfy the dungeon captive, nor will glowing pictures of the 'far off unattained' atone to woman for the wrongs which bow her spirit to the dust." [79]

Although Lydia Sigourney remained grossly ignorant of woman's plight, *Harper's* magazine, wrote another *Una* contributor, was beginning to see the light. In her article "How Fares Our Course" (August 1854), Frances D. Gage, an active feminist organizer, called American journals the best gauges of public opinion. Among them, *Harper's* had been feminism's most "violent" and "uncompromising" foe, printing "squibs, burlesques, caricatures and slanders to be read and copied and recorded by millions." Gage then borrowed that journal's strategy and drew an amusing caricature illustrating how *Harper's* molded public opinion and generated new critiques of the feminist persuasion:

> And the bloated demagogue, who had just swallowed his six courses at some fashionable restaurant, gulped down his pint of champaigne [*sic*], and sits himself down in some fashionable reading room, with his heels higher than his head (more brains in them perhaps), . . . takes Harper from his pocket, and smokes and reads . . . and sagely concludes he could not love a masculine intellectual woman, and shrugs his shoulders . . . with deep disgust at the bare idea of . . . Antoinette L. Brown; and forthwith he seizes his pen, and writes out his honest convictions for Harper or Putnam, or the Knickerbocker; or he rushes into the lecture room and proclaims his ideas of "woman's sphere" to admiring audiences, and tells them, "That it will never do for women to be educated and enlightened, to learn to think and to act for themselves. If they do, *men won't love them.*" [80]

Now that even *Harper's* had, like Charles Dickens, begun to acknowledge the legal disabilities women faced and to "prate" about women's wrongs, Gage concluded that feminists should take heart and act with renewed vigor. They should, Gage thought, strive to live up to that "sneer" of their enemies, the epithet "strong minded women," and illustrate the "mightly wisdom" it concealed—"that we may prove ourselves strong minded; faithful in truth and right . . . till we shall have breathed our testimony . . . " and until they had taken the field. [81]

Sarah J. Hale and *Godey's Lady's Book* fared no better than did *Harper's* in *The Una's* pages. In her letter to the editor, a "southern lady" from Memphis, Tennessee, attacked an article by a southern sister in *Godey's*, including in her attack copious quotations from the article and a critique of the magazine in general, for its unenlightened view of women's condition. [82] Davis assessed Hale and *Woman's Record* with an equally cold eye. Of Hale's encyclopedia Davis concluded that the value of the information was undermined by the context Hale had provided. The world would benefit from its contents, she declared, but "the world does not want it written thus."

Davis's primary objection to Hale's method was the "value judgments" the compiler had appended to each entry. Such a book might be subversive to its author's intent, Davis added, for its view of women was so absurdly restricted and conventional. They were merely "porcelain clay" for Hale regardless of how their lives contradicted her ideal. Thus paradoxically the book only served "to rouse our consciences" and generate "protest" against such simpleminded conceptions of woman's nature. It seemed to Davis that Sarah Hale had missed everything of significance in her epoch; only the publication of her encyclopedia testified to her existence. One might assume, Davis wrote, that Hale "had been passing the last twenty years with Rip Van Winkle, if her ponderous records of women did not lie before us." Even so, she lived in a different world: "We think she has shut herself into the enchanted castle, and knows not how women of the nineteenth century have meddled with the earth." [83]

Turning to female literature more congenial to the feminist spirit, *The Una* entered the controversy over "Fanny Fern's" *Ruth Hall* (1854). In this novel and in a collection of extremely candid essays, *Fern Leaves* (1854), Sarah Willis, sister of the acclaimed literatus and bon vivant, Nathaniel Parker Willis, had exposed the nether side of the cult of "ideal womanhood." In addition, many thought she had exposed the idiosyncrasies, the secret failings of her family and friends, and above all, her overt hostility to her male relatives, to male domination in general, and to its supporting ideology of true femininity. Her chosen nom de plume symbolized, as the historian Ann Wood has recently written, "Fanny Fern's" literary strategy and her dual, devious, even schizophrenic relationship to the tradition of womanhood she so brutally parodied. Although all her writings reflected this double vision, she remained as unconscious of her own motives as did the "female scribblers" she attacked.[84] Sarah Willis was one half true woman, "fern," and one half the gadfly of that sensibility, for, she wrote, "I never saw a 'Fanny' yet that wasn't as mischievous as Satan." [85] In *Ruth Hall*, divided into two parts like Willis's personality, "fern" is ousted by "Fanny" or, as one female reviewer scornfully renamed the book, by *Ruthless Hall*. A narrative of the trials, sufferings, and exultant triumph of a woman writer—a barely fictionalized Sarah Willis—the novel explicitly and joyfully rejects the literary rationale of the female "scribbler." Priding herself upon reflecting the very qualities and motives that strategy sought to suppress, "Ruth Hall" luxuriated in her newly found aggressive nature. Candidly, she explored the motives that compelled her to seek literary success—money, fame, and self-esteem—and celebrated her triumph in the literary marketplace. Appropriately, the book was a bestseller and a sensation. Hawthorne praised it for its honesty and vitality, for speaking directly to the realities of the female experience, which the "scribblers" he abhorred always evaded. [86] "Scribblers," quite naturally, damned it for the qualities Hawthorne most admired. Elizabeth Cady Stanton loved the novel and wrote a rave review for *The Una* of February 1855.

Here at last was a "literary woman" Elizabeth Cady Stanton could admire without qualification, a woman who had, she wrote, by some mysterious and miraculous process transcended the bonds of "ideal femininity" and exposed them as symbols of female slavery—one whose "consciousness" had so blossomed that she recognized that "her legal protectors [were] her tyrants" and painted them as they were. With her characteristic irony, Stanton attacked the *National Anti-Slavery Standard* for giving *Ruth Hall* a bad review. Abolitionists, of all people, should take it seriously, for the book was really "a slave narrative" such as the ones abolitionists treated with such dignity and respect. They should listen to "Ruth Hall," Stanton advised, as if they were hearing "the words of a Frederick Douglass." [87] Like Hawthorne, she rejoiced in the fact that a woman had published an honest account of her life and had succeeded in portraying men and women realistically.

Hoping that *Ruth Hall* marked the birthdate of a genuine female literature, Stanton threw down the gauntlet to male novelists and to all outspoken critics of the book:

> Men have given us all their experience, from Moses down to the last village newspaper; and how much that is palatable have they said of woman? And now that woman has seized the brush, and brought forth on the canvas a few specimens of dwarfed and meagre manhood, lo! what a furor of love and reverence has seized our world of editors and critics! You who have ridiculed your mothers, wives and sisters since you first began to put pen to paper, talk not of "filial irreverence." This is but a beginning, gentlemen. If you do not wish us to paint you wolves, get into lambs' clothing as quickly as possible.[88]

Two months later co-editor Caroline Dall reviewed both the novel and Stanton's article, emphasizing that *The Una* was unwilling to "endorse all the deductions that naturally flow-[ed]" from Stanton's review, however admirable she found Stanton's "fearlessness" in voicing her own opinions. Judged by purely literary standards the novel was a failure, just as "slovenly" a production as critics pronounced it; and Stanton, by ignoring such criteria, had, Dall insisted, told only half the story of *Ruth Hall* and had also distorted its significance. "By no means" could the book be considered the "work of a ripe and well-trained woman." To Dall it was a fiasco and a curiosity. It was not an "autobiography," as many critics claimed, although it did contain what Dall considered cruel caricatures of "Fanny Fern's" relatives—her brother, for example, was immediately recognizable as the foppish Hyacinth, who sabotaged "Ruth Hall's" literary endeavors at every opportunity. The closest analogy Dall could summon for the book was that it was like "the play of Hamlet with the part of Hamlet left out."[89]

Perplexed perhaps by its author's contradictory identity as both rebel and "true woman," Dall could not see the relationship between the two parts of the book. The author merely ranted, Dall wrote, and was unable to maintain any distance from her subject. The book was a tale of sound and fury told by a woman whose artistic failure had significance for the feminist movement. For, most important of all, Dall saw in Sarah Willis basic character flaws that would, she believed, unfit her for the role of feminist spokeswoman or symbol. In fact, the real problem according to Dall was that "Fanny Fern" had no character: she was a cruel, cynical woman who, like her brother Nathaniel, had no convictions on any subject. Such a person obviously did not belong within "the phalanx of related inquiry"; she would be not merely unconvincing as a feminist advocate but dangerous to the spirit of that enterprise. Dall, in summing up her reservations about *Ruth Hall* and "Fanny Fern," hoped that neither book nor author would become identified with American feminism: "Let no one think us indifferent to suffering; we feel for them deeply; but Heaven shield the cause from making a reformer, conscious or unconscious, out of a Fanny Fern." [90]

In contrast to its critical assessment of *Ruth Hall, The Una* recommended without qualification Elizabeth Oakes Smith's feminist novel, *Bertha and Lily* (1854). Davis pronounced it excellent as a whole but reserved her warmest words for the book's last section in which she thought the author "had become more and more thoroughly imbued with the spirit of her own philosophy, and had grown calm in its holy influence, while she felt that her ideal world was her real." [91] Smith's ideal world, of course, was one that granted women social and intellectual autonomy; like the heroine of her poem, *The Sinless Child*, the saintlike Bertha transcends a past of deprivation and suffering, gaining romantic self-hood in the process. In addition, Bertha becomes not only symbol but spokeswoman for the feminist persuasion.

Perhaps thinking of Hawthorne's Hester Prynne—*Bertha and Lily* reads in many ways like a sequel to *The Scarlet Letter*— Smith, in a sense, returned Hester to America as Bertha and reunited her with her long-lost illegitimate daughter Lily, the Pearl of Smith's novel. Although the book contains some rather vicious portraits of women, such as the New England shrew, "Defiance," who makes life miserable for the long suffering Bertha, the overriding message and tone of *Bertha and*

*Lily* made it impossible for its author to be accused of cynicism and inhumanity—the basis of *The Una*'s case against *Ruth Hall* and "Fanny Fern."

Of all the literary women whose lives and works were extolled in *The Una*, Margaret Fuller always remained first in the hearts and minds of editors and contributors. "In America, Margaret Fuller has never yet had a rival, and we doubt very much whether she has ever had one in the Old World," Caroline Dall announced to *The Una*'s readers in July 1855.[92] Although many had blamed Fuller for not offering any constructive criticism upon the woman question in *Woman in the Nineteenth Century*, their objections were dismissed as irrelevant in Dall's article. Fuller's critics, Dall wrote, had misjudged her arguments and intentions. Fuller's vision was one of total transformation of woman's character, and she had offered her book as a mere beginning, a preliminary outline of the problems confronting women. Therefore, Dall thought it ridiculous to demand more of the book and added that its lasting importance would be in the heavy demands Fuller's work placed upon women to work out their own destiny:

> It demands of women that they shall think,—quite as much that they think well. It requires of them that they be no longer slaves—no longer pets and playthings as well. It may be long before we grow hardy enough to reject the pleasant phrases of our life for the sake of the profitable—to put aside a tenderness that cherishes, because we know it debilitates us. Happy those who do it of their own free choice—not waiting until urged on by the shocks of relentless fate.[93]

However fortunate a woman who achieved autonomy might be, the intellectual woman, including Margaret Fuller, was an outsider—a hero and a martyr whose romantic image often haunted issues of *The Una*. In each of its frequent investigations and analyses of woman's nature and history, *The Una* presented this image and touched upon the question of woman's intellectual potential, thus offering its contribution to the cultural debate upon that question. In *The Una* of March 1,

1853, Paulina Wright Davis confronted this vast subject in the first of her series, "The Intellect of Woman."

It was *The Una*'s policy, she wrote, to accept all "natural differences" between the sexes (physical strength in particular) and to reject all arguments that assumed that the exclusion of women from certain fields of activity implied that they were therefore incapable of achievement in such areas. Outlining this age-old strategy, marked for Davis by its "carelessness of logic and slippery generalities of reasoning," she urged readers to learn how to recognize this argument; it was the same whether one was speaking of women, slaves, or any other "oppressed" group:

> The oppressor asserts the incapacity of the oppressed for higher and better conditions. He urges besides, the slave's contentment with his station, and never fails to add that he is better and happier in bondage than he could be in freedom. History is cited to prove that he is better circumstanced than ever before. Exemption from the cares and risks of self-government is played off against all privations which are inflicted, and all the progress which is hindered; and holy writ, Jewish and Pagan, are twisted into authority for the support of this system.[94]

What history really demonstrated about the intellectual potential and achievements of women was quite different, according to Davis's analysis. Women's status in general had declined; they no longer played many significant roles, which they had done in the past. Even their past achievements had been accomplished in the face of such great obstacles that they deserved a "double honor" for their heroic feats of endeavor. The question of woman's intellect and the concept of the intellectual woman must, Davis wrote, be placed into this perspective to be understood. Then one was in a position to answer the taunts of the opposition.

That common query, "Where are all the female geniuses?"— already a cliché by 1853—became moot when one considered the history of the social oppression of women and their intellectual triumphs in the past: "If the range and compass of her work are limited anywhere, it is just where her education and opportunities have been crippled and smothered by the system which enslaves her." Davis's romantic definition of art and experience added depth to her equally romantic insistence that cultural change through time, the process of history, had left its mark on woman. The life of the mind was an organic process that must be perceived as a changing and complex phenomenon; it was, Davis implied, ridiculous to speak of woman's innate ability or lack of ability if nothing else in the mind or the universe could be characterized in such simplistic terms. Experience itself required a context to be understood—all of it must be "related to form an integral life"—and education should reflect and develop its dynamic nature. Only individuals who had not been cut off from experience and an education that enriched it could, Davis stated, achieve the sublime stature of the artist. Only a person familiar with the whole of life could qualify, since "no single faculty of the human intellect can be educated to perfection by itself," because "the whole soul must be brought up in compact array to the achievements of its highest enterprises." [95] Therefore, the "slumbering genius of our sex" could only be awakened, Davis concluded, if women themselves were allowed to come to life:

> The enriching experiences, the informing observations of the life that is flowing around us, [are] almost hidden from our eyes, [life's] excitements are denied to our imagination, its strifes to our ambition; and how can we compete with our highly favored rivals for an equal rank in what they call literature and art? [96]

Davis called female achievers, intellectual and otherwise, "female adventurers" in conflict with "false opinions and all the established order and institutions, laws and customs of society." In spite of—perhaps because of—the obstacles women faced, their intellectual achievements suggested that men and women shared the same "natural genius." If both sexes enjoyed the same opportunities to develop it, one could hardly place limits upon woman's intellectual future, and Davis invited her readers to "imagine what she might be with all circumstances favoring her heroism and helping her capacities."

Davis then called for a moratorium upon the old debate over femininity and intellect until the horizons of women had been extended to match the excellence of their past performance in history. In the third article in her series, Davis urged men in particular to look around them and behold the emergent life of women—to view "the sex as a prospective creation—that womanhood is to be unfolded and realized in the future and that the past is neither its measure nor its prophecy." [97]

*The Una* did not dwell exclusively upon woman's past or her future possibilities; it kept a shrewd eye trained upon the present condition of women in America and upon the progress of the feminist movement. In a convention address reprinted in *The Una* of September 1853, Paulina Wright Davis reported that the "Woman's Movement" was progressing splendidly; it was, she said, the greatest feat in the entire "history of public opinion." [98] With its goals and principles firmly established in conventions, the movement should continue to hold these meetings and proceed immediately upon "the parallel line of *Action*," addressing itself to the question of women's economic plight in America:

> We must take up the bread problem and solve the problem of industrial independence by extending and enriching the varieties of work that women shall do, and so carry on their personal emancipation, while their civil and social enfranchisement makes its way in the sentiments of men. In a word we must buy ourselves out of bondage, and work our way into liberty and honor. [99]

Thus, for Davis, feminist goals were as interrelated, as impossible to compartmentalize, as nature and humanity were to the romantic mind. She could not speak of women's social, economic, and political roles as if they existed on separate planes. History too was inseparable from woman's contemporary status and relevant to her economic dilemma which Davis called the "bread problem." Analogies from the past provided, for Davis, clear perspectives upon the reality of woman's condition in her time. Unlike Elizabeth Oakes Smith, who had found the very idea of a medieval woman's lot extremely uncongenial to women in the nineteenth century, Davis pronounced the Middle Ages superior to contemporary America in the options it offered to women. A return to the Middle Ages would, Davis wrote, paradoxically be a journey of progress. Then, women had been, for example, physicians and manuscript copiers, positions of authority for which the nineteenth century offered no equivalents for women. Contemporary women had no "function," Davis concluded; "manufactures" had taken over her traditional duties, removed them from home to factory. Nothing was left for women to do except to enter the "factory and the schoolroom at *slave* wages." As the traditional world of women no longer existed, it was only logical to Davis that they wished to find the "position which belongs to us in the new world. . . ." [100]

Since "woman's sphere" was still so extremely restricted, especially in America, it was ridiculous to speak of "emancipated" women, declared *The Una*'s editors. In an article entitled "Emancipated Women," Dall called that phrase a contradiction in terms: ". . . The term as applied, has no meaning, for there is no class of women who can claim, in the present stage of the movement, that they are 'set free from bondage, slavery, servitude, subjection, or dependence,' which is the definition given by Webster of the word 'emancipated'." [101]

This misnomer had been coined, Dall believed, by the Swedish feminist Frederica Bremer, whose faulty English might have been responsible for the choice of such an "inexpressive" term. It was also, in Dall's opinion, a phrase most "offensive to good taste," like all "cant phrases belonging to any set, sect, or class." Although *The Una* had never admired the phrase "woman's rights" for this reason, they continued to use it, for "no other term can be found which covers the whole ground we must occupy in this discussion." [102] It was *The Una*'s basic strategy, according to this article, to ignore fashionable "cant" and "slang" unless they revealed new perspectives on the problems feminism faced and indicated changes in public opinion concerning the movement and the condition of women in American society.

Regardless of their lowly status, women did have an influence on society, for better or worse, wrote Caroline Dall in her series, "The Duties and Influences of Women" (August and September 1854). Of all the various types of influence women had always exerted, Dall called their "atmospheric" influence the most widely understood and easily "justified." When "a woman of talent or genius, without a positive attainment of illustrious reputation for herself, stimulates others to attain it; and, like Napoleon, perceives at once what every bystander is capable of, and requires his utmost of him," she is exercising her "atmospheric" influence—for good or evil, as the myriad historical examples she cited suggested. Contemporary America, Dall continued, "offered two of the most remarkable examples of the excess and deficiency of this sort of influence"—Margaret Fuller and Elizabeth Peabody. Dall found Margaret Fuller wanting only in the capacity for empathy. Any woman "deficient in self-assertion" suffered a total loss of whatever self-esteem she had after a meeting with Margaret. If—and only if—one was admitted into her circle, "acknowledged" by her, did Fuller indeed "become a mighty stimulus." Peabody, on the contrary, brought out the best in everyone she met: "No one ever left her without having risen in his own self-respect and hers." This "stimulus" was, Dall concluded, Peabody's greatest "legacy to her country"—greater than all the fruits of her "generous culture, profound research, and Oriental learning." Her spirit would never pale in Dall's "iron" memory, for "radiant as the summer sunlight . . . is the beautiful smile of appreciation with which she welcomed the struggling, half-delivered thought." [103]

In 1859 Caroline Dall, now without the forum provided by the extinct *Una*, continued her explorations of America's intellectual women in a speech prepared for delivery at the Ninth National Woman's Rights Convention in New York City. She never gave that address. Elizabeth Cady Stanton remembered that Caroline Dall had planned to speak of Mary Wollstonecraft and "to show that what she did in the old world, Margaret Fuller had done in the new." The crowd was too impatient and restless to listen and soon drowned out her words, and she "sat down without speaking of Margaret Fuller." [104] That same year Paulina Wright Davis sailed to Europe to study art. The role of the intellectual within the "phalanx of associated inquiry" was becoming more problematic. Perhaps the essentially lonely enterprise conducted by all intellectuals was doubly lonely for intellectual women within the feminist movement. Perhaps they did not belong there at all. Stanton herself recorded the decline and fall of her own influence in post-Civil War America. Many might still consider her the "mother of them all" but others were wary of her participation, afraid that her thoughts might alienate feminism's new constituency. Stanton converted her own sense of displacement into an eloquent soliloquy on solitude in which the vocabulary of romanticism came to her aid and comfort. Prepared for delivery at the National American convention in 1892, her address on individuality and solitude was the last one she delivered in person to a feminist convention. Now seventy-six years old, Elizabeth Cady Stanton sounded very much like Lydia Maria Child describing the female experience as the human condition: "The isolation of every human soul," Stanton began, was the "strongest reason" for opening all opportunities to women:

> The talk of sheltering woman from the fierce storms of life is the sheerest mockery, for they beat on her from every point of the compass, just as they do on man, and with more fatal results, for he has been trained to protect himself, to resist, to conquer. Whatever the theories may be of woman's dependence on man, in the supreme moments of her life he can not bear her burdens. . . . We may have many friends, love, kindness, sympathy and charity to smooth our pathway in everyday life, but in the tragedies and triumphs of human experience each mortal stands alone.[105]

# (5)

# The "Woman of Letters" in Transition

*All great acquisitions come from voluntary thought, and voluntary thought alone.*

—Elizabeth Palmer Peabody

*Daughter of Memory! who her watch doth keep*
*O'er dark Oblivion's land of shade and dream,*
*Peers down into the realm of ancient Sleep,*
*Where Thought uprises with a sudden gleam*
*And lights the devious path 'twixt Be and Seem;*
*Mythologist! that dost thy legend steep*
*Plenteously with opiate and anodyne,*
*Inweaving fact with fable, line with line,*
*Entangling anecdote and episode,*
*Mindful of all that all men meant or said,—*
*We follow, pleased, thy labyrinthine road,*
*By Ariadne's skein and lesson led:*
*For thou has wrought so excellently well,*
*Thou drop'st more casual truth than sages tell.*

—A. Bronson Alcott, "To Elizabeth Peabody"

*Scholars were very generous to each other then, and they had need to be, for they could not tell how soon they might have to ask for the favors they granted.*

—Caroline Healey Dall

Elizabeth Palmer Peabody        *The Schlesinger Library, Radcliffe College*

While outspoken feminist thinkers found it difficult to make their ideas persuasive to the public, women engaged more quietly in writing history and literary criticism or in translating foreign literature experienced fewer problems. They could more easily identify their intellectual pursuits with the tenets of "true womanhood," and they usually remained aloof from the most controversial reform stances. Instead, they managed to function in a culturally acceptable role—the "woman of letters."

Because of the "appropriateness" of her work and the attention commanded by occasional popular successes, the "woman of letters" was most instrumental in enlarging the intellectual territory of American women. At the same time, she was often most discontented with the role she had elaborated. She was too intellectually adventurous to abide by any procedures implicit in history, translation, and literary criticism that meshed nicely with the tenets of ideal femininity.

For these "venturous conservatives" seeking to combine intellect and "true womanhood" without compromise, history, literary and aesthetic criticism, and translation offered excellent possibilities for resolving this dilemma. These disciplines seemed, in addition, to promise shelter—havens from calamity where women would be neither unsexed nor disqualified as thinkers. Each area had methodological procedures and historical precedents that women could use as safeguards, often as masking devices for their own intellectual assertiveness. The strategy of the "woman of letters" thus paralleled that of the "scribbler"; the former, however, did not have to base her case upon domesticity. History and literature served her as illustrations of female submissiveness, dependence, and passivity. Translation, as Harriet Martineau had noted while observing the hordes of American women learning languages, was a harmless pastime, a passive activity—or so it seemed. Female literary critics were engaged in a similarly feminine undertaking—admiring "great" works of literature, which by definition were masculine creations. History offered a mask of objectivity and a wealth of data that also seemed to require sensitive and diligent exploration and presentation, not aggressive acts of interpretation. This approach especially held true for romantic historians, who believed that their empathetic re-creations of the past would convey the essence of a historical epoch. Thus, compilation was its own reward for female historians in the mid-nineteenth century, implicit proof of both feminine and scholarly excellence.

In addition, the romantic orientation common to most "women of letters" could easily be interpreted as a passive appreciation of life and art. Since cold "reason" was the romantic's enemy and an attribute always denied to female minds, the characteristically romantic "habit of wonder" was easily reconciled with traditional notions of feminine sensibility. Thus the romantic revolution, which called forth the intellectual talents of antebellum women, seemed to guarantee their "true womanhood" as well.

Yet, the "woman of letters," like the intellectual feminist, appeared doomed to extinction or exile. Although literary critics, in particular, had tried to create intellectual communities similar to Margaret Fuller's version of an American salon, the social roles they had elaborated increasingly lost their appeal as the decade of the 1850s drew to a close. Only Sarah Helen Whitman of Providence, Rhode Island, seemed content as an American "Corinne"—and as an exclusively literary intellectual—on the eve of the Civil War. She was the last priestess of the antebellum generation. Later, of course, she was joined by many others—most of whom, however, preferred the pleasure of their own company and lived, like Emily Dickinson, a life of exile in America, watching a transformed America from their particular and often isolated regional vantage points.[1]

The work of the antebellum "woman of letters" reflects the dynamic nature of her search for a congenial intellectual style; the successes and failures of women writing history, literary criticism, and translations measure both their excellence and their discontent with circumscribed intellectual terrains. Socially and intellectually, they attempted to infuse vitality into stances that seemed to them decadent at worst and static at best. Most had abandoned the role of "woman of letters" even as they sought to transform it.

### 1. The "Woman of Letters" as Translator:
*From Passivity to Politics and Pedagogy*

Most significant historians of women, intellectual feminists, or "women of letters" between 1830 and 1860 were polylingual by the time they reached their teens. Margaret Fuller, with her extraordinary grasp of languages, was the rule, not the exception.[2] Encouraged, usually by their fathers, to master several ancient and modern tongues, these young women found themselves in a most advantageous position when the romantic revolution began to transform both their own and America's intellectual life. Their knowledge of languages served as a passport to the world of romanticism, both intellectually and socially, and often ensured their own development as romantic thinkers.

The romantic interest in contemporary German and other foreign literatures created an American market for translations that offered Margaret Fuller, Elizabeth Ellet, and Mary Booth, among others, their first intellectual opportunities. This skill also benefited female linguists socially, opening exclusively male intellectual milieus to them out of necessity. In this wider context they could enrich their own knowledge. Elizabeth Peabody and Margaret Fuller were named charter members of the Transcendentalist Club from its inception. Many male members of that circle were not only ignorant of the German language but, as Fuller and others had noted during her "Conversations," also quite deficient in the Greek and Latin they had supposedly learned at Harvard. Peabody would read aloud to William Ellery Channing for hours at a stretch, often from Goethe's *Wilhelm Meister*.[3] In turn, he discussed contemporary and ancient philosophy with her and introduced her to Coleridge and Wordsworth, idols from whom he had absorbed romantic principles. Knowing each other was indeed a liberal education for Peabody and Channing, and it is impossible to say, as with all real friendships, who gained the most by this association.

Like Margaret Fuller, most women romantics abandoned translation as their primary intellectual concern, but sectional conflict gave new vitality and relevance to the female translator's role during the 1850s and at the outbreak of the Civil War. Political strife and convictions rather than the pleasures of romantic theory caused two women to refashion the role of translator into a political stance. At the start of the Civil War, Mary Louise Booth of New York City translated Count Agénor de Gasparin's *The Uprising of a Great People* (1861), an enthusiastic endorsement of the Union cause, after persuading Charles Scribner that her translation might benefit the war effort. Scribner, afraid the fighting would end before the work could be published, accepted it with one condition: Booth must complete the translation in one week. Working twenty hours a day, she met the deadline.[4]

For this and other translations during the war she won the praise of President Lincoln, and Senator Charles Sumner said of her translation of Gasparin, "It is worth a whole phalanx in the cause of human freedom."[5] A member of the Kentucky branch of the United States Sanitary Commission wrote to her in 1862, urging her to do more translations and calling her work "a treasure to me, and a noble contribution to American readers." Other members of the Sanitary Commission in Louisville, described by the correspondent as "our leading spirits in the ranks of prophets," were, he declared, equally impressed and cheered by Booth's work.[6]

In contrast to Margaret Fuller, Mary Booth began her career as a translator on a most prosaic level by rendering into English a French technical treatise, *The Marble-Workers' Manual*, in 1856. As a girl on Long Island, New York, Mary often dreamed of the "main chance" the metropolis was sure to offer, and at the age of eighteen she moved to Manhattan, bent on pursuing a literary career. Supporting herself as a seamstress, a vest maker, in particular, she wrote at night and published several articles without remuneration. Eventually she was hired by *The New York Times* to write articles on education and women's activities. Booth was an active feminist during the 1850s, and during that decade she translated almost forty French books, including selections from Pascal, Joseph Méry's *André Chénier* (1857), and Victor Cousin's *Secret History of the French Court under Richelieu and Mazarin* (1859). Her own extensive (850 pages) *History of New York,* the city she loved, was completed in 1867. Booth continued to achieve the success of which she always dreamed, becoming in 1868 the editor of *Harper's Bazaar,* a post she held until her death in 1889.

Mary Booth deplored the spirit of sectionalism; hers was a

national vision. In a letter to Longfellow she referred to the photograph of him and Charles Sumner entitled "Poetry and Politics of New England," objecting to that regional designation. She admired seeing the "conjunction of two truly representative men," but felt she must "protest as a New Yorker the limitation"—why were they not called Americans instead of New Englanders? "I hope some day to see these geographical distinctions blotted out . . . and to live under a broader dispensation—the consanguinity of a whole country. . . ." [7] As she later wrote, in her *History of New York*, she saw New York City as a cosmopolitan center where American civilization might blossom, creating a sense of unity and culture truly national in its scope and vitality:

> That it is in her power, through her immense resources, her boundless wealth, her buoyant elasticity, her composite population, the vast array of talent which lies at her disposal, and most of all, by the breadth, cosmopolitanism and geniality of the character of her people, to mould herself into what she will—to become the Athens of America, the centre of culture and of art—must be evident to all. [8]

In contrast to Booth's national conception of American culture, Louisa Cheves McCord of Charleston, South Carolina, viewed America from a sectional vantage point. In 1848, at her husband's urging, she put her skills to work for the "mind of the Old South." She became, as an admiring biographer later phrased it, "the votaress of political economy." [9] Translating a series of works by the French economist Frédéric Bastiat, she was able to get published his argument against the protective tariff, "Sophismes Economiques," in *Putnam's* and his recent article, "Justice and Fraternity," from the *Journal des Economistes* in the July 1849, issue of the *Southern Quarterly Review*. The latter, introduced by a statement of McCord's principles, conjured up the "run-mad fancies" that had ended in the French Revolution, an event strongly deprecated by the Frenchman Bastiat. Unless such arguments as he offered were heeded, McCord warned, that "wild dream of 'fraternity' and socialism" would surely corrupt America and chaos would come again. It might already be too late; even now "Free-soilers, barn-burners, anti-renters, abolitionists stare us in the face at every turn, and frightful to the thinking mind is the anarchy which must follow should they have their way." According to her, America's greatest danger was its youth and gullibility, its relative openness toward and tolerance for dissenters. "The mind is free, but the mind is swayable." [10] Works like Bastiat's would, she hoped, act as countervailing forces against the anarchists.

For Bastiat, for McCord, and for her father before her, "justice" and "fraternity" were hollow abstractions unless translated into economic and political terms, namely laissez-faire and states' rights. She recalled that as a child she had "two grand passions—for her father and for her State." [11] Now she could serve them both without fear of losing her "true womanhood." Although it is difficult to imagine a more unsuitable field for a nineteenth-century woman than economic theory,[12] McCord, well aware of this, also knew that the crisis facing the South warranted and justified her participation. Her credentials as a "true woman" were never questioned. They proved to be, in fact, as useful as her knowledge of French and economics, for she soon broadened her attack, on the basis of her feminine credentials, to discredit *Uncle Tom's Cabin* as well as American feminists and British women who sympathized with American feminists and American abolitionists. [13]

Louisa McCord was the Southern Elizabeth Cady Stanton. Although they represented different worlds and would have disagreed on everything one could name, they shared a biting, ironic, and colloquial style that reflected their intellectual energy and argumentative skills. As extremely convincing to her supporters as Stanton, McCord was likewise not one to mince words. She quickly became a symbol for Southerners; *De Bow's Review*, to which she contributed articles, called her a "brilliant anomaly," [14] but the popularity of the views she so forthrightly and ruthlessly defended made that a compliment in disguise. To most contemporaries, she seems to have appeared as she did to a close friend, "Roman, always Roman, and never Corinthian, always Doric." [15]

Born in 1810 in Charleston, Louisa Cheves was one of fourteen children. Her father, Langdon Cheves, was a wealthy lawyer who had had a successful career in state and national politics. When Louisa was nine years old her father was appointed president of the Bank of the United States by President Monroe. The family accordingly moved to Philadelphia, where Louisa was sent to female academies. She was, however, far more interested in what her brothers were learning at home from their tutors, especially mathematics. Eavesdropping on their lessons, she secretly attempted to solve the equations given them. When her father caught her listening at the keyhole, he concluded that such determination warranted her receiving the same mathematical knowledge as her brothers.[16] Likewise, economics and politics were subjects she could investigate at home. They were the favorite topics of conversation in her father's household. Webster, Calhoun, and Clay were household words to the young girl, who absorbed their views as easily as she had absorbed mathematical equations— and with equal passion.

After the family returned to Charleston in 1829, Louisa's older sister was an instant success in the social whirl of the city and soon married. Louisa must have been given up as an old maid by Charleston society, for she did not marry until 1840, when she was twenty-nine. The groom, David McCord, was thirteen years her senior and a widower who shared her political views, and brought ten children to the marriage. A Columbia, South Carolina, banker and lawyer, he had served in the state legislature and was now editing a nullification newspaper. David McCord was, according to a recent assessment, a "handsome, intelligent, hot-tempered man not at all afraid of an intellectual wife."[17] The couple had three children of their own and, from 1848 until David's death in 1855, they both wrote articles that often appeared in the same issue of *De Bow's* or the *Southern Quarterly Review*.[18]

Louisa McCord described her role as translator of economic treatises as a most important duty that "those who are ahead in the race of knowledge," owed to their fellow citizens, who were confronted on every side by "specious formula[s]."[19] For

McCord, hers was the worst of times for thinkers and everyone else: "The fashion of our age is *cant*, a whining pretension
to goodness. Ultra in everything, it condemns and tosses
aside . . . each sober thinker." The latter should, she emphasized, attempt to clarify social issues for the public. One crucial
stance was to "*popularize* (allow us the word) popularize political economy." [20]

Henry C. Carey's "The Slave Trade, domestic and foreign;
why it exists, and how it may be extinguished," brought forth
McCord's best talents; her attack upon his support of a protective tariff to develop "an American system" of internal manufactures and his abolitionist sympathies demonstrated how effectively she could use various reformist positions to cancel
out each other, discrediting the proponents of one—and all.
Her strategy relied heavily upon the feminists she despised;
they were the wedge she used to drive reformers apart and ex-
pose their faulty logic. This was, of course, exactly the role
feminists played historically, of which they were well aware at
the time.

Why was Carey, "the great medicine man with his charms
and his rattles," not a feminist? [21] To McCord he sounded as
foolish as they did: his "rant about progressive slavery would
better suit the style of argument of an Antoinette Brown
. . . than that of a grave political economist." Moreover,
McCord characterized both feminists and abolitionists as
ignorant, effeminate, or unsexed idiots among whom Carey
most certainly belonged, side by side with "Mrs. Stowe, Lucretia Mott, Gerrit Smith, and all the other old women,
breeched and unbreeched, who go into hysterics of agony over
the evils of a system, of which they know absolutely and literally nothing." All of them were, McCord implied, totally provincial—especially Carey, whose greatest error was "assuming
two or three states to be the whole country."

Most important of all, however, it seemed to McCord, as it
had to Elizabeth Cady Stanton, that on both logical and moral
grounds any self-respecting abolitionist would support feminism as well. Since Carey did not, McCord concluded that he
occupied a totally inconsistent intellectual and moral position,

regardless of her views of both reforms. It is impossible to say which she found the more ridiculous, but both feminism and abolitionism served her well in her attempts to argue that slavery and "true womanhood" were laws of nature that, if transgressed, would destroy the social order.[22] As feminists did, McCord also saw many parallels between slaves and women and implied that her definition of slavery might well apply to women, with few qualifications. Slavery was, McCord wrote, "the involuntary legal subjection of any individual to another." She argued that other characteristics attributed to the "peculiar institution" were mere connotations added by know-nothing reformers like Carey, for slavery did "not imply oppression on the part of the ruler, nor suffering on that . . . of the slave." [23] If one looked at slavery realistically, she concluded, it was obvious that both women and slaves fared best under the present social order.

Louisa McCord, as a Southern mind, did not believe for a moment in the dominant cultural myths that her Northern neighbors cherished. Her critique of Carey in *De Bow's Review* concluded with a startlingly candid exposition of her cynical view of the American experience—a striking illustration of the Southern mind and its almost total separation from that other country, the rest of America. Well before the war, Louisa Cheves McCord had no ties left to sever from the Union. "Perfect freedom," she declared, was "incompatible" with the very idea of society; "equal freedom" was a dream "never seriously aimed at by any government." Certainly, the Founding Fathers, being reasonable men, had never considered supporting such a "preposterous" notion. McCord effectively pointed out that most signers of the Declaration of Independence were themselves slaveowners who obviously did not plan to emancipate slaves or women by granting them legal and political rights. Feminist reference to that document was therefore absurd:

> Antoinette Brown, Sojourner Truth & Company, do talk of it; but no reasoning man, (we beg the ladies' pardon, we mean no exclusion of them, the term man signifying with us, human being,) no reasoning individual ever imagined so anomalous a state of

society. Mr. Jefferson's great humbug flourish of "free and equal," has made trouble enough. . . .[24]

Although Louisa McCord obviously remained unconvinced by the Jacksonian Persuasion, her intellectual strategy also relied upon the spirit of romanticism. For many Southern minds the South was romanticism incarnate, a region whose uniqueness and essence had been established by sublimely heroic individuals who now sought to preserve its integrity. Louisa McCord viewed herself as a participant in this symbolic cultural drama. In addition to her translating work, she wished to be remembered as the author of a five-act verse tragedy, *Caius Gracchus*, in which the virtues of the Old South were transposed to a setting remote in time but not in spirit, the early days of the Roman Republic. In that drama, woman asserted her strength and power for the glory of the republic and then declared she was merely man's helpmate.[25] Heralding the appearance of *Caius Gracchus* in 1851, the *Southern Quarterly Review* ignored its artistic failings and pronounced it a unique female production: "A tragedy by a Southron, and a lady, is surely no such ordinary event, that we should pass it with indifference." [26]

As a spokeswoman for the Southern persuasion, Louisa McCord had used economic theory, art, and the art of translation to defend "the mind of the South" and the "cult of true womanhood." All her works testify that she saw her role as that of social redeemer. Her poem, "Woman's Progress," implied that hers was a truly regenerative and "progressive" vision, unlike that of the feminists she attacked as ". . . our modern female Reverends,/Learned M. D. 's, and lecturing damsels." They thirsted after attention merely "To feed their hungry vanity, and bring/Unnoticed charms before the gaping crowd." [27] The rhetorical question at the beginning of the poem suggests that McCord, in contrast to those she viewed as harbingers of chaos, wished her own work might symbolize woman's excellence to posterity as well as to her contemporaries:

And is this progress!—Are these noisy tongues—
In fierce contention raised and angry war—
Fit boast for Womanhood? You shrewish things,
In wordy boisterous debate,—are these
Perfected woman's exponents to show
Her model virtues to a later age? [28]

Far to the north and in ideological contrast to Louisa Mc-
Cord, the irrepressible Elizabeth Palmer Peabody began her
public intellectual career as a translator. Like Margaret Fuller,
she covered most of the mental terrain, visible and invisible,
of antebellum America. Born in 1804 in Billerica, Massachusetts, the firstborn of seven children, Elizabeth spent her
childhood in Salem, Massachusetts, where the family moved
when her father gave up his post as schoolmaster at Phillips
Andover Academy to become a dentist. He taught Elizabeth
Latin and Greek and encouraged her to master romance languages. By the time she reached her twenties she was fluent in
French, Italian, and German, and often attended informal language classes in Boston.

In 1830 she published an anonymous translation of the
Baron Joseph de Gérando's *Self-Education*, which was reissued
in 1832 with a preface signed by Peabody and again in 1860
with Peabody identified as the translator. This French work,
very popular in New England, asserted the values of self-
cultivation, which Elizabeth Peabody had absorbed from her
parents, her mother in particular, and from romantic thought.
Declaring that "moral progress is a career open to all," de
Gérando had written that "self-education alone raises us
above the vulgar," emphasizing that "the character of great
men is always partly their own work." [29]

Also a translator and schoolteacher, Elizabeth's mother had
likewise stressed intellectual activity and development as important nurturers of individuality and character. [30] Elizabeth
had acted upon these principles at the early age of eighteen,
setting off in 1822 to teach school in Boston. Her younger sister Sophia, a semi-invalid whose illness and sense of depen-

dence were evidently carefully nurtured by Mrs. Peabody, remained at home in Salem until marriage to Nathaniel Hawthorne removed her from her mother's control.[31] In contrast, Elizabeth always urged Sophia, as she had been urged by their mother, to develop her intellectual potential and artistic talent. Writing to Sophia from the new world of Boston, Elizabeth insisted that *"no considerations* should hinder us from cultivating to the highest degree *circumstances* will *possibly* allow of, our *intellectual faculties."* [32]

Rejecting all but the most noble and moral considerations, Elizabeth outlined the true purpose of acquiring knowledge: ". . . you do not study for the sake of being admired, for the sake of attracting attention, nay *even* so much for the pleasure it will afford you as for the good effect it has upon yr mind, considered in its influence upon yr own moral character, and upon society as it is around you." [33] She had learned at her mother's knee that, as Emerson later asserted, "the world exists for the education of each man"—and woman.[34]

Elizabeth Peabody's entire life was an illustration of these lofty principles. She remained totally absorbed in, and absolutely fascinated by, the intellectual life she led so spiritedly until her death at ninety. As an old woman she became one of Boston's curiosities. Thomas Wentworth Higginson, seeing her fall into a deep snowdrift, came to her rescue and recalled that Peabody, undaunted, immediately took up the thread of their last conversation, urging justice for the American Indian.[35] Often so absorbed in thought that she was totally oblivious to her surroundings, she reportedly collided with trees on the Boston Common.

As a young woman, she impressed many acquaintances with her learning and her vitality. Theodore Parker remembered her as "a woman of most astounding powers," with "a many-sidedness and a largeness of soul quite unusual; rare qualities of head and heart." [36] Horace Mann, who married her sister Mary, christened Elizabeth "Miss Thesaura" when he sought her advice upon ancient history.[37] Her nephew, Julian Hawthorne, remembered her in a rhapsodic account of her intellectual stature as "a thesaurus of all knowledge":

She was probably the most learned person in the world—certainly the most learned woman, in an era of feminine pundits .... Greek, Latin, Sanskrit, and Hebrew were household tongues with Aunt Lizzie. And not content with knowing things, she wanted everybody else to know them, and had invented ingenious ways of instructing them.[38]

Although her nephew certainly exaggerated the extent of Peabody's linguistic fluency, she had studied the languages he listed and many more. In 1835, for example, she was investigating Sanskrit, Icelandic, Chinese, and Hebrew and wished to learn the Basque tongue. Her numerous translations of Greek, German, and Italian works included Plato's *Phaedo* and *Crito*, Berni's *Angelica Sleeps* for *The Dial* (1840), and J. P. Richter's "Recollections of the Most Beautiful Hours," for her own short-lived educational journal, *The Family School Magazine* (1836). And, in 1842 Peabody published Margaret Fuller's translation of the correspondence between Günderode and Bettina von Arnim. Sounding much like Günderode describing the distinction between imagination and fancy, Peabody revealed in her preface to Fuller's translation why she found these figures so fascinating, declaring that only the pure heart and mind, perhaps only a romantic mind, could appreciate them:

To those who have eyes to see, and hearts to understand the deep leadings of the two characters, these leaves present a treasury of sweetest satisfactions, of lively suggestions;—to the obtuse, the vulgar, and the frivolous, they will seem sheer folly, the cobweb tissues of a misled fancy, the bubbles on waters yet undrained. They will be much or nothing to the reader, according to the degree in which he has sought, felt, and lived a pure, a private, and aspiring life.[39]

For Peabody, knowing languages not only allowed one to share the experiences of women like Bettina and Günderode but to discover the essence of foreign cultures in their history and literature directly, without the interference of an alien tongue. In her organic view of the interrelatedness of all natural phenomena and fields of human knowledge, language itself was the key to those spiritual realms that the artist-hero might synthesize with the worlds of nature and history. As it did to Emerson, the very nature of language symbolized to Peabody nature's process; language both distinguished men from nature and made possible those acts of symbolic perception that reunited humanity with nature and with history in a work of art.

Although Elizabeth Peabody, with many other intellectual worlds to conquer, engaged in translation work only sporadically, her plastic sense of the nature of language and its possibilities were most important to her other myriad intellectual adventures and accomplishments—she was what Emerson called an "analogist," the student of "relations in all objects." [40] Contained in a lecture delivered late in her career, her definition of language is the best illustration of Peabody's intellectual method and debt to romantic thought:

Language is the element in which the intellectual nature makes a sphere wherein to live and move and have its being. What breath is to the material body, making man alive in nature, language is to the social body, making it alive in history. [41]

When she discovered the educational theories and pedagogical techniques of Friedrich Froebel in the late 1850s, Elizabeth Peabody synthesized her knowledge of several intellectual fields in the kindergarten movement of which she became the American pioneer and chief intellectual exponent. [42] Always fascinated in her own teaching career by the problems involved in teaching children foreign languages, she gave such studies an important place in her analysis of an ideal educational curriculum. If language study was presented to children as an exercise of imagination, intellect, and free will, it might be possible for every child to be a romantic artist, inspired by what she termed the greatest of all intellectual motivations, the self-generated rewards of "voluntary thought." [43]

## 2. The "Woman of Letters" as Historian

Between 1830 and 1860 both male and female intellectuals found that writing history was a method of stabilizing experience by creating a usable past in chronicles of the American experience and records of other world cultures. However, no woman ventured into a territory of a Bancroft, Prescott, or Parkman in antebellum America. Sweeping historical interpretations were, by cultural definition, left to masculine minds.

Lydia Maria Child's massive *The Progress of Religious Ideas Through Successive Ages* (1855), which she hoped to have stand as her greatest work, deliberately lacked any tendentious arguments. Religious tolerance, Child wrote, specifically forbade a biased approach to the past. Bigotry and controversy had obscured the world's religious heritage. For those who wished to view it without distortion Child offered her encyclopedia. It was not for those who were "conscious of bigoted attachment to any creed, or theory": "Whether they are bigoted Christians, or bigoted infidels, its tone will be likely to displease them." [44]

Child's romantic orientation was also responsible for her views of religion and the types of questions she asked of its history. Calling her approach a "candid method," she searched through history for the truth about the world's religions, from "the most ancient Hindoo record to the complete establishment of the Catholic church." As a youth she had been "offended" by the way "Christian writers" dismissed other faiths as " 'childish fables' or 'filthy superstitions.' " Accounts by religious skeptics were equally biased. She had always wished to meet a real "Brahmin, or Mohammedan, that I might learn, in some degree, how their religions appeared to *them*." Although she knew she could never recapture their worlds, "separated from them by the lapse of ages," she hoped to tell the story of the "process" of religious history, a history that, as it "struggl[ed] through theological mazes, furnish[ed] the most curious chapter in the strange history of mankind." The greatest lesson in that story was, she wrote, that *"theology"* was not synonymous with *"religion."* [45] The former seemed to discourage organic interpretations; the latter was, in contrast, an illustration of process and change. Like William E. Channing and Theodore Parker, Child hoped to rekindle the living spirit of Christianity.

Child's approach to religious history offered a mask of objectivity and a wealth of data that seemed to require, above all, diligent study and organization—not aggressive acts of interpretation, for these had been primarily responsible for obscuring the nature of the religious past and present. Thus, for Child, compilation was satisfying in itself; it offered, in addition, implicit proof of both "true womanhood" and scholarly ability. In supporting these proofs, her romantic orientation to history furnished the kind of rationale for writing it that Mercy Otis Warren had used to justify her history of the American Revolution. The mind of the female historian was unfortunately buried under the abundant detail she had presented in her earnest search for the truth about the world's religions.[46] Since the past should be allowed to speak in its own voice without the historian's intrusion, data had become its own excuse for being.

Child emphasized that hers was a "simple" account, not the work of a profound thinker; and, as she had done in her letter to Margaret Fuller, Child denied that she was a "learned person." She turned that pretended liability into what she hoped was the book's chief virtue:

> In the course of my investigations, I have frequently observed that a great amount of erudition becomes a veil of thick clouds between the subject and the reader. Moreover, learned men can rarely have such freedom from any sectarian bias, as the circumstances of my life have produced in me.[47]

After all, she concluded, it was a general audience, not a community of scholars, who were most in need of her work. For such readers, clarity and "conciseness" mattered more than elaborate erudition, which merely hid the past from both reader and writer.

Writing history textbooks for children and young adults, a popular alternative to writing the historical encyclopedia, appealed to another prominent woman intellectual and to other women engaged, as she was, in educational work. Like the educationist Emma Willard of Troy Seminary, Elizabeth Peabody tried her hand at writing history textbooks. She published *First Steps to the Study of History* in 1832, and in the same year inaugurated her series of historical seminars for adult women, the model and prototype of Fuller's "Conversations." During the 1830s she also wrote a religious history text, *Key to the History of the Hebrews,* and an outline of a civilization she idolized, *Keys to Grecian History,* the two traditions her work always attempted to synthesize. Continuing her "historical conferences" for women in Boston and Salem throughout the 1830s and 1840s, she often advised Harvard students on their reading and allowed several to follow her course "*sub rosa.*" [48]

A pioneer in so many intellectual fields, she could be considered America's first professor of history, for, as she later recalled, when she started her "historical conferences," "there was . . . no professor of history in any college in the United States." [49] The "conferences" were held twice weekly for six months. The fifty-session course on ancient history was a great success, Peabody recalled. Each woman took a different country and presented the results of her readings from assigned texts and other researches. Peabody described her teaching role as supplier of details and synthesizer of the "contemporaneous developments of humanity" that had occurred in the civilizations under study. [50] The class was so interesting that sessions often lasted for four hours. Like Fuller, Peabody attempted to re-create the past, relate it to the present, and encourage maximum participation from class members.

From 1850 to 1860 Elizabeth Peabody promoted historical studies in normal schools and published more texts designed for the classroom. A meeting with Polish refugees was responsible for the private publication of Peabody's compilation, *The Crimes of the House of Austria against Mankind. Proved by Ex-*

*tracts from the Histories of Coxe, Schiller, Robertson, Gratten, and Sismondi, with Mrs. M. L. Putnam's History of the Constitution of Hungary and its Relations with Austria.* These associations also led to her discovery of General Jozef Bem's "historical chart," which she welcomed as a pedagogical device, a key that might unlock the past and revivify historical events for pupils almost instantaneously. In 1852 she published Bem's *Polish-American System of Chronology* and enthusiastically argued its merits, urging teachers to adopt it and to watch their pupils master, through the use of color charts, the broad outline of world history and its most significant specific events and dates. In 1856 she published a history of the United States using this system.[51] Unfortunately, perhaps, no one in America was as impressed with Bem's method as Elizabeth Peabody. Such an approach appealed to her conception of history as plastic, of culture as process, and seemed to promise almost immediate discovery and mastery of the past for eager students to whom whole new worlds of thought would accordingly be revealed.

Elizabeth Peabody's mother, herself a teacher, had impressed upon her daughter the importance of history and of the contribution a woman might make as a teacher. Teaching was, Mrs. Peabody evidently felt, best left to women like herself and her daughters, for she had persuaded her husband, to his permanent chagrin, to give up that calling for the "main chance" of dentistry.[52] Like Catharine Beecher, Mrs. Peabody thought that teaching was "the highest and the proper activity of every American woman who loved her country." [53]

Elizabeth, who attended her mother's Salem school as a child, recalled that one of her mother's most effective techniques was the manner in which she "filled the mind with heroic images" and emphasized that "moral education" was the "essence of all education." Consequently, Elizabeth wrote that she "never thought of any intellectual acquisition nor of any artistic power except as subservient to moral and social ends." [54] Such views by no means entailed shunning the life of the mind. Instead, they made thorough intellectual cultivation a moral imperative, an almost religious activity.

Moreover, Elizabeth saw in her mother's classroom that

thinking was, or should be, a self-generating and organic activity that the ideal teacher should, like a midwife, bring forth in her pupils: "It seems to me that the self-activity of the mind was cultivated by my mother's method in her school . . . . Not so much was poured in—rather—more was brought out." [55] Her early absorption of such ideals helped make Elizabeth Peabody's intellectual life a continuous sequence, unbeset with conflicting orientations, for her mother's teachings meshed perfectly with the romantic thought she discovered in the late 1820s and, later, with the educational theory of her idol, Friedrich Froebel, whom she called the "cosmopolite prophet of the nineteenth century." [56] She superimposed aesthetic and educational theories and ideals influenced by romantic thought on the lessons of her earliest years, never abandoning the historical perspective that her mother originally taught her to value.

Elizabeth Peabody had begun her own teaching career at the age of sixteen, first at her mother's Salem school. In 1821 she set forth alone "in a high heroic mood" to pursue a teaching career in Boston in order to raise money for her brothers' college educations. [57] Heroism was not enough to ensure financial success, however, and in 1823 she accepted a position as governess for a wealthy Maine family, teaching the children of Benjamin Vaughn in Halowell. Life was most pleasant in the Vaughn household—particularly in the library, whose ten thousand volumes rivaled Harvard's twelve thousand tomes. Elizabeth Peabody continued her voracious reading there, not missing an opportunity to utilize the Vaughn's vast collection. Thus, for Peabody, the accredited female role of teacher was both intellectually and socially liberating. It allowed her to further and deepen her knowledge and commitment to an intellectual life. After she returned to Boston and opened a school with her sister Mary in Brookline, her position led to her rewarding friendship with William Ellery Channing, whose daughter and son were among her pupils; her position also led to her association with Bronson Alcott in his educational venture, The Temple School, with which Margaret Fuller had also been involved.

Peabody's relationships with Channing and Alcott resulted in her assumption of another historical role—that of recorder of contemporary social and intellectual history. Her work in this area reveals how she shrewdly yet unconsciously exploited the female role of "copyist" or amanuensis to her advantage. Recording a master's thoughts, an appropriately feminine stance, developed her intellectual strength and independence. She seems to have been blessed with an "iron memory," like Caroline Healey Dall. Consequently, she recalled and wrote down everything of any consequence to her and to the intellectual life of her era, leaving two documents that revivify the period for posterity: *Record of Mr. Alcott's School, Exemplifying The Principles and Methods of Moral Culture* (1835), and *Reminiscences of Rev. William Ellery Channing, D. D.* (1880), an excellent and usually unacknowledged source of information concerning New England's intellectual culture in mid-century.[58] A biographer of Alcott said of her *Record of Mr. Alcott's School:* "Merely as an example of what may be called intellectual good manners and of the complete conquest of professional jealousy, the little book speaks well of the two persons chiefly concerned." [59] The comment applies equally to her memoir of Channing.

In her preface to the first edition, Peabody noted that her motive for preserving a record of Alcott's teaching methods and student responses was to keep concrete evidence of those rather remarkable days, a "way of verifying to herself and others the principles acted upon." Although Peabody came to disagree with certain of Alcott's pedagogical techniques and voiced her reservations in subsequent editions of *Record of Mr. Alcott's School,* she always emphasized that she agreed with Alcott upon the principles and the ends of education— that "education must be moral, intellectual and spiritual, as well as physical, from the beginning of life." Some people might consider it "rather out of place to bring philosophy to bear upon taking care of babies," Peabody wrote in her conclusion; yet she insisted, as both her mother, Alcott, and her soon-to-be-discovered prophet Froebel did, that infancy was the "starting point of education." [60]

As a romantic intellectual, Peabody glorified the spontaneity and "habit of wonder" she attributed to childhood. She wished education to enhance, rather than inhibit, children's perceptions of the world and themselves. These perceptions reflected the organicism that characterized nature's process, and children were thus, by definition, closer to nature and more reflective of its dynamics than adults. Making an analogy between the "organization of human soul" and that of plant life, Peabody declared that educators should remember this similarity and the conception of individuality that applied to both humanity and nature. According to their particular constitutions each might require different nourishment and nurture to flourish. Alcott's educational theory was, she wrote, designed to "follow the natural order of the mind." Having begun with an investigation of children's speech patterns, he had discovered a hallowed romantic doctrine, probably from Coleridge: imagination was the "faculty which [had] formed language." [61] Such an important faculty required tender care and proper "food" to keep it alive. Peabody then defined the imagination with a conciseness often missing from other romantic works:

> It is the concentration of profound feeling, reason, of the perception of outward nature into one act of the mind, and prepares the soul for vigourous effort in all the various departments of its activity. [62]

Imagination should not be confused with mere "Fancy," Peabody insisted, as Margaret Fuller had also emphasized in her translation of "Bettine Brentano and Her Friend Günderode." Only when the imagination was starved and perverted from its natural course did such an aberration occur. The proper kind of education would, Peabody hoped, keep the sublime imaginative faculty from decay and decadence.

Elizabeth Peabody's self-effacing preface to *Record of Mr. Alcott's School*, like Lydia Maria Child's apologia for her history of religion, stressed that the book's merit was its practical and nontheoretical nature, definitions of imagination notwithstanding:

This little book makes no high pretensions. . . . It will perhaps be more useful than if it were a more elaborate performance; for many will take up the record of an actual school, and endeavor to understand its principles and plans, who would shrink from undertaking to master a work professing to sweep, from zenith to nadir, a subject which has its roots and issues in eternity, as this great subject of education certainly has.[63]

The appropriately feminine role of recorder obscured Peabody's crucial importance to Alcott's venture. She had suggested the idea to Alcott initially, recruited students and volunteered her own intellectual expertise to give solidity to the enterprise. Far from joining Alcott's established school, she was, as a recent article points out, the "first promoter, the chief recorder, and the last defender" of The Temple School.[64] When Alcott's publication of *Conversations Upon the Gospel* jolted Boston, Elizabeth and her sister Mary supported Alcott, although their loyalty brought them into the conflict with Boston's guardians of morality and necessitated a move back to their parents' home in Salem in 1836.

Elizabeth's support is all the more remarkable since she began to doubt Alcott's effectiveness during her years at the school. She wrote Mary, then teaching in Cuba, about her doubts and voiced them to Alcott himself. Initially Alcott had seemed to her a true hero, "destined . . . to make an era in society," . . . "a beautiful and very great mind." In 1835 she began to think his supposedly organic method was most "unnatural," requiring "too much self-control" from his young pupils. Moreover, their personal relationship became strained when, perhaps as payment for her teaching, Elizabeth moved into the Alcott household. From her reports of life there as a visitor, it is clear that *Little Women* was a work of fiction. Her first meal with the Alcotts proved less than congenial and convinced her that silence on topics even remotely controversial was the best policy. Reacting to her comment at the table that living two hundred years was a most unappealing thought, her host declared Elizabeth "suicidal" and launched a lengthy attack upon all physicians, whom she felt obliged to defend.

Alcott quickly dismissed her words as those of a poor observer. Finding Mrs. Alcott's nature equally tempestuous and unpleasant, Elizabeth wrote Mary that she would find it far "more comfortable to live on the top of a whirlwind than to live with her."[65]

Elizabeth Peabody's friendship with William Ellery Channing, Unitarian minister and "man of letters," whom Margaret Fuller had called New England's finest mind, was a living model of Peabody's educational ideals. Where Alcott had proved a disappointment, Elizabeth's relationship with Channing succeeded, almost as if they were living out the principles soon to be advocated in The Temple School. The romantic "habit of wonder" characterized their friendship, intellectual orientation, and conversation.

Published in the 1880s from copious notes and journal entries written during the 1830s, Peabody's memoir of Channing is her own intellectual autobiography as well. It captures the intellectual milieu in which the two "kindred spirits" moved in the Boston and Cambridge of the 1830s—an informal intellectual history of their age. It is, in addition, a valuable record of religious history, for Peabody knew exactly which churchmen were fighting with each other and why. She described and analyzed the creeds various clergymen were trying to reject or revise, specifically identifying the parties involved. The fact that the *Reminiscences* is her story as well as Channing's reveals that theirs was by no means merely a mentor–pupil relationship. "Instead of subjecting my mind," she wrote, "he gave it liberty to grow with his,—thus acting as my educator without thinking of doing so."[66]

William Ellery Channing abhorred most of all an "imitator," a disciple who merely absorbed and repeated everything he said, Peabody declared.[67] Although he had been a physical wreck since early childhood, he seemed to Peabody forever young, symbolizing to her his own favorite principle of growth. After their first long conversation in 1829, Channing told his wife how Elizabeth had likewise represented youth and vitality to him, realizing to his astonishment and delight, that an almost total stranger had completely trusted him with a candid revelation of her hopes, fears, and dreams for the future.[68]

In addition to his other admirable traits, Channing seems to have been almost congenitally incapable of condescension. Such qualities made him the kind of man with whom an intellectually ambitous young woman might have a rewarding friendship. It was Channing, Peabody recalled, who introduced her not only to the concept of "transcendentalism" in Coleridge's poetry but to Wordsworth's verse as well.[69] They read and discussed, among sources too numerous to cite in full, such works as Plato, Sismondi's history of Mohammedanism, and Gibbon's *Decline and Fall of the Roman Empire*. And they agreed that Locke's conception of a child's mind as a tabula rasa was totally erroneous. Their extended conversations covered such wide-ranging topics as religion, history, philosophy, art, literature, educational theory, cooking, fashion, Boston mores and manners, child-rearing, feminism, female ideals and social roles, as well as American government and politics. Peabody characterized their discussions as true conversations, informal and "delicious," for Channing never stooped to "*orate*."[70] He probably represented to Peabody what Sir Philip Sidney symbolized to Margaret Fuller—a synthesis of action and contemplation, a "man of ideals" and an "ideal man"—Fuller's sublime accolade.

Channing thought history should play a major and early role in education. If children read works like Plutarch's *Lives* and biographies of significant individuals, their sense of the past would become rich and usable. He recommended this course of reading because, as Peabody wrote, he believed that "the immediate causes of historical events are to be found in gifted, energetic persons, who show that men are responsible for the catastrophes of history."[71] Channing viewed the institutions and extant knowledge in any given culture as organically interrelated and searched through history for societies that had most closely reflected this romantic ideal. Such a society nurtured the individuality of all its members without subordinating them to social authority. The individual and society were thus mutually compatible and self-reinforcing, dualities synthesized into a harmonious whole that reflected the ideal models of all aspects of humanity and the cosmos. An individual family, a particular community, a nation, or the family of cultures that made up human society symbolized to Channing the organization of all nature that formed an organic whole: "The worlds of matter and mind are too intimately connected to admit of partition." [72] In the life and ideals of Jesus, Channing found his greatest inspiration. The "essence of Jesus' character was *love*," an abstraction until one attempted to "realize the *life* that this thought defines." Then, Channing wrote, the revelation of Christ might make one spiritually "alive," seeing Christ "as the liberator from all limitations, even from that last one of one's own individuality." [73]

Channing brought Peabody in contact with a small group much interested in education who met weekly beginning in the fall of 1827. Among those present were: Channing and his wife; Jonathan Phillips; Charles Follen, the German scholar and teacher; Peabody and her sister Mary. When Joseph Tuckerman later joined the group the women stopped attending, Peabody noted cryptically, but she initially found a true spirit of intellectual community in the coterie. In addition, the group seemed to dramatize the tensions between individualism and social authority, which Channing and Peabody so often discussed. Observing both the compatibility and the intellectual conflicts apparent among Channing, Follen, and Phillips, Peabody viewed these men as concrete illustrations of the historical process, of innovation, continuity, and conflict. "Three minds so harmonious but so utterly diverse in their turn and discipline, and . . . entirely self-determined and independent" served as a diagram of the possibilities and problems of social organization. [74]

Phillips represented to her a delightful yet threatening form of individualism. Among the many unhappy childhoods recounted by New Englanders, his was perhaps the most somber. Totally oppressed by the Calvinist tenet of human depravity, pronounced "hopelessly diseased" by the family doctor when he was fifteen, Phillips discovered in the same year the glories of nature and possibilities of human freedom. "An idea flashed up within my heart that I was a free agent who might have something to say in regard to my own destiny . . . ," he had told Peabody.[75] From that day, she wrote, he began to live, becoming an uncompromising foe of all forms of authority. In contrast to his own temperament, Channing had noted Phillips's dry wit and "sad eloquence": "His was an imagination which hung the whole universe in crape." For Phillips, Peabody continued, "the universe was not a temple, as it was to Dr. Channing, but a dungeon; and his friend could not answer his terrible *pessimism*." [76] In contrast, Dr. Follen seemed the representative of social authority and an advocate of "socialism." Although the three adhered to—Phillips most of all—the same goal of "moral and intellectual freedom," Peabody declared that Channing alone seemed to "strike the golden mean" between Phillips's "all-demolishing *individualism* and Dr. Follen's tendencies to *socialism*." He symbolized to Peabody "the idea of a generous culture of the imagination" nourished "by a study of history. . . ." [77]

Integrating the ideas and experiences gleaned from Channing and his friends and her reading in romantic literature, Peabody wrote and published her own re-creations of the usable past. In "Ego-theism, the Atheism of Today," published in 1836 in *The Religious Magazine*, she criticized transcendentalists for dismissing history and promoting an excessively individualistic ethic. She recommended that the egoists, steeped in philosophies of Kant and Hegel, read Plato, from whom these philosophers had gained many ideas, perverting many original doctrines in the process.[78] Peabody found in history two ideal societies, one Greek, one Christian, against which she measured and judged contemporary societies and the communitarian ventures of her era.[79] As she was not content, like Child, to collect historical data, her knowledge, her shrewd view of American culture, and her willingness to exercise judgment make her historical essays, usually contrasting past societies with contemporary America, the most interesting and important ones written by a woman in antebellum America.

In an 1841 essay for *The Dial*, "Christ's Idea of Society,"

Peabody echoed Child's criticism of standard religious history. These copious sources had, Peabody lamented, almost embalmed the spirit and ideals of Jesus. Like Parker, Emerson, and Channing, Elizabeth Peabody wanted to recover and re-create Jesus as a man, as an individual whose values and vitality she thought had been destroyed both by historical accounts and the conventional reverence with which Christians beheld their savior. To "catch the subject in a natural point of view" and to discover Christ's conception of society and social organization was extremely difficult. Ecclesiastical history offered no help; the best approach was to follow "*his method* of Life and Thought." [80]

Jesus did believe, argued Peabody, that the kingdom of God could have earthly manifestations, that men could "*begin* to love and assist each other," that at last this community would prevail. His was an inclusive social vision, which to Peabody entailed a complete reorganization of society as a prerequisite for redemption. Christ was a supreme individual who respected other individuals; indeed, "he alone has respected all men, even the lost and dead." Unlike many others who professed to be Christians, he never "intended to cut men to a pattern." [81]

At the heart of Christ's social ideal, as Peabody conceived it, was an organic interpretation of society. Individual development and social harmony should exist simultaneously, thus ensuring both continuity and growth. She found her own primary interest, education, to be a crucial part of Christ's social vision. It was, in fact, what she called "the ground Idea," a process that illustrated the basic principles of Christ's life and thought, "to call forth man in his fellow and child." [82] Only a society with such an educational process could be termed truly Christian, and therefore truly human:

> The organization which shall give freedom to this loving creative spirit, glimpses of which were severally called the Law in Rome, the Ideal in Greece, Freedom and Manliness in Northern Europe, and Christ by the earnest disciples of Jesus of Nazareth, is at once the true human society, and the only university of Education worthy of the name. [83]

In Karl Otfried Mueller's *History and Antiquities of the Doric Race,* Elizabeth Peabody discovered an actual society that she thought most closely reflected Christ's social vision. In "The Dorian Measure, With a Modern Application," issued in pamphlet form in 1848 and published in Peabody's own short-lived periodical *Aesthetic Papers* in 1849, she analyzed the dynamics of that civilization, emphasizing that it had a particular relevance to her own time. "When so many nations seem to be waking up to reassert that individuality, and, more than all, when the idea is started that the object of Providence in societies is to produce unities of life, to which the individuals that compose them shall each contribute something, even as every limb and fibre of the physical system contributes to the wholeness of the body of a man," one should inquire within the "records of history" if any past culture had reflected this organic ideal. Although historians still disputed their origins, the Dorians, like their god Apollo, were "the children of the creative wisdom and mystery." The aims of Doric culture as she described them closely paralleled Peabody's romantic cultural ideal—"to have a society perfectly organized to express the beauty of the most beautiful." [84]

For the Dorians, Peabody wrote, government was subordinate to education; their educational system itself ensured social harmony. For them and for Peabody, education *was* government. Doric education developed whole men and women, sensitive to beauty from an early age. Music and dancing were included, along with gymnastics, to produce a fully rounded program of individual cultivation. In addition, women were held in high esteem and granted important roles in society. Life became art for all citizens, regardless of sex, and this orientation ensured the harmonious and artistic functioning of all their institutions. Such a culture suggested to Peabody what the concept of "order" should signify. Never mere "subjection," true social order was "an arrangement around a centre," the educational process itself, whereby all individuals received sustenance and support. [85]

Peabody urged American educators to adopt many features of the Doric system, especially their inclusion of the arts within the curriculum of secondary education. Moreover, an attempt to re-create aspects of this Greek culture seemed to Peabody the best way to create a truly Christian nation, to make Christ's idea of society thrive in an actual culture. Since the origins of America were essentially religious and the "oracle which directed it was deeper in the breasts of the Pilgrims than they themselves knew, or could adequately unfold," Peabody thought that the United States was in a most advantageous position to become the first truly Christian nation of modern times. Appropriately for a romantic intellectual, she viewed the Constitution and the institutions of American government in symbolic terms that "correspond[ed] to the spiritual constitution of man, and [had] elasticity to admit his growth." In her idealistic conception, "universal suffrage" reflected man's passionate, earthly nature; the "legislative and judicial departments" represented the "Will" of the people.[86] Thus, she dreamed that America might synthesize Greek and Christian thought, marking a new "birthdate of mankind." In this laboratory of the spirit, Plato's vision of the ideal republic, the Doric measure, and Christ's idea of society might be combined.

To Peabody, Greek and Christian thought were far from visionary, for both stressed, as did Apollo, that "life [was] antagonism, action and re-action."[87] She urged the "self-righteous of modern time, who may not learn of Christ," to "meditate this lesson promulgated in Greece," the virtue of intellectual and moral courage and "contact" with the world:

> The Greeks dared to look the prime difficulty, the great mystery of life, in the face, and reverently to bow before it . . . . The Greek was inspired by Apollo to go up man-like, and act, with eyes wide open to the expiation that was to follow; and which, in its turn, he also suffered man-like, without subterfuge or meaching.[88]

Castigating those who preserved their false virtue, "people of sickly morality" who evaded action and confrontation "for fear of doing wrong," Peabody summoned her readers to action, urging them to banish all fears. The alternative was a living death, she warned, in which knowledge and imagination also perished, for "the Muses will never follow you." [89] Thus, for Elizabeth Peabody, a knowledge of history entailed a "modern application" of the truths she found operative in past societies. Research and comparison of ancient and modern cultures were themselves moral acts of the highest order, crucial aids in the regeneration of all modern societies around the world, and especially America.

Peabody's extravagant expectations of history, characteristic of a romantic intellectual's faith in what she termed that "rich and vast science," [90] were extended to "woman's sphere," where she thought history might also accomplish miracles. For her, history was not only "the proper discipline for the intellect of a republican woman," but it was also the most "notable intellectual discipline" for the American woman to master. It was to women what law and medicine were to men. When in 1855 *The Una* asked her to contribute a series of historical essays, Peabody responded enthusiastically. Her letter of acceptance, grandly entitled "The Philosophy of History in the Education of Republican Men and Women," appeared in the issue of February 1855. A knowledge of history was indispensable for all Americans, regardless of sex, she declared, in order for them to be worthy citizens. It was especially appropriate for women, however, because of their domestic role. Within the family circle women watched at close range the historical process in action, the ideally supportive relationships between husband, wife, and children. This organic conception of the family, a replica in miniature of the organization of society, nature, and the cosmos, illustrated the basic lesson of "Divine Providence," the unfolding of each person's individuality. History would, Peabody hoped, broaden woman's perspective, giving her a new vantage point from which to observe the same processes at work in the family that had occurred in the larger worlds of ancient and modern times. Such knowledge would enable her to become an expert judge of character, excellence, and, conversely, infamy; good judgment was both imperative and closely related to her familial role. Her children and all American society would be the beneficiaries, because woman "inevitably gave society its character," for better or worse.

Peabody evidently felt that women were at present directly in need of history. The family and the role of women within it warranted a pessimistic response from the usually sanguine Peabody. She described the tensions and aggressions apparent within families in Asian "despotism[s]" that practiced "polygamy," deploring the unnatural roles assumed by all family members and the resulting oppression of children imprisoned in that situation. Instead of symbolizing natural harmony and growth, the family reflected tyranny, strife, and corruption. She wrote that under such conditions women as wives became destructive within the family, forcing fathers to assume tyrannical postures, and, as mothers, stifling their offspring. In that closed world of the family, women had no relation to the outside world; they seemed to despise other women and to corrupt not only their own children but society as well.

Although Peabody was referring to women in the "distant climes" of the East, it is clear that she had the American family in mind too, for she immediately returned to the American scene after her description of corrupt Eastern practices, urging that an immediate study and application of the lessons of history be undertaken by American women and the "youth of both sexes." [91] After all, the Mormons in Utah were at that moment practicing polygamy, she noted. If their women had known history, Peabody felt certain they never would have assumed such an unnatural and socially destructive role. One has merely to substitute "America" for "Asia" to learn what Peabody probably thought of the American family of her era. A single meal at the Bronson Alcott's might possibly have been sufficient evidence for anybody that something was terribly wrong with "the family tie"—that there were many affinities between republican American and Eastern despotisms.

Women also needed history, in Peabody's analysis, in order to try to live up to the almost impossible demands placed upon them. If women did not know more about a greater variety of subjects than men, women were considered abject failures. Peabody evidently believed that being a "true woman" was too difficult a task for any human to fulfill. Since she thought it impossible to do everything well, Peabody felt that most women probably considered themselves failures. Although they were supposed to be well versed in many subjects, truly intellectual abilities and achievements were liabilities: "Practical wisdom is required of her, and this in the most difficult and delicate social combinations; and should she fail anywhere, if she has any scientific attainment, or artistic faculty, instead of its standing her instead, as an excuse, it is censured as an aggravation and offence." [92]

Her series of *Una* articles was designed to add to woman's "practical wisdom." Entitled "Lessons of God's Providence as It May Be Traced in History," the essays were primarily descriptive, offering outlines of ancient cultures and underlining the principles of growth and organicism that Peabody identified with "divine providence." She urged women to view history through a symbolic lens and to analyze particular cultural myths as "symbolic statements" with "an inner meaning" that revealed the essence of that culture. [93] Myths were crucially important to historical understanding and should never be dismissed as mere "fiction[s]." For Peabody the larger the role myth and symbol played in a society, the higher it ranked in the scale of civilization. Accordingly, she recommended to her readers a detailed study of ancient art and culture for its "stupendous grandeur and beauty" and its "rich[ness] of expression." [94]

From her mother, from Channing and his circle, and from such romantic works as Herder's *The Spirit of Hebrew Poetry*, which Peabody had used in her "historical conferences" for women, she had developed her romantic strategy of investigating history, as she did all other branches of knowledge, for the spiritual truths it might reveal. Although Harriet Martineau had indirectly accused her of "passivity" as she had branded Margaret Fuller a "gorgeous pedant," [95] Peabody clearly did not consider the role of historian in this light. Analyzing past cultures and social structures was for her not an idle amusement, because such an activity entailed contrast and comparison with contemporary societies. Then, "a modern application," a re-creation of ancient models, might regenerate human culture. History for her was thus a powerful social force, and her own work demonstrates that, as a historian, Elizabeth Peabody was also a force in history. Unlike other intellectual women engaged in historical work, she alone dared to interpret the past in light of the present and explicitly reveal what she thought her contemporaries should learn from history.

### 3. The "Woman of Letters" as Philosopher and Critic of Literature and the Arts

"The mind of Schiller, exuberant and discursive, was intuitively romantic," declared Elizabeth Ellet in her 1839 study of the artist whom she considered the best dramatist of the age.[96] Primarily a descriptive treatise, Ellet's *The Characters of Schiller* began with a definition of romanticism in which the author cited with approval Schlegel's distinction between the classic and romantic and referred to Coleridge's formulation of those contrasting orientations. In agreement with both the English and German critics, Ellet wrote that the essence of the classical poetic genius was practical and concrete, "deal[ing] with the immediate impression of objects upon the senses." Filtering his impressions through his "imagination," the romantic genius was a manipulator of symbols and a virtuoso at fusing art and nature in new syntheses. "Unfettered by the material form," he could execute "the most rapid and fantastic combinations, the most excursive flights." Poetic activity was itself a challenge and a delight, for the remotest objects tempted the poet to make comparisons and analogies to resolve the most stubborn polarities. Thus, each poetic feat was heroic: "No abyss was too profound for his active and far reaching intellect, no height too lofty for his soaring spirit." For Ellet, the distinguishing traits of the romantic genius were "manliness and simplicity." His perceptive eye worshipped excellence most of all, and his keenest desire was to attain that highest standard.

Other significant "women of letters" between 1830 and 1860 shared Ellet's conception of the romantic genius. Like most romantic intellectuals engaged in aesthetic, literary, and philosophical criticism, these women were preoccupied with semantic strategies for relating art and life. Lydia Maria Child, also an admirer of Schiller, translated passages from his works in her journal. The artist's genius, she wrote, made him representative and made his work symbolic of the realm of spirit, that ideal world of Kantian noumena and Platonic ideas. The "province of the actual," was not his domain. While lesser mortals remained "here at home," "*he* strive[d] from the union of the possible with the unavoidable, to bring out the ideal." [97] Above all, for Schiller and for Child, the artist had a divine mission. His was much more than a talent to amuse:

> The artist, it is true, is the *son* of his Age; but pity for him if he is its *pupil*, or even its favorite. Let some beneficent Divinity snatch him when a suckling from the breast of his mother, and nurse him with the milk of a better time; that he may ripen to his full stature beneath a distant Grecian sky. After having grown to manhood, let him return, a foreign shape, into his century; not, however, to delight it by his presence; but dreadful, like the son of Agamemnon, to purify it.[98]

In 1830, Margaret Fuller wrote a similar paean to genius, which rendered the romantic artist a divinely masculine hero. "Such a man would suddenly dilate into a form of Pride, Power and Glory,—a centre, round which asking, aimless hearts might rally,—a man fitted to act as interpreter to the one tale of many-languaged eyes." [99]

Only such a sensitive and powerful perceiver could create beauty, Child wrote in a short essay for *The Dial*, "What Is Beauty?" With an epigraph from Bettina von Arnim extolling love and wisdom as the divine secrets of the universe, Child defined beauty as an organic synthesis of love and truth, the "two great Creative Principles" that symbolized both the nature and process of the "Divine Mind," the world of spirit. "Mere analysis," she continued, could only "dissect" beauty.

"Thought standing *alone*" created pale and inferior works of criticism: "A primal color is gone, and its painting is deficient."[100] Critics were only contemptuous beings, Child confided in a letter. She classified them along with Calvinists "as the two classes that especially annoy me," and revealed how difficult it was to refrain from denouncing them: ". . . it requires all the grace I have, not to pour out the phials of my aversion upon them, in pointed speech."[101]

Elizabeth Oakes Smith also ranked the role of artist far above the critic's, placing ultimate value upon the creative act. Her popular lyceum lecture, "Genius," was an account of an evening spent at Emerson's home where that topic was the subject of a most intense, lengthy discussion, and was declared transcendent.[102] Emerson symbolized the romantic genius to Smith, and she referred to him as the "Sage of Concord" without that tint of irony that colored Fuller's portrayals or Child's disappointment at Emerson's "want of continuity." No matter how profound and brilliant he was, Child had written, "he [had] no thread to string his pearls upon."[103]

Like Fuller, Child felt that those of Emerson's lectures she attended seemed to summon men to the hallowed halls of genius, leaving women in that world of the "commonplace" far below the summits where men created art.[104] She rationalized her exclusion as an opportunity, quoting Bettina von Arnim's paean to the freedom bestowed upon the insignificant, who need not scale the formidable heights of art but merely "narrate" things as they are without striving for significance or profundity.[105] However, Child would not be satisfied with this compromise and always worshipped the artistic life. Writing in 1844 that her life had been too "fragmentary, and therefore without important result," she vowed to "devote the remainder of my life to the attainment of literary excellence," adding wryly that her correspondent might well think she had been "smitten with what Milton calls 'the last infirmity of noble minds.' "[106]

In the correspondence and criticism of the "women of letters" the creative artist shines through, resplendent in his poetic power, the supremely moral *man*. Ellet, Child, Fuller,

Smith—all defined themselves as women outside the category they most admired as romantic intellectuals. As if by cultural fiat, the function of literary "women of letters" was to analyze, not create, romantic art. Thus, Margaret Fuller's self-fulfilling prophecy to this effect was borne out in the lives and works of other women intellectuals in antebellum America. Their social and intellectual orientations, in combination, had created an apparently unbridgeable gap between "woman's sphere" and the far-ranging, even unlimited, terrain of the artist-hero. Yet, the "woman of letters" fought desperately and unsuccessfully against the cultural consensus voiced by Sarah Hale and reinforced by romantic theory, that held, as Hale had declared, that "the path of poetry" was narrow for women and as broad as the horizon for the "Lords of creation." [107] Like the modern poet E. E. Cummings, the "woman of letters" believed that negation was the destiny of those who were not artists.

The heady religion of art generated by romantic thought had affected increasing numbers of women in the mid-nineteenth century and found its social expression in the cult of female friendships and correspondence in which many "women of letters" also participated. However, "women of letters" were too intellectually ambitious and talented to find the cult of friendship and correspondence with kindred spirits sufficiently satisfying as outlets for self-expression. Notwithstanding the discrepancies between the role of artist-hero and the female experience, women like Child, Smith, and Fuller plunged into that "world elsewhere," imaginative literature. In the midst of the American literary "renaissance" and the "flowering of the New England Mind," these women seemed to wither artistically, destroyed by the very intellectual tradition that had originally brought them and American literature to artistic maturity. The poetry and fiction of the "women of letters" is eloquent testimony of their shortcomings as literary artists. Moreover, the poetry and prose fiction written by these intellectuals was haunted by this fear, a self-conscious anxiety that, no matter how hard they tried, creative writing was for them synonymous with failure.

Although Lydia Maria Child was a pioneering writer of the

historical romance in America, her inability to create convincing characters marred each of her novels, from *Hobomok* to her last work of fiction, *The Romance of the Republic* (1878), her greatest novelistic failure. Like Louisa McCord's ponderous verse drama, *Caius Gracchus* (1855), Child's *Philothea* was a "romance"; she hinted at the presence of truth glimmering within, her warning to America to act immediately to save the Republic from degeneracy and decay. A long discourse on the evils of slavery, the nature of democracy, and the status of women in the ornately rendered setting of Periclean Athens, the book is a potpourri of exotic description, Platonic idealism, and contemporary and ancient social theory. The characters seem to exist for the sake of such abstract discussions. Although their own problems vanish in a contrived and cheerful denouement, none of the intellectual contradictions they ponder are resolved. Their long conversation is dully rendered, as is the characterization of the sublimely moral Constantia who shares more than her Christian name with an earlier heroine— Charles Brockden Brown's Constantia in *Ormand*—distinguished and isolated from other women by her brains, purity, intense seriousness, and piety. Among the slaves and courtesans of Athens, Constantia's virtue is transcendent and boring, as the author was probably aware.[108]

The author of *Philothea* seems acutely, even obsessively, aware of the dangers that romanticism posed for her own temperament and talent. The same ambivalence to the orientation that marks Child's correspondence mars her fictional ventures. In *Philothea* she had subverted the romance unconsciously. Afraid of being too "aesthetic" or too "intellectual," she could not use the vocabulary of romanticism with conviction. Unlike Hawthorne, who shared her fears and her ambivalence toward art, she could not find what he styled that "neutral ground" where "fact and fancy meet." [109] This liability led to her great success as a journalist, in another pioneering literary venture, recently styled "personal journalism." Her *Letters from New York* (1843) explicitly satirized the romantic theory that she found both convincing and somehow inapplicable to her own intellectual role and to contemporary America. By surrounding the popular terms of philosophical idealism with vivid descriptions of life in the metropolis, she found her own voice in an appropriately romantic synthesis. Perhaps, like Margaret Fuller, she had found support for her skepticism of Emerson's remoteness and discontinuity on the sidewalks of New York City, for the syntax Child employed reveals that, unlike Emerson, she was incapable of moving from the emblematic natural fact to metaphysical speculation and synthesis without subjecting that cognitive style to an often blatant irony.

Elizabeth Oakes Smith was fatally drawn to fiction too. The feminist heroine of her *Bertha and Lily; or, the Romance of Beechwood Glynn* (1854) resembles Child's Constantia as a model of virtue scarcely distinguishable from American recreations of Samuel Richardson's Clarissa Harlowe, not to mention his own moral heroine. Bertha's discussions of woman's plight, the condition that she so sublimely overcame, form the rhetorical center of Smith's book. Thus, like Child's *Philothea*, Smith's *Bertha and Lily* merges with that sentimental tradition of the domestic novel that both authors disdained. Although Child continued to write novels in this vein, Smith solved her fictional dilemma by abandoning the world of artistic fiction and writing the first "dime novel," *The Newsboy*, a genre in which she no longer had to be self-conscious about her artistic ability. She could not, however, abandon the realm of romantic art completely, for she continued to write poetry. Although she was usually more successful as a poet than as a novelist, Smith's best poems lack the vitality that distinguish her essays. Even that favorite male pseudonym she employed, "Ernst Helfenstein," could not, as both mask and support, give Smith the power she exhibited in works like *Woman and Her Needs*. Although *The Sinless Child* is a skillfully wrought celebration of her emergent identity, it too lacked the authority of her essays.

Margaret Fuller's ventures into verse had more disastrous artistic results. Although a poem written in memory of her father will have a certain resonance for all toilers in the fields of knowledge, the beginning couplet needs no further comment: "With fevered brow and tortured brain/The founts of intellect I drain." [110] Fuller's fictional sketches of romantically inclined young women destroyed by society, symbols of the alienated individual that Fuller alternately cherished and rejected as her own self-image, were mere abstractions. Writing to a friend in 1843, Fuller attached a revealing moral to her tale, "Mariana." Although persecuted by society and severed from the "common womanly lot," her heroine found that isolation was a blessing in disguise. It allowed her to "decipher the great poem of the universe," to attempt to fulfill the "destiny of the thinker, and (shall I say it?) of the poetic priestess, sibylline, dwelling in the cave or amid the Lybian sands. . . ." [111] Margaret Fuller, splendidly equipped to play the former role and painfully aware of her meager creative talents, always yearned to symbolize the literary artist as priestess, although she knew that role was not her destiny.

Although Fuller and other "women of letters" failed in their artistic ventures, one of their contemporaries became "the poetic priestess" incarnate. Sarah Helen Whitman of Providence, Rhode Island, was the best literary artist among "women of letters" between 1830 and 1860, and her essays rank with those of Margaret Fuller and Elizabeth Peabody as the most important literary criticism produced by women—and men—in the period. Sarah Whitman's essay on Emerson, although much praised by her contemporaries, is still not considered a major contribution to American romanticism. Her close friend, George William Curtis, later editor of the *Century* magazine, pronounced her essay the best analysis of Emerson's thought he had read. [112] Published in the *United States Magazine and Democratic Review* (June 1845), and signed only by "a Disciple," the article was soon recognized as Whitman's work by most Boston and Providence literati. Emerson admired it too, yet thought the signature inappropriate. [113] He knew from the essay that its author was no effusive disciple but an immensely learned critic.

Better versed in the technicalities of German philosophy than most American intellectuals, Sarah Whitman could effortlessly place Emerson's work within that tradition, bringing out subtle contrasts between his thought and that of the German romantics he admired. It was the elegance and ease with which Whitman could handle Kant, Fichte, Schelling, Spinoza—to name only a few of the philosophers she discussed—that most appealed to George W. Curtis. He was amazed that anyone, especially a woman, could present complex metaphysics in such a natural manner. Curtis correctly observed that Whitman made even Emerson's thought seem more systematic than it actually was. A condensed history of philosophy rendered with precision and clarity, her essay, Curtis noted, was far more interesting than turgid academic treatises on the subject.[114]

Whitman surveyed the evolution of self-consciousness in history and the attempt of philosophers to solve the new problems that each metaphysical system engendered. She pinpointed the late eighteenth century as a time of intellectual crisis, a "Chaos of partial and opposing systems." From the bankruptcy of all forms of materialist philosophy and the new problems posed by Kantian idealism, Whitman wrote, Schelling "freed himself by a daring and sublime hypothesis," a new assertion of the unity of mental and natural phenomena, and "a bold affirmation of absolute cognition." Kant had severed all relations between the noumenal and phenomenal worlds he posited, having sundered subject from object, the thinker from the thought. To Whitman, his ethics and epistemology thus revealed there to be no bridge between the real and ideal realms. Schelling's new synthesis reintegrated "all antagonisms" even "the great antagonism of matter and spirit, the insuperable problem in every dualistic system." All phenomena were made newly alive in Schelling's philosophy. Schelling's was the first convincing philosophical incorporation of the idea of progress as the gradual development in humanity of this "inherent energy." [115]

Defining American transcendentalism as the New England expression of "this philosophy of identity" elaborated in German philosophy, Sarah Whitman identified Emerson's Essays as a supreme and sublime expression of these ideas.[116] Although his thought so closely resembled that of Schelling and the modern German school, Whitman was disappointed that

Emerson seemed to have derived his ideas from Neoplatonists like Plotinus. Emerson's failure to take advantage of Schelling's equal emphasis of real and ideal had resulted in an overemphasis on the latter. This was, according to Whitman, the "only flaw in Emerson's crystalline intellect." [117]

Although many derided his intellect as feeble, and pronounced his writings and lectures discontinuous, contradictory, and often ineffable, Whitman believed his critics were ignorant of the true nature of his "affirmative" and "oracular" thought. It seemed ridiculous to her that anyone should ask for proof of his ideas. Whitman urged her readers to appreciate the way Emerson gave "adequate and beautiful expression to the most profound and cherished aspirations of the age," and to admire his "novel statements of the most familiar phenomena of life," delivered with "strange force and directness." To Whitman, Emerson seemed destined to be the greatest philosopher-poet of the nineteenth century: "No man is better adapted than Emerson to comprehend the spirit of the age and to interpret its mission." Each of his essays reflected the organicism inherent in mind, nature, and culture, which Whitman called "formative energy, . . . that harmonious adaptation of parts which marks the development of organic structure." [118] The same expansive energy and unlimited progress at the heart of nature personified for Whitman the spirit of the nineteenth century, which Emerson, as a romantic prophet, might symbolize in his life and art.

Demonstrating no personal predilection for the role of romantic hero, she revealed in her essay on Emerson her close identification with what she had described as "the essence of her age." In her brilliant description of the nineteenth-century mind, Sarah Helen Whitman revealed that, for her, the century was romanticism incarnate:

It is mystic and devout, yet patient and diligent in research. An age in which mighty secrets have been won from nature by the ceaseless questioning of her solitary votaries, in which science seems about to restore to us all that the imagination has from time to time surrendered to the narrow skepticism of the understanding. Already she has whispered to us the secret law of Nature's boldest miracles,—she has imparted to us a spell by which we may restore the oracles of the past, and has initiated us into the possible modes and conditions of a more spiritual and sublimated existence.[119]

When Sarah Helen Whitman was present, a friend recalled, everyone in the room "felt that noble and beautiful things were possible." A "woman of unusual charm" and beauty, she was noted for her unconventional romantic attire, the veils and scarves she usually wore and the fan she always carried.[120] Not only the most prominent "woman of letters" in Providence, she was also a welcome addition to most literary gatherings in New York and Boston. Undergraduates at nearby Brown University, including John Hay, often visited her home, finding her company delightful and stimulating. She was an encouraging critic and friend to the many young students of Brown with artistic ambitions. Even after men like Hay and George William Curtis left school, they continued to correspond with Whitman.

Many contemporaries noted that she seemed perennially young, even shortly before her death in 1878 at the age of seventy-five. "One never realized that she was an old lady," Professor Bailey of Brown remembered, crediting this youthfulness to her "rare devotion to youth of either sex." Recalling many hours he had spent in her home, Bailey remembered her sitting room where the lighting was dim and paintings were illuminated with "inverted lampshades." In this "weird and somber" setting, his hostess, always wearing a veil, "delighted in passing literary squibs." Her humor seemed to thrive, even in such an incongruous setting: "She would indeed poke goodhumored fun at her best friends, or most treasured beliefs, meaning no harm, and expecting the same treatment of herself. Like Hood, Lamb, Holmes, Thackeray, and others, she loved a pun, but to have it passable, it must be very good. . . . " Knowing of her meager finances, Bailey was amazed she could live, as Child did, on practically no income. Sarah Whitman and her eccentric sister, Anna, whom Whitman cared for in their home, located most appropriately on Benevolent Street, lived from hand to mouth. With no domestic help, Bailey recalled, they "ate like the gods when there was food, not always nectar and ambrosia, and when they felt like it." [121]

Sarah Whitman lived in Providence most of her life. Born there in 1803, she was the second of five children, only three of whom survived infancy. Her father, Nicholas Power, was a dashing figure and a wanderer whose Irish ancestry included the Nicholas Power who had helped Roger Williams create his Rhode Island colony. Whitman, proud of such lineage, valued the principle of the freedom of conscience upheld by this ancestor. Her father personified such freedom in a more extreme form. After receiving two degrees from what would become Brown University, he started a successful mercantile business in Providence. Made bankrupt by the War of 1812, he sailed away, abandoning his family for eighteen years. When he returned to Providence, to the shock and dismay of the family, Sarah's eccentric sister immortalized the event in doggerel:

> Mr. Nicholas Power left home in a sailing vessel
> for St. Kitts,
> When he returned, he frightened his family out
> of their wits. [122]

From early childhood, Sarah exhibited a more decided poetic talent than her sister, Anna, and an insatiable intellectual appetite. Ignoring the warnings of relatives, and reading the wicked Byron, she plunged into the artistic world of fiction and poetry they considered so dangerous. Attending several female academies, she was encouraged to study Italian, French, and German literature and to write poetry. In 1828, she married a young Bostonian, John Winslow Whitman, "dreamer, an amateur inventor, and an improvident lawyer," who wrote poetry under the pseudonym "Ichabod" and co-edited, among other magazines, the *Boston Spectator*, in which Sarah was first published. [123] He shared and encouraged her literary aspirations until his early death in 1833.

Although Sarah Whitman left Boston, returning to Providence to live with her mother and sister, Anna, she remained in contact with the intellectuals of Boston and Cambridge where she had discovered and joined the caravan of New England romantics. Interested in most reformist ventures of the period, including Alcott's school, Ripley's Brook Farm, and American feminism, she did not, however, play an active part in these experiments before 1860; but after the Civil War she assumed an active role in the woman's movement. Hailed as the first "literary woman" of Rhode Island to join the state suffrage organization, she became its vice-president in 1868.

"Helen of a thousand dreams," Edgar Allan Poe called her, remembering the sight of her on one moonlit evening, a vision he could not forget.[124] To Whitman, Poe was the personification of the romantic artist. Their extraordinary courtship began with a light-hearted exchange of compliments, a favorite literary convention of the period. Her valentine poem to Poe appeared in the New York *Home Journal* (March 1848) and won her a poetic response in his "To Helen." By the following autumn, Poe was trying to convince Whitman to marry him, and her misgivings about his irregular life were gradually put at rest. In November they were engaged, and in letters to his fiancée, Poe shared with her his dream of the literary power that might be theirs. If she were as ambitious as he believed, and his partner as well, they could establish an "aristocracy of intellect" in America, secure its "supremacy" and then lead and control it—"Would it not be 'glorious,' *darling*."  [125] Visions of future bliss soon vanished after a series of unbearable public and private scenes with a drunken and tortured Poe. Although Whitman ended their engagement, she continued to support Poe long after his tragic death. Vindicating his aristic excellence and personal reputation was the difficult measure of her commitment to the romantic sensibility and to the man who had loved her so strangely.

In 1860 she published *Poe and His Critics,* in which she analyzed him as the victim of the era's conflicting intellectual positions:

The negation of Carlyle, and the boundless affirmation of Emerson served but to stimulate without satisfying the intellect. The liberal ethics of Fourier, with his elaborate social economies, and systems of petrified harmony, were leading his disciples through forlorn enterprises to hopeless failures. A divine dissatisfaction was everywhere apparent.[126]

Unlike Emerson or Carlyle, who at last uttered the "everlasting Yea," Poe symbolized "the pervading skepticism of the time." He was a romantic hero of a very different sort than Emerson. Poe transformed the organicism and energy that to Emerson were the benevolent principles of the universe into frightening symbols of chaos and "nothingness." Any reader willing to "follow the vast reaches of his thought" would find in Poe's poem, "The Universe," what Whitman called "a form of unbelief far more appalling than that expressed in the gloomy pantheism of India." For Poe, "the central, creative soul is alternately not diffused only, but merged and *lost*, in the universe, and the universe in it. . . ." Carrying the disillusionment and alienation of Byron, Goethe, Shelley, and Keats to their ultimate extension, Poe had plunged into the maelstrom, swallowed up in his own symbol of chaos: "Sadder and lonelier, and more unbelieving than any of these, Edgar Poe came to sound the very depths of the abyss. The unrest and the faithlessness of the age culminated in him." [127]

To Sarah Whitman, Poe's life was as tragic as his art, for a single look into its "mournful corridors" would "appall the boldest heart." Whitman wrote that Theodore Parker's noble assertion, "every man of genius has to hew out for himself, from the hard marbles of life, the white statue of tranquility," merely highlighted Poe's fragmented, tortured life. Instead of a finished statue, he had left to posterity a "melancholy torso," which she urged her readers to view "with pity and reverent awe." [128]

Sarah Whitman was able to achieve the sense of tranquility that forever eluded Edgar Allan Poe. The last priestess among "women of letters" in antebellum America, Whitman had fused her critical and artistic talents into an appropriately romantic synthesis, an act that proved impossible for Ellet, Child, Smith, and Fuller, whose artistic aspirations were forever frustrated. While these intellectuals played the role of "women of letters," they felt that it could not symbolize the very essence of their individuality, the sublime self that they cherished as romantic intellectuals. Since Whitman was able to combine the roles of critic and artist so skillfully, she found this intellectual style and social role totally satisfying. In contrast to the lives of most American intellectuals between 1830 and 1860, hers was marked by serenity instead of conflict. Perhaps it was this sense of self-fulfillment that enabled her to play the literary mentor as well as the "Corinne" implicit in the "woman of letters" role by genuinely encouraging and supporting the artistic endeavors of both promising talents and mere enthusiasts.

Elizabeth Peabody was also a most adept and enthusiastic literary mentor. Her myriad intellectual interests and talents probably prevented her from aspiring to the role of creative artist, which she analyzed so well. Among her many pursuits, she was, like Sarah Whitman, not averse to being an American "Corinne." She had, in addition, that rare ability to judge new literary talent and the unflagging energy to search for it. She discovered the mystic poet, Jones Very, and convinced Emerson to act as editor and publisher of the 1839 edition of Very's *Poems and Essays*. Her most important discovery was Nathaniel Hawthorne, whose anonymous tales she had read in the *New England Review* between 1830 and 1836. Convinced that these stories were from the same pen, she found in 1837 that the author lived in her hometown of Salem. Hawthorne's *Twice-Told Tales* were published that March, and Peabody arranged to meet the author she so admired in her Salem home the next November. That evening (immortalized in Henry James's *Hawthorne*) while the guests nervously hovered over Homer's *Iliad*, eyes glued to Flaxman's engravings, Elizabeth expressed to Hawthorne her admiration for his anonymous tales. Hawthorne told her that he wished she had found him out sooner—that he often "felt like a man talking to himself in a dark place," without benefit of praise or criticism.[129]

Elizabeth Peabody promoted Hawthorne's career at every opportunity. Through her friend George Bancroft, Hawthorne received his post at the Salem Custom House, where he began *The Scarlet Letter*. In 1853, Peabody wrote an enthusiastic review of *The House of the Seven Gables* and *The Blithedale Romance* for *The North American Review*. To her, Hawthorne was impossible to classify, for his was a unique talent and literary style. Not "poetic" or euphonious in any conventional sense, his prose was often "crisp and harsh," devoid of literary allusions. More familiar with the "driest of chronicles" than with great art, Hawthorne had found his greatest inspiration in New England history. In spite of these artistic deficiencies, Peabody declared him a poet. His genius was to "create out of nothing—to place before the imagination objects and personages which derive their verisimilitude not from their resemblance to the actual, but from their self-coherency."[130]

It was most difficult for Peabody to pinpoint the nature of his artistic power, for he was an utter failure in terms of contemporary conventions of prose fiction. Since she judged him incapable of narration or "plain story telling," Peabody pointed out that "the most paltry tale-maker" or journalist could "easily excel him in what we might term the mechanical portion of his art." His plots were totally unconvincing, either too laborious or too simple, his dialogue unnatural and improbable. Each of his productions seemed curiously unfinished, incomplete, even fragmentary. Hawthorne and his art, she wrote, existed "independently" of the artistic conventions so clumsily rendered by him. Prevented from "presenting a naked thought" by his own brilliance, he was instead impelled by an imagination that "warmed with textures and tints strange, fantastic, sometimes sombre, sometimes radiant." His work had philosophical not artistic unity, she concluded, for Hawthorne could make a single thought dominate an entire novel or tale. It was even possible to remove sentences at random as independent units from most of his writings and enjoy their power to convey "ideas clearly defined and vividly expressed by imagery which at once astonishes by its novelty, charms by its aptness, and dazzles by its beauty." [131] Thus, to Peabody, Hawthorne's genius lay in each sentence, and she could not recall any other author, living or dead, whose prose could be dissected without violating its syntax, imagery, or sense.

Peabody's greatest artist-hero, however, was the painter Washington Allston, who was also obsessed with the stylistic qualities of his medium. As an old man in Cambridge, with his flowing white hair and his gentle and dreamy manner, Allston symbolized the artistic life for his many admirers. To Peabody, the majesty of Milton's line best matched Allston's character and genius: "The true poet is himself a heroic poem." [132] In *Emerson's Magazine* of October 1857, she published an account of their final visit, "Last Evening with Allston," an embarrassing effusion most uncharacteristic of Elizabeth Peabody. Like those "women of letters" who idolized the artist-hero and attempted to write poetry and fiction, Peabody lapsed into sentimentality when she contemplated the very idea and image of Washington Allston. After hearing him recite several of his own verses, Peabody felt that she had been admitted to the innermost chamber of Allston's sacrosanct genius. In the sublime silence that followed his reading, they recognized each other as "kindred spirits," transported into "that electric sphere which needs no words." Even in death Allston was majestic, almost Christlike, and Peabody, viewing his remains, remembered his last words to her: "God bless you. Go on to perfection, my child." [133]

Seeking perfection as a committed "woman of letters," Elizabeth Peabody opened her famous West Street Bookshop in Boston during 1840. The entire Peabody family had moved from Salem that year, and in their new home Elizabeth set up shop in the front parlor, while her father, now a homeopathic physician, practiced "medicine" in the rear of the house. Convinced that Boston needed what Margaret Fuller termed an "intellectual center," Peabody envisioned an oasis of contemporary European and British literature. After soliciting funds for her venture from wealthy friends, she opened her shop and circulating library, the only place in Boston where one could buy French and German books.

With her characteristic devotion to excellence, she insisted that "no *worthless books* . . . nothing of a secondary quality," would be found on her shelves.[134] The little center for avantgarde culture quickly became a salonlike meeting place for New England romantics, famous and obscure, who continually stopped in to discuss the pressing metaphysical and social questions of the day. Not only was *The Dial* conceived in the bookstore, but it was there that Ripley first disclosed his plans for establishing Brook Farm. On Wednesday nights, a small coterie of the interested could even participate in Margaret Fuller's "Conversations" at Peabody's place. For ten years, until she closed its doors in 1850, the West Street Bookstore was a romantic institution devoted to the propagation of that new revelation.

"Insatiable in her love for knowledge and for helping others to it," [135] Peabody could not be satisfied as a passive proprietor, and she soon became a publisher too,the first woman in Boston and most probably in America to assume this role. Channing's emancipation pamphlet, other abolitionist writings, three of Hawthorne's children's books, and *The Dial* (temporarily in 1842), form a partial list of her West Street publications. Her experience as literary mentor, promoter, and publisher led to another literary role—editor and publisher of her own periodical, *Aesthetic Papers*. Although the first issue in May 1849, was also the last, Peabody's venture was itself a sublimely romantic gesture, and her prospectus reflected her romantic orientation, her desire to resolve all polarities and conflicts—literary, cultural, and social—into an ultimate synthesis of diversity:

> The Editor wishes to assemble, upon the high aesthetic ground (away from the regions of strife, in any bad sense), writers of different schools,—that the antagonistic views of Philosophy, of Individual and of Social Culture which prevail among the various divisions of the Church, and of the Scientific and Literary world, may be brought together, and a white radiance of love and wisdom be evolved from the union of the many-colored rays, that shall cultivate an harmonious intellectual and moral life in our country.[136]

The contents of *Aesthetic Papers* definitely symbolized and reflected romantic diversity and the progression from nature to the world of spirit. The diverse orientations of the contributors also revealed why Peabody's dream of a new unity was destined to fail. Amid analyses of language, criticism, natural history, and music, as well as Peabody's own historical essay, "Dorian Measure," and Hawthorne's "Main Street," Thoreau's *Essay on Civil Disobedience* made its literary debut. Highlighting the conflict between the individual and society that Peabody hoped to resolve, Thoreau's essay seemed to dismiss her vision of an organic and aesthetically harmonious culture as merely a romantic illusion.

The failure of *Aesthetic Papers*, ironically, was due in large measure to its extremely aesthetic nature. It had been produced and written by the small band of New England intellectuals, never a cohesive group, whose sense of community was derived from their devotion to romantic thought, however their applications and emphases might vary. By 1849 the group had begun to scatter, leaving Peabody's journal without even the small audience for whom it was designed.[137] Finding it impossible to sustain and support the spirit of romanticism in New England, Elizabeth Peabody deserted the role of literary "woman of letters" and returned to history and educational theory for the next decade. In 1859, with her discovery of Froebel, she glimpsed new possibilities for her own intellectual future and in the next year admitted pupils to her experimental kindergarten in Boston. By focusing her knowledge and experience upon educational theory and practice in the American kindergarten movement, she was thus able to forge a unique romantic synthesis for herself, which she had never been able to create as a "woman of letters."

The American "woman of letters," unable to produce a romantic literary genius from her own ranks comparable to the sublime male artists she studied, had written about the majestic romantic heroes of America, England, and Germany. She had found at the heart of the romantic theory that seemed so congenial to her talents the splendidly masculine image with which she could have no "elective affinities." With such knowledge and after many struggles, artistic and critical, the "woman of letters" came to "know her place." Only Sarah Helen Whitman seemed content to remain there, undisturbed by the frustrations others had experienced.

Even those who abandoned the "woman of letters" world in search of more vital intellectual stances assumed appropriately feminine roles, duly accredited as part of "woman's sphere." Elizabeth Peabody became, once again, a teacher of children; and Louisa McCord achieved renown as an American Florence Nightingale during the Civil War.[138] Elizabeth Oakes Smith's lecturing career, interrupted by her failing health, came to a close on the eve of the hostilities. Only Margaret Fuller continued until her death to seek new ways of "acting out her nature" as a romantic symbol of the "woman of letters."

# Epilogue

*We are associated in adolescent and adult life with some friends, who, like skies and waters, are coextensive with our idea.*

—Ralph Waldo Emerson

*In the eighteenth century that age of manners and of formal morals it was believed that the temper of a woman was determined by the turn of her features; later, in the beginning nineteenth, the period of inner spiritual illumination it was accepted that the features were moulded by the temper of the soul within; still later in the nineteenth century when the science of heredity had decided that everything proves something different, it was discovered that generalizations must be as complicated as the facts and the problem of interrelation was not to be so simply solved.*

—Gertrude Stein

The story of the American woman is, in many ways, the record of her attempts to be an American. The options, obstacles, and opportunities that were hers by cultural consensus, her own agitation or appropriation of new modes of action, have differed in each period of the nation's history. The story of the American woman as intellectual in the mid-nineteenth century forms a part of this larger narrative. Although Sarah J. Hale had blanched at the possibility, the emergence of a recognizable group of female intellectuals—not all of whom shared the feminist persuasion she loathed—was a natural outgrowth of the American experience during this period. America's intellectual women between 1830 and 1860 were striving intensely, and often self-consciously, to become representative American women. Even the Southerner Louisa Mc-Cord based her life and work on another definition of America; she too sought to symbolize and support her culture and defend its "peculiar institution." The Grimké sisters, on the other hand, as southern exiles, came to share the cultural orientation of their northern counterparts who were born and raised in New England or rural New York.

As children and young women, few of these future intellectuals experienced insurmountable conflicts between intellectual activity and "true womanhood"; no one succeeded in stopping them from pursuing a life of the mind. Usually left to their own devices, they browsed in the family library, often teaching themselves how to read. Each soon revealed her intellectual precocity to astonished and sometimes admiring parents. Frequently, their fathers enthusiastically endorsed and encouraged their efforts. Lawyers, in particular, transmitted standards of professional excellence and expertise to their daughters.[1] Only Timothy Fuller became tyrannical in his zeal to give Margaret a thorough grounding in the best thoughts of mankind, presiding over her studies without allowing any intrusions from his submissive wife. More assertive mothers, like Elizabeth Oakes Smith's, warned their daughters that too much learning might make them unfit for their "main chance" of marriage. Conversely, Elizabeth Peabody's mother, emphasizing the value of intellectual cultivation and personal independence, urged her daughter not to marry. In those instances where both parents disapproved of their child's intellectual development, the children found a way, right under their parents' noses, to pursue a life of the mind, often alone and on their own terms. Accordingly, even as an adult, painfully aware of all aspects of "the woman question" as it occupied American culture, an intellectual feminist like Caroline Healey Dall believed that other women could overcome obstacles as she had, given sufficient fortitude, energy, and self-reliance.

For their limited formal education, these young women usually attended female academies where they learned embroidery, music, and other feminine arts. They had, however, always learned more at home, even if they attended more rigorous academic institutions. At coeducational preparatory schools designed to ready young men for college, they often outshone their male schoolmates, as Margaret Fuller did, impressing the other students with their knowledge of languages and literature. When male friends left for colleges like Harvard or Union, where even learned girls were not admitted, some young women chose to accompany them in order to be privately tutored by college professors (primarily at Harvard); and several remained, like Fuller and Dall, in such close contact with young Harvard men that they often felt like undergraduates too. Among intellectual women in the period, only Elizabeth Cady Stanton received a close approximation of a college education, and she judged her term at Troy Seminary as the most desolate period of her life.

Stanton and the other young women who were to become intellectuals represented a fund of mental energy that could not be fully utilized in the roles then available to women. Most found "scribbling" or teaching equally unappealing. Teaching the young, especially, was not thought of as a learned profession. Even Sarah Hale, who hoped that women could raise standards and find their "temple of fame" in the schoolroom, openly admitted the truth of the popular saying, "only a dunce will keep a school from choice." [2] Elizabeth Oakes Smith and Elizabeth Peabody were the only young women in this generation of intellectuals who aspired to a teaching career. Smith's mother squelched her dream while Peabody's mother made her daughter value that role above all others. For the rest, such options were so depressing that, as the "cult of true womanhood" dictated, marriage often seemed the brightest possibility life would offer them. Only Elizabeth Peabody, Sarah Grimké, and Mary Louise Booth never married.

Although by the 1840s many feminists were urging women

to consider carefully what marriage would force them to give up, especially whatever legal status they might have, the marriages of the majority of intellectual women in the mid-nineteenth century seem to have been relatively comfortable and congenial relationships that supported, and in many cases, initiated, the women's public intellectual endeavors. In most of their marriages, the question of submissiveness did not come up, for a variety of reasons. In general, the intellectual woman who married found a great deal of freedom within marriage because she had married a man who was either very supportive to her extra-domestic activities, too busy to care what she was doing, or sometimes totally reliant upon her talents to bring in extra income. His occupation was often the same as her father's—but several of the young lawyer husbands had intellectual inclinations, talents, and reformist sympathies that interfered with their law practice. The most striking example was Lydia Maria Child's husband, David, an ardent abolitionist author who recklessly gave away his slender legal fees to any worthy cause or needy individual crossing his path. As his wife well knew, the old adage, "a fool and his money are soon parted," was only too applicable to David, however delightful and intelligent he was as her life's companion.[3] During most of their marriage she was the sole breadwinner. Also financially unstable, although not in such spectacular fashion, Seba Smith, journalist and humorist, had to rely upon his wife's talents even though he heartily disapproved of the feminist persuasion she argued so eloquently. Thus, for Child, Smith, and Caroline Healey Dall (abandoned by her minister husband), life in what has been termed the "era of precarious fortunes" worked to their intellectual advantage. More successful providers, like Antoinette Brown's husband and both husbands of Paulina Wright Davis, all merchants, shared their wives' commitment to the women's rights movement.

Contrary to the popular assumption that intellectual activity might "unsex" them, most of these women had children. And the few who did not marry or have children of their own, publicly and privately supported the ideal of motherhood. In addition, most of these mothers could rely upon some form of relief from domesticity, which allowed them time for their intellectual endeavors. As a result, none seemed to mind playing a domestic role and being a "true" mother. Elizabeth Cady Stanton, with her large brood of seven, relied upon a faithful nurse for help, although during her first year in Seneca Falls, with three infants and a large house, she had no domestic assistance. Stanton, in particular, enjoyed her children, mostly boys, giving them a great deal of freedom and finding rather unique ways to make them behave without resorting to tyranny. Once, when her three eldest sons had taken up cursing at the dinner table, the feminist Lucretia Mott, the very epitome of feminine gentility, suggested a most successful cure: she and Elizabeth would curse throughout the next meal. When the Stanton boys heard Lucretia Mott asking, "Wilt thee have some damned chicken?" and their mother's outrageous reply, they begged her to give up the habit, agreeing to reform themselves, if only she would too.[4]

The religious faith of intellectual women was subject to continual transformations.[5] Their religious orientations reflect the pluralistic nature of American faiths before the Civil War, and the changing nature of their religious allegiances reveal that such a lack of consensus was a form of liberation, not only for American culture in general, but especially for the woman intellectual in America. Like most Americans, they abandoned the harsh theology of John Calvin. As New England Unitarians, Dall, Fuller, and Child escaped the fire and brimstone that had plagued Stanton and Davis as children in rural New York. From the family farm in upstate New York, Antoinette Brown was touched by the evangelistic genius of Charles G. Finney, but, after her years at Oberlin, she too turned to the Unitarian faith. Elizabeth Ellet and the Grimké sisters, originally Episcopalians, deserted that faith, becoming Catholic and Quakers, respectively. None held really unorthodox religious stances—except when these stances are viewed from an overall cultural perspective—for each rejected the increasingly popular paths to salvation offered by the proliferating sects of evangelical protestantism. The Quaker and Unitarian faiths, in particular, left their adherents free to think about other questions besides their own salvation, allowing intellectual women who embraced these doctrines the liberty to confront the major intellectual questions of their era. Unitarianism was perhaps too benignly liberating for its own good: as it did for so many New England romantics, it led intellectual women from the folds of organized religion in any form, and prepared them for the romantic revolution that became their new faith. In many senses, as Elizabeth Oakes Smith phrased it, God had "given them the new." [6]

Not submissive in marriage, not oriented exclusively toward domesticity, not as institutionally pious as "true" women were supposed to be, intellectual women between 1830 and 1860 veered far from the ideal. The personal freedom so many achieved, within and without marriage, allowed them to engage in intellectual activity and become active participants in the Jacksonian Persuasion. To pursue their own form of upward mobility, these "venturous conservatives" had sought to reconcile old and new, to make "new" and "true" woman mean the same thing. Since, as intellectuals, they were dealing with more difficult problems than the "female scribbler," their attempts to integrate intellect with womanhood were more complex. Wishing to confront intellectual traditions and social issues as analysts and interpreters of both theory and practice, they bypassed the comfortable world of the "female scribbler," accompanied only by a sense of mission, a desire to redeem and reconstruct American culture, and a faith that their own intellectual journeys might offer unquestionable proof of their representative womanhood. Childhood, family background, regional and religious affiliations, and other accepted modes of action for women determined the nature and structure of their intellectual response to the Jacksonian Persuasion.

Intellectual women in this period who spent their lives thinking about woman, charting her future course, schematizing and justifying their own intellectual roles, revealed that, like Emerson, they had found their own voice in talking about themselves. As investigators of the nature of woman, historians and feminists discovered, as did other American explorers, that the process of exploration was both their major concern and cognitive style. In modifying Crèvecour's question to fit their own sex, their generation, and themselves—"who is this American, this new woman?"—each of the intellectual women in this period, self-consciously American and self-consciously female, sought to reassure herself that she was an ideal woman and an ideal American, in terms of her particular definitions of feminine and cultural identity. Since they all lived in mid-nineteenth-century America, none of them could successfully maintain clear definitions or static conceptions of nationality, sex, or intellect. To Margaret Fuller, the meaning of America, if it had a meaning, seemed to lie in that continuous movement she called "energy." The other members of America's first generation of women intellectuals agreed.

Stable concepts of either "ideal femininity" or intellect were increasingly inapplicable to the changing concepts of America's social energy and European romanticism, an intellectual revolution also based upon energy and change. None of the new American women could have imagined Jane Austen's stable world. As their voices began to be heard, they registered and analyzed the intellectual and social forces of change with the new vocabulary of romanticism. Symmetrical blueprints for present and future, like Catharine Beecher's, failed to explain to them either the nature and aspirations of women or those of American culture. Women like Margaret Fuller and Lydia Maria Child, responding to the dictates of the romantic orientation, might find themselves victims of intellectual flux, spinning out to a frontier of uncertainty at the edges of American culture. Yet, even there, intellectuals, male and female, were engaged in the same vast drama of transcendence and expansion that characterized antebellum America.

After the Civil War the social roles and intellectual stances of American women reflected a new America, transformed not only by science, technology, and the rise of a business civilization, but also beset with pressing social problems. Analyzing the consequences and casualties of industrial America, Jane Addams helped make social work a profession and saw work in that field as a "subjective necessity" for American college women with nothing to do with their educations after graduation.[7] The "Seven Sisters" colleges in New England began their rise to equal status with men's institutions of higher learning. Vassar's opening in 1865 launched that drive to excellence, and the founding of Bryn Mawr in 1885 marked the success of this educational experiment. Returning from Germany with a doctorate and a thesis on *Sir Gawain and The Green Knight*, Martha Carey Thomas became Bryn Mawr's first president and attempted to make it a citadel for intellectual women. Scientific and tough-minded, President Thomas wrote essays in reply to every criticism of educated and intellectual women that crossed her desk and published her work in America's major educational reviews. Other "new women," professionally trained in the sciences, also taught at New England's women's colleges. Even women without scientific training were drawn to varieties of scientific work. Calling herself a "sociologist," Charlotte Perkins Gilman argued the logic and economics of feminism in the 1890s. In summing up her century, she seemed a symbol of her age. Young Gertrude Stein, a Johns Hopkins medical student and former pupil of William James, when asked to address a Baltimore ladies' club on the "college woman," was at a loss for words and promptly appropriated Gilman's vocabulary.[8]

Members of America's first generation of intellectual women could see few connections between their experience and that of intellectual women in the later nineteenth century. Feminists, with their burgeoning organizational structures, seemed to have no time for intellectuals of either sex, young or old. The business of institutionalized feminism was apparently business. Tactical maneuvers to get the franchise too often eclipsed intellectual strategies designed to persuade society of the intrinsic merit of women as individuals. Even that "scientific" intellectual, Charlotte Perkins Gilman, like Elizabeth Cady Stanton, was no longer welcomed within the "phalanx of associated inquiry." The women who had begun their intellectual careers during the 1830s saw, in the later nineteenth century, young women going to women's colleges in New England, where it was rumored the degree was equal to that granted in any male institution of higher learning; and they also witnessed the entry of women into previously all-male colleges. Female literary intellectuals could now get advanced degrees—usually in Europe—return to America, and teach in women's colleges. Many of the most talented young college women seemed more scientifically oriented than the antebellum intellectual woman dreamed possible.

Noticing that few of these new professionals married, the older intellectual woman could not decide whether marriage itself or the emerging structure of academia was responsible for this new style among her younger counterparts. Even with all the new options, it seemed to be increasingly difficult to combine female and intellectual roles. This was the great paradox to her, when she thought about women. And she had always been thinking about them, wondering why intellectual activity had been branded as unfeminine. After all, some of her best friends were men—even male intellectuals—and she had devoted a great deal of intellectual and social energy to proving that both roles were compatible. Such efforts, as well as her intellectual achievements and those of her post-Civil War counterparts, were always ignored during the heated discussion of woman's mind and social role that resumed after the Civil War and continued throughout the century. In 1874 Dr. Clarke's best selling *Sex and Education* once again severed all links between intellect and womanhood, highlighting the confusion that prevailed, and still prevails, over what an intellectual is, why anyone in his right mind would choose to be one, and whether women would lose their minds if they tried.

Like all American thinkers, the woman intellectual attempted to analyze the new century that was fast approaching and to understand her own life as a nineteenth-century woman and intellectual in relation to the future. She was as perplexed as Henry Adams by the new lines of force at work in America. Having always conceived of America in terms of energy and fluidity, she wondered whether this very energy was beginning to create a pattern of increasingly rigid social institutions, as strong as the shiny rails of iron that now crossed the continent. She wondered whether American women of the future, especially women intellectuals, might find themselves in a sharper and more defined conflict with the new America than women of her own era had experienced. She perished with that thought.

# Notes

## INTRODUCTION

1. Christopher Lasch, "Mabel Dodge Luhan: Sex as Politics," *The New Radicalism in America, 1889–1963: The Intellectual as a Social Type* (New York: Random House, Vintage Books, 1967), pp. 104–41.

2. John McCormick, *The Middle Distance: A Comparative History of American Imaginative Literature, 1919–1932* (New York: The Free Press, 1971), p. 1.

3. Tom Wolfe, *Radical Chic & Mau-Mauing the Flak Catchers* (New York: Farrar, Straus & Giroux, 1970), pp. 25–27.

4. The most useful contemporary source on the etymological and social origins of the noun "intellectual" and its association with French radicals of the late nineteenth century is Victor Brombert's *The Intellectual Hero: Studies in the French Novel, 1880–1955* (Philadelphia: Lippincott, 1961).

5. Seymour M. Lipset, "American Intellectuals, Their Politics and Status," *Daedalus* (Summer 1959), p. 311. Other useful articles appeared in the Summer 1962 *Daedalus*, which was devoted to the theme of intellectualism. Several of these essays have been reprinted in the best anthology of articles concerning this subject, *On Intellectuals: Theoretical Studies/Case Studies*, Philip Rieff, ed. (Garden City, N.Y.: Doubleday, Anchor Books, 1970).

6. For these general descriptions of intellectual activity, see Richard Hofstadter, *Anti-Intellectualism in American Life* (New York: Random House, Vintage Books, 1962). Also see Marcus Cunliffe, "Intellectuals: The United States," *Encounter* (May 1955) for a historical portrait and definition of "intellectual." The most useful sociological analyses are in Joseph A. Schumpeter's classic, *Capitalism, Socialism and Democracy*, 3d ed. (New York: Harper & Row, Harper Torchbooks, 1962), pp. 145–54, and Lewis A. Coser's *Men of Ideas: A Sociologist's View* (New York: The Free Press, 1970).

7. For a recent synopsis of anthropological research upon women, see Sherry B. Ortner, "Is Female to Male as Nature is to Culture?", *Feminist Studies* 1 (1972):5–33.

8. Barbara Welter, "The Cult of True Womanhood, 1820–1860," *American Quarterly* 18 (Summer 1966):151–75. Although the term "true woman" was in common use in the nineteenth century, Welter deserves credit for bringing it to the attention of cultural historians in this lucidly argued and carefully documented analysis of the concept of ideal femininity.

9. *Ibid.*

10. Morse Peckham, *Romanticism: The Culture of the Nineteenth Century* (New York: George Braziller, 1965), p. 15. In addition to this book, Peckham's other brilliant interpretations of romanticism have been most helpful to me. See Peckham's *Beyond the Tragic Vision: The Quest for Identity in the Nineteenth Century* (New York: George Braziller, 1962), and his recent collection of essays, *The Triumph of Romanticism* (Columbia, S.C.: University of South Carolina Press, 1970).

11. Peckham, *Tragic Vision*, p. 185.

12. René Wellek, "The Minor Transcendentalists and German Philosophy," *New England Quarterly* (1943), pp. 652–80.

13. *Ibid.*

14. An original interpretation of Channing's definitional strategy is presented in Dave Hickey's "William Ellery Channing and American Literature." (Unpublished manuscript courtesy of the author).

15. Tony Tanner, *The Reign of Wonder: Naivety and Reality in American Literature* (London: Cambridge University Press, 1965). Tanner analyzes the stylistic manifestations of these concepts in the works of American writers from Emerson to Stein.

16. Peckham, *Tragic Vision*, p. 182.

17. For the best analyses of the far-ranging impact of romanticism on American culture in the nineteenth century, see William H. Goetzmann's *Army Exploration in the American West, 1803–1863* (New Haven: Yale University Press, 1959), especially pp. 17–21, and the same author's more comprehensive work, *Exploration and Empire: The Explorer and the Scientist in the Winning of the American West* (New York: Alfred A. Knopf, 1966).

18. Gerda Lerner, "The Lady and the Mill Girl: Changes in the Status of Women in the Age of Jackson," *Mid-Continent American Studies Journal* 10 (1969):9.

19. Elizabeth Cady Stanton, *Eighty Years and More: Reminiscences, 1815–1897* (1898; reprint ed., New York: Schocken Books, 1971). Stanton wanted to attend Clark University with her brothers and male friends and did not relish attending Troy Seminary. Her doubts confirmed, she found that institution intellectually and socially confining and vowed that no daughter of hers would undergo what she called the torture of life in a "girl's school."

## CHAPTER ONE

1. Barbara Welter, "The Cult of True Womanhood, 1820–1860," *American Quarterly* 18 (Summer 1966):151–75.

2. Arthur O. Lovejoy, *The Great Chain of Being: A Study of the History of An Idea* (New York: Harper & Row, Harper Torchbooks, 1960). Lovejoy's work and Peter Gay's brilliant two-volume study, *The Enlightenment: An Interpretation* (New York: Alfred A. Knopf, 1967, 1969) are indispensable sources for any student of eighteenth-century intellectual history.

3. See Morse Peckham, *Romanticism: The Culture of the Nineteenth Century* (New York: George Braziller, 1965), and *Beyond the Tragic Vision: The Quest for Identity in the Nineteenth Century* (New York: George Braziller, 1962) for discussions of the way in which the eighteenth-century cult of sensibility and sentimentality provided a psychological safety valve for those living according to the strict orientation of Enlightenment rationalism.

4. Peckham, *Romanticism*, p. 17.

5. See Ethel Rolt Wheeler, *Famous Blue-Stockings* (London: Methuen & Co., 1910). Also see Bonamy Dobrée, *English Literature in the Early Eighteenth Century*, *The Oxford History of English Literature* (New York: Oxford University Press, 1959), and the *Oxford Companion to English Literature*.

6. Christopher J. Herold, *Mistress to An Age: A Life of Madame de Staël* (New York: Bobbs-Merrill, 1958), p. 229.

7. Quoted in *ibid.*, p. 360.

8. From de Staël, *De la Littérature* as quoted in *ibid.*, p. 360.

9. Quoted in Caroline Ticknor, *Hawthorne and His Publisher* (Boston: Houghton Mifflin, 1913), pp. 141–43.

10. Marvin Meyers, *The Jacksonian Persuasion: Politics and Belief* (New York: Alfred A. Knopf, Vintage Books, 1960).

11. The preceding quotations are from Margaret Coxe, *The Young Lady's Companion* (Cincinnati, 1846), pp. vi, 128, 6, 79, 89.

12. *Ibid.*, p. 129.

13. *Ibid.*, p. 89.

14. *Ibid.*

15. Barbara Welter, "Anti-Intellectualism and the American Woman, 1800–1860," *Mid-America* 48 (1966):258–70. Although Welter presents a convincing and well-documented case for her conclusion that few Americans thought that intellect and "true womanhood" had any affinities, my research in periodicals and in ladies' manuals suggests that all ties had not been severed. Writers famous and obscure, tailoring their work for an audience of "true women" and often supporting higher education for women were, like Margaret Coxe, sometimes sanguine about a synthesis of mind and femininity which would create a paradigmatic American woman, the glory of the Republic. Among less optimistic arbiters of femininity and educationists, confusion and ambivalence might reign, but most of them diligently kept trying to unite intellect and femininity in a culturally acceptable resolution.

16. Quoted in Thomas Woody, *A History of Women's Education in the United States,* 2 vols. (New York: The Science Press, 1929)1:155. Woody's study is still the basic and most exhaustive reference work on women's education, and his magnificent bibliography is in itself a major contribution to women's studies.

17. Quoted in Welter, "Anti-Intellectualism," p. 260.

18. Quoted in Woody, *Women's Education* 1:154–55.

19. Quoted in Welter, "Anti-Intellectualism," p. 259.

20. For a detailed and entertaining account of the anti-intellectualism of "female scribblers" see Leslie A. Fiedler, *Love and Death in the American Novel,* 2d rev. ed. (New York: Stein & Day, 1966). Helen Papishvily's *All The Happy Endings* (New York: Harper & Bros., 1956) analyzes many "domestic" novels and demonstrates through textual analysis how this seemingly passive genre became a weapon of power in the hands of women, a countervailing force against male supremacy in which women could assert their own strength and superiority.

21. Quoted in Ann D. Wood, "The 'Scribbling Women' and Fanny Fern: Why Women Wrote," *American Quarterly* 23 (1971):6. I am indebted to this astute analysis of the motives of "scribbling women" and the rationale they cleverly employed to legitimatize their professional undertakings as essentially "feminine" pastimes. For a related exploration of these themes, see Wood's recent article, "Mrs. Sigourney and the Sensibility of the Inner Space," *New England Quarterly* 45 (1972):163–81.

22. Wood, "Why Women Wrote," p. 6.

23. Quoted in *ibid.*, p. 7.

24. Eleanor Flexner, *Century of Struggle: The Woman's Rights Movement in the United States* (New York: Atheneum, 1968) p. 23.

25. See analyses of Beecher and Lyon below.

26. Mabel Newcomer, *A Century of Higher Education for Women* (New York: Harper & Bros., 1959), p. 20.

27. Quoted in *ibid.*

28. Quoted in Gamaliel Bradford, *Portraits of American Women* (Boston: Houghton Mifflin, 1919), p. 89.

29. *Ibid.*, p. 70.

30. *Ibid.*, p. 90.

31. *Ibid.*

32. *Ibid.*, p. 153.

33. Beth Bradford Gilchrist, *The Life of Mary Lyon* (Boston: Houghton Mifflin, 1910), pp. 150, 316.

34. Barbara Cross uses this adjective to describe Beecher in *The Educated Woman in America: Selected Writings of Catharine Beecher, Margaret Fuller and M. Carey Thomas* (New York: Teachers College Press, Columbia University, 1965), p. 9.

35. Catharine Beecher, "An Essay on the Education of Female Teachers" (1835), quoted in Cross, *Educated Woman,* p. 68.

36. Catharine Beecher and Harriet Beecher Stowe, *The New Housekeeper's Manual*, quoted in *ibid.*, p. 12.

37. Catharine Beecher, "Female Teachers," quoted in *ibid.*, p. 71.

38. *Ibid.*, p. 75.

39. The quotations which follow are from "Man's Mental Superiority Over Woman, Referrable to Physical Causes Only," *The Ladies' Magazine* 2:367–70.

40. The quotations which follow are from "The Intellectual Character of Woman," *Ladies' Magazine* 2:146–50.

41. The quotations which follow are from Caleb Atwater, "Female Education," *The Ladies' Repository, and Gatherings of the West: A Monthly Periodical Devoted to Literature and Religion* 1(1828):11.

42. Jos. M'D. Matthews, "Substance of a Report on 'Female Education,' Presented to the 'College of Teachers,' in Cincinnati, October, 1840," *The Ladies Repository* 1:51.

43. "The Social Condition of Woman," *North American Review* 42 (1836):511–12.

44. *Ibid.*, p. 513.

45. *Ibid.*

46. The quotations which follow are from Sarah J. Hale, "Authoresses.—No. I," *Ladies' Magazine* 2:30–31.

47. Hale, "Authoresses.—No. II," *Ladies' Magazine* 1:143.

48. Hale, "The *Bas* and the *Bleu*: Sketches of American Character," *Ladies Magazine* 1:305.

49. Hale, Review of *Bluestocking Hall*, *Ladies' Magazine* 1:143.

50. The quotations which follow are from Harriet Martineau, *Society in America*, 2 vols. (London: Saunders & Otley, 1837), 2:226–28.

51. Quoted in Elizabeth Cady Stanton, Susan B. Anthony, and Mathilda Jocelyn Gage, *The History of Woman Suffrage*, vol. 1, 2d ed. (Rochester: Charles Mann, 1889), pp. 802–3, 808.

52. Quoted in *ibid.*, pp. 517, 852.

53. Quoted in *ibid.*, p. 853.

54. *Ibid.*

55. *Ibid.*, pp. 556–67.

56. Antoinette Brown, "Address to the 'Mob Convention,' " New York City, September 6–7, 1853, quoted in *ibid.*, p. 553.

## CHAPTER TWO

1. Sarah J. Hale, *Ladies' Magazine* 2 (1829):142.

2. Sarah J. Hale, *Woman's Record: or Sketches of All Distinguished Women from "The Beginning" Till A. D. 1850* (New York, 1853), p. 669. See also the Rev. Mr. Harrington's villification—"they are only semi-women, mental hermaphrodites"—of Mary Wollstonecraft, Frances Wright, and Harriet Martineau in *The Ladies' Companion* 9 (1838):293.

3. *Ibid.*, p. 383, and Horace Greeley, *Recollections of a Busy Life* (New York, 1868), p. 178.

4. Maria Weston Chapman, ed., *Harriet Martineau's Autobiography*, 2 vols. (Boston: Houghton Mifflin, 1877) 1:381.

5. Quoted in Perry Miller, ed., *Margaret Fuller, American Romantic: A Selection from Her Writings and Correspondence* (New York: Anchor Books, 1963), p. 192.

6. Henry James, *William Wetmore Story and His Friends: From Letters, Diaries, and Recollections,* one vol. ed. (1903; reprint, ed., New York: Grove Press, 1957), pp. 127–28.

7. Margaret Fuller to James Nathan as quoted in Miller, *Margaret Fuller,* pp. 202–03.

8. Thomas Carlyle to Ralph Waldo Emerson, 7 May 1852. From *The Correspondence of Thomas Carlyle and Ralph Waldo Emerson: Supplementary Letters* (Boston: Ticknor & Co., 1886).

9. *Ibid.*

10. Germaine Greer, *The Female Eunuch* (New York: Bantam Books, 1972).

11. Margaret Fuller, "Commonplace Book," n.d., Fuller Papers, Houghton Library, Harvard University. By permission of the Harvard College Library. Disillusioned with the dearth of true men in her era, Fuller wrote the following in 1841: "I wish I were a man, and then there would be *one*. I weary in this playground of boys, proud and happy in their balls and marbles." Women lived who were far superior to even the "best" of men, who were "so unripe, the wisest so ignoble, the truest so cold." Fuller noted that the thought of Sir Philip Sidney and a belief that God could not possibly have botched his own creation saved her from total despair: "Like a desperate gamester I feel, at moments, as I cling to the belief that he [the Deity] cannot have lost this great throw of Man, when the lesser hazards have ended so successfully. Men disappoint me so, I disappoint myself so, yet courage, patience, shuffle the cards . . . . There was . . . a Sidney,—we need the old counters still." [Quoted in Thomas Wentworth Higginson, *Margaret Fuller Ossoli,* American Men of Letters Series, Charles Dudley Warner, ed. (Boston: Houghton Mifflin, 1884), pp. 111–12.]

12. Higginson, *Margaret Fuller,* p. 11.

13. *Ibid.*

14. Margaret's brother Arthur, the heroic subject of Richard Fuller's memoir, *Chaplain Fuller,* officially relinquished his post as Chaplain of the Sixteenth Regiment of Massachusetts Volunteers due to illness and exhaustion on December 10, 1862. His discharge, effective immediately, made his wife ineligible for a pension in case of his death. The very next day the virtuous chaplain lost his life when he joined volunteers attacking Confederate sharpshooters during the Battle of Fredericksburg.

15. Miller, *Margaret Fuller,* p. x.

16. Higginson, *Margaret Fuller,* p. 17.

17. *Ibid.*, p. 19.

18. Ralph Waldo Emerson, William Henry Channing, and James Freeman Clarke, eds., *The Memoirs of Margaret Fuller Ossoli*, 2 vols. (Boston: Phillips, Sampson and Co., 1852) 1:15.

19. Fuller, *Chaplain Fuller*, p. 9.

20. Emerson et al., eds., *Memoirs of Margaret Fuller*, 1:18.

21. *Ibid.*

22. See Margaret Fuller's fictional sketch of the brilliant and doomed "Mariana," in *Life Without and Life Within; Or, Reviews, Narratives, Essays and Poems*, Arthur B. Fuller, ed. (Boston: Roberts Brothers, 1874) pp. 258–76. "Leila" was one of Fuller's favorite poetic personae. She wrote the following poem in her diary in 1844 (quoted in Higginson, *Margaret Fuller*, p. 102):

Leila, of all demanding heart
By each and every left apart;
Leila, of all pursuing mind
From each goal left far behind;
Strive on, Leila, to the end,
Let not thy native courage bend;
Strive on, Leila, day by day,
Though bleeding feet stain all the way;
Do men reject thee and despise?—
An angel in thy bosom lies
And to thy death its birth replies.

For a more fortunate intellectual heroine, see Fuller's fictional creation, "Miranda," in *Woman in the Nineteenth Century*, who "took her place easily not only in the world of organized being, but in the world of mind." Clearly an ideal woman to Fuller, Miranda, noble, dignified, serene, "intellectual without boldness," "fortunate in a total absence of those charms which might have drawn to her bewildering flatteries," was a symbol of the self-reliance Fuller was trying to achieve, an autonomy which she considered essential to all women's future development. For Fuller, every woman should say, with herself and her heroine: "I must depend on myself as the only constant friend." (Quoted in Miller, *Margaret Fuller*, pp. 151–52.)

23. Higginson, *Margaret Fuller*, p. 27.

24. *Ibid.*, p. 25.

25. [Baronne de Staël-Holstein] Anne Louise Necker, Madame de Staël, *Corinne: Or Italy*, trans. Elizabeth Hill (New York: A. L. Burt & Co., 1807), pp. 234–36.

26. Quoted in Helene G. Baer, "Mrs. Child and Miss Fuller," *New England Quarterly* (June 1953), p. 250.

27. Edith Wharton, *The House of Mirth* (New York: Charles Scribner's Sons, 1905).

28. Christopher Lasch and William R. Taylor, "Two 'Kindred Spirits': Sorority and Family in New England, 1839–1846," *New England Quarterly* 36 (1963):23–42.

29. *Ibid.*, p. 31.
30. *Ibid.*, p. 33.
31. Quoted in *ibid.*, p. 34.
32. Quoted in Julia Ward Howe, *Margaret Fuller (Marchesa Ossoli)*, (Boston, 1883), p. 28.
33. Quoted in Miller, *Margaret Fuller*, p. 35.
34. *Ibid.*, p. 35.
35. Fuller, *Chaplain Fuller*, p. 31.
36. Alice Felt Tyler, *Freedom's Ferment: Phases of American Social History from the Colonial Period to the Outbreak of the Civil War* (New York: Harper & Row, Harper Torchbooks, 1962), p. 247. For a detailed description, see Elizabeth Palmer Peabody, *Record of Mr. Alcott's School, Exemplifying the Principles and Methods of Moral Culture,* 3d ed. rev. (1835; Boston: Roberts Brothers, 1874).
37. Howe, *Margaret Fuller,* p. 61.
38. Edward A. Hoyt and Loriman S. Brigham, "Glimpses of Margaret Fuller: The Green Street School and Florence," *New England Quarterly* 29 (March 1956):87.
39. *Ibid.*, p. 95.
40. *Ibid.*, p. 88.
41. Margaret Fuller to Caroline Tappan, 16 November 1837, Fuller Papers, Houghton Library, Harvard University. By permission of the Harvard College Library.
42. Margaret Fuller to Caroline Tappan, 3 January 1838, Fuller Papers, Houghton Library, Harvard University. By permission of the Harvard College Library.
43. Emerson et al., eds., *Memoirs of Margaret Fuller* 1:324.
44. Higginson, *Margaret Fuller,* p. 116. Also see Howe, *Margaret Fuller;* and a detailed record of the "Conversations" can be found in Caroline Healey Dall, *Margaret Fuller and Her Friends, Or, Ten Conversations with Margaret Fuller Upon the Mythology of the Greeks and its Expression in Art* (Boston: Roberts Brothers, 1895).
45. Quoted in Higginson, *Margaret Fuller,* p. 117.
46. Quoted in Bradford, *Portraits of American Women,* p. 141.
47. Emerson et al., eds., *Memoirs of Margaret Fuller,* 1:326.
48. Miller, *Margaret Fuller,* p. 57.
49. The following quotations are from Margaret Fuller and Ralph Waldo Emerson, "The Editors to the Reader," *The Dial: A Magazine for Literature, Philosophy and Religion* (July 1840; reprint ed., 4 vols., New York: Russell & Russell, 1961), 1:1–2.
50. See Lovejoy, "Romanticism and the Principle of Plenitude," *The Great Chain of Being,* chap. 10.
51. *Ibid.*, pp. 294–96.
52. Fuller and Emerson, "To the Reader," *The Dial* 1:2, 4.
53. See Peckham, *Romanticism* and *Beyond the Tragic Vision.*

54. Fuller, "A Short Essay on Critics," *The Dial* 1:6–7.
55. Miller, *Margaret Fuller*, p. 79.
56. Fuller, "Goethe," *The Dial* 2 (July 1841):1–2.
57. *Ibid.*, pp. 97–98.
58. *Ibid.*, p. 6.
59. *Ibid.*, pp. 20–21.
60. Fuller, "Bettine Brentano and Her Friend Günderode," *The Dial* 2 (January 1842):313–57.
61. *Ibid.*, p. 322.
62. Fuller, "Commonplace Book," Fuller Papers, Houghton Library, Harvard University. By permission of the Harvard College Library.
63. Fuller, "Bettine," *The Dial* 2:320.
64. Quoted in *ibid.*, pp. 354–55.
65. Fuller, "Essay on Critics," *The Dial* 1 (July 1840):10.
66. Fuller, *New York Daily Tribune*, 8 September 1845.
67. Quoted in Julian Hawthorne, ed., *Nathaniel Hawthorne and His Wife*, 2 vols. (Boston: J. R. Osgood, 1885) 1:262.
68. Quoted in Emerson et al., eds., *Memoirs of Margaret Fuller*, 2:58.
69. Quoted in Julian Hawthorne, *Nathaniel Hawthorne and His Wife*, 1:261. Hawthorne confided in his journal that "It was such an awful joke, that she should have resolved—in all sincerity, no doubt—to make herself the greatest, wisest, best woman of the age. And to that end she set to work on her strong, heavy, unpliable, and in many respects, defective and evil nature, and adorned it with a mosaic of admirable qualities such as she chose to possess; putting in here a splendid talent and there a moral excellence, and polishing each separate piece, and the whole together, till it seemed to shine afar and dazzle all who saw it. She took credit to herself for having been her own Redeemer, if not her own Creator."
70. From Fuller, *Summer on the Lakes* (Boston, 1844) as quoted in Miller, *Margaret Fuller*, pp. 121–23.
71. Margaret Fuller to Caroline Sturgis Shaw, 20 November 1845, Fuller Papers, Houghton Library, Harvard University. By permission of the Harvard College Library.
72. George William Curtis remembered meeting Margaret Fuller shortly after her journey and was disappointed that *Summer on the Lakes* did not reflect her sense of humor: "Those who think of this accomplished woman as a mere *bas bleu*, a pedant, a solemn Minerva, should have heard the peals of laughter which her profuse and racy humor drew from old and young. The Easy Chair remembers stepping into Noah Gerrish's West Roxbury omnibus one afternoon in Cornhill, in Boston, to drive out the nine miles to Brook Farm. The only other passenger was Miss Fuller, then freshly returned from her 'summer on the lakes,' and never was a long, jolting journey more lightened and shortened than by her witty and vivid sketches of life and character. Her quick and shrewd observation is shown in the book, but the book has none of the comedy of the *croquis* of persons which her sparkling humor threw

off, and which she too enjoyed with the utmost hilarity, joining heartily in the laughter . . . ." Quoted in the "Easy Chair," *Harper's Magazine* (March 1882).

73. Fuller, *Woman in the Nineteenth Century, and Kindred Papers Relating to the Sphere, Condition and Duties of Woman,* Arthur B. Fuller, ed. (1845; reprint ed., Boston: Roberts Brothers, 1884), pp. 168–69, 115–16.

74. *Ibid.,* pp. 24, 172, 174, 19.

75. *Ibid.,* pp. 80–81.

76. *Ibid.,* pp. 115, 94.

77. *Ibid.,* pp. 115, 103–4.

78. *Ibid.,* pp. 141, 115.

79. For a discussion of dysfunctionalism in American prose styles, see Richard Poirier's excellent *A World Elsewhere: The Place of Style in American Literature* (New York: Oxford University Press, 1968). Other useful sources are Tony Tanner's *The Reign of Wonder* and Peckham's works, including his controversial *Man's Rage for Chaos: Biology, Behavior and the Arts* (Philadelphia: Chilton Books, 1965).

80. Quoted in Miller, *Margaret Fuller,* p. 117.

81. *Ibid.,* pp. xi–xii.

82. See Perry Miller's excellent study of the New York literary milieu in mid-century in *The Raven and the Whale* (New York: Harcourt, Brace & World, 1956). Higginson used the phrase "tomahawk theory" to describe the type of criticism written by New York literati. (Higginson, *Margaret Fuller,* p. 216.)

83. Quoted in Higginson, *Margaret Fuller,* p. 218.

84. Fuller, "American Literature; Its Position in the Present Time and Prospects for the Future," *Papers on Art, Literature, and the Drama,* Arthur B. Fuller, ed. (1846; enl. ed., Boston: Roberts Brothers, 1889), p. 314.

85. Fuller, *New York Daily Tribune,* 29 May 1845.

86. *Ibid.,* 1 May 1845; 7 June 1845.

87. *Ibid.,* 1 May 1845.

88. *Ibid.,* 4 July 1845; and "Letter 23," 29 March 1848.

89. *Ibid.,* 19 May 1845.

90. Fuller, "American Literature," *Papers on Art,* p. 300.

91. *Ibid.,* p. 308.

92. Fuller, *New York Daily Tribune,* 11 July 1845.

93. *Ibid.*

94. Fuller, "American Literature," *Papers on Art,* p. 304.

95. Fuller, *New York Daily Tribune,* 7 December 1844.

96. *Ibid.,* 10 September 1845.

97. *Ibid.,* 8 September 1845.

98. *Ibid.,* 4 July 1845.

99. Fuller to Nathan, 23 March 1845, in *Love-Letters of Margaret Fuller,* ed. Julia Ward Howe (New York, 1903), pp. 18–19.

100. Fuller, "Letter 18," *New York Daily Tribune,* November 1847. Quoted in Miller, *Margaret Fuller,* p. 270.

101. Quoted in Miller, *Margaret Fuller,* p. 273.

102. *Ibid.*, pp. 270–71.

103. Quoted in Emerson et al., eds., *Memoirs of Margaret Fuller*, 2:224–25.

104. For a full description of Ossoli's noble lineage and a sensitive portrayal of his almost idyllic relationship with Fuller, see Joseph Jay Deiss, *The Roman Years of Margaret Fuller* (New York: Thomas Y. Crowell, 1969).

105. Fuller to Emelyn Story, 30 November 1849. Quoted in Miller, *Margaret Fuller*, p. 301.

106. Fuller to Elizabeth Hoar, 18 January 1847. Quoted in Miller, *Margaret Fuller*, pp. 261–65.

107. Fuller to "George Sand." Reprinted in *Woman in the Nineteenth Century*, p. 228.

108. *Ibid.*, p. 45.

109. Writing of male reactions to her fictional sketches of Mariana and Miranda, Fuller noted that men could safely "admire, at poetic distance, that powerful nature that would alarm them so in real life . . . . Imagine those eyes, with glassy curiosity looking out for Mariana! Nobody dreams of its being like me; they all thought Miranda was, in the 'Great Lawsuit.' People seem to think that not more than one phase of character can be shown in one life." (Quoted in Higginson, *Margaret Fuller*, p. 198.)

110. Fuller to Emerson [?], n.d. Quoted in Emerson et al., eds., *Memoirs* 1:98–101.

## CHAPTER THREE

1. Abigail Adams to John Adams, 1776. Quoted in Ishbel Ross, *Sons of Adam, Daughters of Eve: The Role of Women in American History* (New York: Harper & Row, 1969), p. 12.

2. Hannah Adams, quoted in Alma Lutz, "Women Record History: 1784–1902," Address read at Radcliffe Women's Archives Workshop, 17 February 1955. Schlesinger Library Collection, Radcliffe College.

3. For a discussion of the historicist impulse generated by romanticism, see Morse Peckham's *Romanticism* and *Beyond the Tragic Vision*.

4. Betty Friedan revivified this concept in *The Feminine Mystique* (New York: W. W. Norton, 1963), an impressionistic, depressing, and often amusing study of the roles and images of women in American popular culture in the 1950s.

5. The quotations which follow are from Elizabeth Oakes Prince Smith, *Woman and Her Needs* (New York: Fowler & Wells, 1851), pp. 24, 82.

6. *Ibid.*, p. 109.

7. *Ibid.*

8. Gerda Lerner, "The Lady and the Mill Girl," *Mid-Continent American Studies Journal* 10 (1969):9.

9. *Ibid.*, p. 10.

10. Christopher Lasch and William R. Taylor, " 'Two Kindred Spirits,' " *New England Quarterly* 36 (1963):23–42.

11. Philippe Ariès traces the emergence of the conjugal family in the late sixteenth century in *Centuries of Childhood: A Social History of Family Life*, trans. Robert Baldick (New York: Alfred A. Knopf, 1962). He argues that both the idea and institution of the family as a "child centered universe" were relatively new historical phenomena whose increasing power was just beginning to be felt in the nineteenth century—that period in which many social historians have characterized the family as a rapidly fragmenting institution.

12. William L. O'Neill's *Everyone Was Brave: A History of Feminism in America* (Chicago: Quadrangle Books, 1971) uses Ariès's thesis to help account for the emergence of American feminism in the 1830s. I am indebted to O'Neill's application of this concept in his analysis of feminism and in his *Divorce in the Progressive Era* (New Haven: Yale University Press, 1967).

13. See Gerda Lerner, *The Grimké Sisters from South Carolina: Pioneers for Woman's Rights and Abolition* (New York: Schocken Books, 1971).

14. See Elizabeth Cady Stanton et al., eds., *The History of Woman Suffrage* 1:chap. 1, and Stanton's *Eighty Years*, p. 81.

15. Stanton, *Eighty Years*, pp. 82–83.

16. Stanton et al. eds., *Woman Suffrage* 1:15–20.

17. Milton Meltzer, *Tongue of Flame: The Life of Lydia Maria Child* (New York: Thomas Y. Crowell Co., 1965), pp. 18, 35.

18. Lydia Maria Child to Francis George and Sarah Blake [Sturgis] Shaw, 23 March 1856. Shaw Family Papers, Houghton Library, Harvard University. By permission of the Harvard College Library.

19. Meltzer, *Tongue of Flame*, p. 112.

20. *Notable American Women, 1608–1950: A Biographical Dictionary*, 3 vols. (Cambridge: Harvard University Press, 1971), s.v. "Child, Lydia Maria."

21. Mrs. D. L. [Lydia Maria] Child, *The History and Condition of Women*, 2 vols. (Boston: John Allen & Cox, 1835) 2:260–61.

22. *Ibid.*, pp. 261, 266–67.

23. Child to Francis George and Sarah Shaw, 23 March 1856, Shaw Family Papers, Houghton Library, Harvard University. By permission of the Harvard College Library.

24. Child, *History and Condition of Women*, 2:208–9.

25. *Ibid.*, pp. 261, 144–45.

26. Lydia Maria Child's personal letter-seal, Loring Collection, New York Public Library.

27. Child, *Memoirs of Madame de Staël and of Madame Roland*, rev. ed. (1847; reprint ed., Auburn, Me.: A. L. Littlefield, 1861), p. 140.

28. *Ibid.*, pp. 107–8.

29. Quoted in *ibid.*, p. 109.

30. The following quotations are from *ibid.*, pp. 109, 240.

31. Quoted in Meltzer, *Tongue of Flame*, pp. 132–33.

32. Lydia Maria Child to Margaret Fuller, 23 August 1844, Fuller Papers,

Houghton Library, Harvard University. By permission of the Harvard College Library.

33. *Ibid.*

34. Child, *De Staël and Roland,* p. 135.

35. Harriet Martineau to Lydia Maria Child, 10 January, n.d., Lydia Maria Child Letters, Houghton Library, Harvard University. By permission of the Harvard College Library.

36. Lydia Maria Child to Convers Francis, 25 October 1857, Lydia Maria Child Papers, New York Public Library.

37. *Ibid.*

38. Lydia Maria Child to Francis George Shaw, 29 May 1843, Shaw Family Papers, Child Correspondence, Houghton Library, Harvard University. By permission of the Harvard College Library.

39. Child to Shaw, 11 July 1847, Shaw Family Papers, Child Correspondence, Houghton Library, Harvard University. By permission of the Harvard College Library.

40. Child to Convers Francis, 25 October 1857, Lydia Maria Child Papers, New York Public Library.

41. Child to Loring, 18 April 1843, Loring Collection, New York Public Library.

42. Child to Sarah Shaw, 23 March 1845, Shaw Family Papers, Child Correspondence, Houghton Library, Harvard University. By permission of the Harvard College Library.

43. Child to Loring; 7 May 1840, 11 April 1841, 31 August 1841, 24 November 1841, 9 March 1842, 6 April 1842, 18 September 1842; Loring Collection, New York Public Library.

44. Child to Francis George and Sarah Shaw, 24 October 1849, Shaw Family Papers, Child Correspondence, Houghton Library, Harvard University. By permission of the Harvard College Library.

45. Elizabeth Fries Lummis Ellet, *Women of the American Revolution,* 4th ed. in 2 vols. (New York: Baker and Scribner, 1850), pp. ix–xi.

46. *Ibid.,* pp. ix–x.

47. *Ibid.,* pp. xi, 14–17.

48. Ellet, *Women of the American Revolution,* p. 22.

49. The following quotations are from Elizabeth Ellet, *Women Artists in All Ages and Countries* (New York: Harper & Bros., 1859), pp. 234, 22–23.

50. *Ibid.,* p. 234.

51. *Ibid.,* p. 245.

52. *Ibid.,* p. 362.

53. *Ibid.,* p. 361.

54. For discussions of the almost byzantine intrigues concerning Poe and other literati in which Ellet played a major role, see Emile Lauvière, *The Strange Life and Strange Loves of Edgar Allan Poe* (Philadelphia: J. B. Lippincott, 1935) and Sidney P. Moss, *Poe's Literary Battles: The Critic in the Context of his Literary Milieu* (Durham, N.C.: Duke University Press, 1963).

55. See Ellet, *Women of the American Revolution* 1:78–85.
56. Elizabeth Oakes Smith, *Woman and Her Needs*, p. 27.
57. *Ibid.*, pp. 27–28, 82, 84, 28.
58. *Ibid.*, p. 10.
59. *Ibid.*
60. *Ibid.*, p. 108.
61. *Ibid.*, p. 109.
62. *Ibid.*, p. 105.
63. Mary Alice Wyman, ed., *Selections from the Autobiography of Elizabeth Oakes Smith* (Lewiston, Me.: Lewiston Journal Co., *ca.* 1924), p. 42.
64. *Ibid.*, pp. 37, 35.
65. *Ibid.*, pp. 22, 24.
66. Elizabeth Oakes Smith, *Diary* entry quoted in Mary Alice Wyman, *Two American Pioneers: Seba Smith and Elizabeth Oakes Smith* (New York: Columbia University Press, 1927), p. 207.
67. Wyman, ed., *Selections*, p. 42.
68. *Ibid.*
69. *Ibid.*, p. 43.
70. Writing his sister in 1852, Seba Smith dismissed his wife's literary career as "filibustering." Her sons objected more violently, and Smith often cut short her speaking engagements because of their disapproval. (Wyman, *Two American Pioneers*, p. 194.)
71. *Ibid.*, p. 167.
72. Smith, "Wife," *Graham's Magazine* (September 1843).
73. Quoted in Wyman, *Two American Pioneers*, p. 207.
74. Smith, "Aurora Leigh," *United States Magazine* (February 1857), p. 182.
75. Smith, journal entry, 21 January 1861, quoted in Wyman, *Two American Pioneers*, pp. 193–94.
76. Smith, *Woman and Her Needs*, pp. 87, 84, 86.
77. *Ibid.*, p. 87.
78. *Ibid.*, p. 88.
79. *Ibid.*, p. 11.
80. Smith, "Massachusetts Constitutional Convention," *The Una* (June 1853), quoted in *Woman Suffrage* 1:254.
81. *Ibid.*
82. Smith, *Woman and Her Needs*, p. 18.

## CHAPTER FOUR

1. Elizabeth Cady Stanton et al., eds., *The History of Woman Suffrage*, 2d ed. in 3 vols. (Rochester: Charles Mann, 1889), 1:68.
2. *Ibid.*
3. *Ibid.*, p. 73.

4. Stanton, *Eighty Years and More: Reminiscences, 1815–1897* (1898; reprint ed., New York: Schocken Books, 1971), pp. 148–50.

5. *Ibid.*, p. 149. See also pp. 190–92 and Appendix, *Woman Suffrage* 1, for excerpts from newspaper accounts of early conventions.

6. The preceding quotations are from Stanton, *Eighty Years,* pp. 152–53.

7. *Ibid.*

8. Gail Parker, in her introduction to the Shocken reprint of *Eighty Years and More,* finds what she calls Stanton's "superiority complex" and her love of amusement rather "repellent" and often self-indulgent, yet decides that such "self-love" is "the only possible basis for a genuinely radical feminism."

9. Frederick W. Gale, a brother of one of Fuller's Green Street School pupils, having met Fuller in Florence in 1849, wrote the following to his sister in his journal about the woman whose life and works he had always derided. Finding her "much older and uglier" than even he had anticipated, he failed to hear that "tone of scorn and contempt which I expected in her conversation." At a subsequent gathering of American expatriates he found her more entertaining: during "a fine supper in which cold turkey, duck, maryonaise [sic], champagne & whisky punch played a prominent part . . . the transcendental ex-editress of the *Dial* devoted herself with unmistakable ardor to them all not even declining that vulgar, but comforting beverage—so unfashionable for Boston blues, *the whisky punch.* I danced two cotillions with her & found her none the worse for the liquor—but merry and agreeable." Quoted in Edward A. Hoyt and Loriman S. Brigham, "Glimpses of Margaret Fuller: The Green Street School and Florence," *New England Quarterly* 29(1956):98.

10. Quoted in Alma Lutz, *Created Equal: A Biography of Elizabeth Cady Stanton, 1815–1902* (New York: The John Day Co., 1940), p. 82.

11. In his address to the Seventh National Woman's Rights Convention, New York City, November 25–26, 1856, Higginson discussed the progress of American feminism and declared that "the reform [was] reversing the ordinary weapons of the sexes, for the women have all the logic, and the men only gossip and slander." (Stanton, *Woman Suffrage* 1:661).

12. *Ibid.*, pp. 60, 77.

13. *Ibid.* Volume I contains lengthy and sometimes entire transcripts of all conventions from 1848 to 1861.

14. *Ibid.*, p. 535.

15. *Ibid.*, p. 242.

16. *Ibid.*

17. See William O'Neill, *Everyone Was Brave: The Rise and Fall of Feminism in America* (Chicago: Quadrangle Books, 1971). Although O'Neill's book is an excellent overview of the social history of feminism and an interesting analysis of the intellectual dilemmas faced and generated by feminists, his study perpetuates the assumption that feminist thought before the Civil War lacked intellectual content.

18. Sarah Grimké, "Letter," Westchester, Pennsylvania Convention, 1852. Quoted in *ibid.*, pp. 353–55.

19. *Ibid.*

20. Paulina Wright Davis, "Presidential Address," (Worcester) Massachusetts National Convention, 1850. Quoted in *ibid.*, p. 217.

21. Davis, "Presidential Address," Syracuse National Convention, 1852. Quoted in *ibid.*, p. 534.

22. Howard Mumford Jones, *The Age of Energy: Varieties of American Experience, 1865–1915* (New York: The Viking Press, 1970). Jones's term applies with equal force to the experience of intellectual women before the Civil War.

23. Davis, "Address," Syracuse Convention, 1852. Quoted in Stanton, *Woman Suffrage* 1:533–34.

24. Elizabeth Oakes Smith, "Address," Syracuse Convention, 1852. *Ibid.*, p. 522.

25. Stanton, "Letter," Syracuse Convention, 1852. *Ibid.*, p. 812.

26. Quoted in *ibid.*, p. 535.

27. Angelina Grimké, "Letter," Syracuse Convention, 1852. *Ibid.*, p. 541.

28. Stanton, "Address to the New York State Legislature," 1854. *Ibid.*, pp. 595–96.

29. *Ibid.*, pp. 596–97, 600, 602, 596.

30. *Ibid.*, p. 595.

31. Antoinette Brown, "Resolutions," Albany Convention, 1854. *Ibid.*, p. 593.

32. Brown, "Resolution," Syracuse Convention, 1852. *Ibid.*, p. 535.

33. Brown, "Address," Syracuse Convention, 1852. *Ibid.*, p. 524.

34. *Ibid.*, p. 553.

35. Brown, "Albany Resolutions," *ibid.*, p. 595.

36. *Ibid.* See also, Stanton, "Second Appeal of 1854," and "Address to the New York State Legislature, 1860," and various Brown addresses already cited.

37. Stanton, "Second Appeal of 1854," *ibid.*, p. 858. See also, Stanton, "I Have All the Rights I Want," *The Una* (March 1855), pp. 38–39.

38. Stanton, "Second Appeal of 1854," *Woman Suffrage* 1:859.

39. Maria Weston Chapman, *Right and Wrong in Boston* (Boston, 1836). Quoted in Harriet Martineau, *The Martyr Age of the United States* (Boston: Jordan, Weeks & Co., 1839), p. 27.

40. Sarah Grimké, *Letters on the Equality of the Sexes and the Condition of Woman* (1838; New York: Source Book Press, 1970), pp. 46, 48.

41. Stanton, "Address to the New York Legislature, 1854," *Woman Suffrage* 1:605.

42. Stanton, "New York," *ibid.*, p. 68.

43. *Ibid.*

44. *Ibid.*

45. Aileen Kraditor, *The Ideas of the Woman Suffrage Movement, 1890 to 1920* (Garden City, N.Y.: Doubleday Anchor Books, 1971), p. 43.

46. Stanton, *Woman Suffrage* 1:387.

47. *Ibid.*, pp. 388, 387.

48. *Ibid.*, p. 388.

49. E. O. Smith, "The Massachusettes Constitutional Convention," quoted in *ibid.*, p. 253.

50. Reverend A. D. Mayo, "The Real Controversy," *The Una* (February 1853), p. 3.

51. Paulina Wright Davis, "Introduction," *The Una* (February 1853), p. 4.

52. Davis, "Prospectus," *ibid.*, p. 1.

53. Lillie B. Chace Wyman and Arthur C. Wyman, eds., *Elizabeth Buffum Chace, 1806–1899*, 2 vols. (1914) 1:120.

54. Stanton, "Reminiscences of Paulina Wright Davis," *Woman Suffrage* 1:286.

55. Wyman and Wyman, eds., *Chace* 1:120.

56. Stanton, "Davis," *Woman Suffrage* 1:283, 284.

57. *Ibid.*, p. 284.

58. *Ibid.*

59. Paulina Wright Davis, "Introduction," *A History of the National Woman's Rights Movement* (1871; reprint ed., New York: Source Book Press, 1970).

60. Barbara Welter, "The Merchant's Daughter: A Tale from Life," *New England Quarterly* (March 1969), 3.

61. Caroline Healey Dall, *Alongside, Being Notes Suggested by "A New England Boyhood" by Doctor Edward Everett Hale* (Boston: Thomas Todd, 1900), pp. 97, 94.

62. *Ibid.*, p. 2.

63. *Ibid.*, p. 30.

64. Quoted in Welter, "Merchant's Daughter," p. 10.

65. Dall, *Alongside*, p. 54.

66. *Ibid.*, pp. 44–45.

67. Quoted in Stephen Nissenbaum, "Caroline Wells Healey Dall," *Notable American Women* 1:428–29.

68. Dall, "Madame de Staël," *The Una* (November 1853), pp. 172–73.

69. Caroline Healey Dall, "To the Reader," *The Una* (February 1855), pp. 25–27.

70. *Ibid.*

71. Dall, *Historical Pictures Retouched; A Volume of Miscellanies* (Boston: Walker, Wise, and Co., 1860), p. 3.

72. *Ibid.*, p. 21.

73. *Ibid.*, pp. 23, 24.

74. *Ibid.*, p. 132.

75. *Ibid.*, pp. 124–25.

76. *Ibid.*, p. 133.

77. *Ibid.*, Preface, pp. v–vii.

78. *Ibid.*, p. vi.

79. Mary F. Love, "Letter to the Editor," *The Una* (June 1854), p. 282.

80. Frances D. Gage, "How Fares Our Cause," *The Una* (June 1854), p. 282.

81. *Ibid.*

82. "A Southern Lady," "Letter to the Editor," *The Una* (September 1854), pp. 11–12.

83. Davis, Review of *Woman's Record, The Una* (February 1853), pp. 11–12.

84. Ann D. Wood, "The 'Scribbling Women' and Fanny Fern: Why Women Wrote," *American Quarterly* 23 (1971):3–25.

85. Quoted in *ibid.*, p. 18.

86. Quoted in *ibid.*, p. 18.

87. Elizabeth Cady Stanton, "Ruth Hall," *The Una* (February 1855), p. 29.

88. *Ibid.*, p. 30.

89. Caroline Healey Dall, "Ruth Hall," *The Una* (March 1855), pp. 42–43.

90. *Ibid.*

91. Paulina Wright Davis, "Bertha and Lily," *The Una* (September 1843), pp. 330–31.

92. Dall, "Margaret Fuller," *The Una* (July 1855), p. 105.

93. *Ibid.*

94. Davis, "The Intellect of Women," *The Una* (March 1, 1853), p. 24.

95. *Ibid.*, p. 25.

96. *Ibid.*

97. *Ibid.*, pp. 24, 26. [See also, Davis, "The Moral Character of Women," *The Una* (June 1, 1853), pp. 72–73.]

98. Davis, "Remarks at the Convention," *The Una* (September 1853), p. 136.

99. *Ibid.*, p. 138.

100. *Ibid.*, pp. 136–37.

101. Dall, "Emancipated Women," *The Una* (June 1854), pp. 280–81.

102. *Ibid.*

103. Dall, "The Duties and Influences of Women," *The Una* (August 1854), pp. 307–9.

104. Dall, "Address," Ninth National Convention, New York City, 1858. Quoted in Stanton, *Woman Suffrage* 1:673–74.

105. Stanton, "Solitude of Self," quoted in Miriam Schneir, ed., *Feminism: The Essential Historical Writings* (New York: Vintage Books, 1972), p. 158.

## CHAPTER FIVE

1. For a social profile reflecting differences between pre- and post-war women writers, see Ann D. Wood, "Literature of Impoverishment: The Women Local Colorists in America, 1865–1914," *Women's Studies: An Interdisciplinary Journal* 1:3–47.

2. Dall, Ellet, Child, Booth, Peabody, and McCord all demonstrated talent and interest in learning other languages as children. In her own teaching career Peabody noted that girls were far more interested in languages than boys. W. E. Channing's son, for example, rebelled at learning Latin, while his young daughter was most enthusiastic and adept at her studies of foreign tongues. See Elizabeth Peabody, *Reminiscences of William Ellery Channing* (Boston: Roberts Brothers, 1880), pp. 257–61; 265–66.

3. *Ibid.*

4. Madelaine B. Stern, "Mary Louise Booth," *Notable American Women, 1607–1950: A Biographical Dictionary.* 3 vols. (Cambridge: The Belknap Press of Harvard University Press, 1971), 1:207.

5. Quoted in *ibid.*

6. T. S. Bell to Mary Louise Booth, 30 December 1862, Mary L. Booth Correspondence, Houghton Library, Harvard University. By permission of the Harvard College Library.

7. Mary L. Booth to Henry Wadsworth Longfellow, 29 December 1863, Booth Correspondence, Houghton Library, Harvard. By permission of the Harvard College Library.

8. Booth, *History of the City of New York*, 7 vols., illustrated. (1867; reprint ed., New York: W. R. C. Clark, 1876), 7:881. (Copy in Manuscript Division, The New York Public Library.)

9. Jessie Melville Fraser, *Louisa Cheves McCord: Woman, Patriot, Scholar* (Columbia, S.C.: University of Carolina Press, 1919), p. 15.

10. Louisa Cheves McCord, "Review of F. Bastiat's 'Justice and Fraternity,' " *Southern Quarterly Review* (July 1849), pp. 369, 371.

11. Quoted in Frazer, *McCord*, p. 8.

12. In *Woman's Record* Sarah J. Hale noted that Louisa McCord had "distinguished herself in what may be styled political literature, a species of writing seldom attempted by woman." Hale approved of all McCord's work, but especially liked her antifeminist articles. In all her essays Hale found evidence of "True Womanhood": "She reasons well; her style is excellent, and flashes of wit, 'temperately bright' as a woman's should be, is please without wounding." Hale, *Woman's Record; Or, Sketches of All Distinguished Women, From the Creation to A.D. 1854*, 2d. ed. rev. and enl. (1855; reprint ed., New York: Source Book Press, 1970), p. 894.

13. McCord, "Review of John Campbell's *Negro-Mania*," *De Bow's Review* (May 1852), pp. 507–24. McCord warned her readers that abolition of slavery would not only destroy civilization but lead to the "extinction" of either the white or the black race. Slavery was exactly tailored to the Negro's nature: "The very virtues of the negro fit him for slavery, and his vices cry aloud for the checks of bondage." (p. 519). See also, McCord, "Diversity of the Races; Its Bearing upon Negro Slavery," *Southern Quarterly Review* (April 1851), pp. 392–419. McCord's response to British women abolitionists, "British Philanthropy and American Slavery," *De Bow's Review* (March 1853), urged the "ladies of England" to ignore the reports of slavery's evils and listen to a "true woman" of the South, speaking for all Southern women. If slavery were really evil, surely the women of the South would have been the first to denounce it: "We can think as women, and feel as women, and act as women, without waiting for the promptings of your appeals, or of Mrs. Stowe's imaginative horrors." For McCord's views upon woman's nature and social role, see her "Enfranchisement of Women," *Southern Quarterly Review* (April 1852) and her review of Elizabeth Oakes Smith's *Woman and Her Needs*, *De Bow's Review* (September 1852), in which McCord declared that intellect and womanhood

were compatible but cultivation of the former was not woman's "highest destiny." McCord's lengthy and venomous critiques of Stowe and her work are in the January and July 1853 issues of the *Southern Quarterly Review*.

14. Review of *Caius Gracchus, De Bow's Review* (1851) 11:224.

15. Quoted in Fraser, *McCord*, p. 15. See Margaret Ferrand Thorp's study, *Female Persuasion: Six Strong-Minded Women* (New Haven: Yale University Press, 1949), pp. 179–215, and Thorp's sketch of McCord in *Notable American Women* 2:450–52 for more descriptions of McCord and a more trustworthy analysis than the almost idolatrous Fraser can provide.

16. Fraser, *McCord*, p. 15.

17. Thorp, "McCord," *Notable American Women* 2:451.

18. Thorp judges McCord's essays superior to her husband's and quotes a legal colleague's description of David McCord's "tedious" courtroom manner, which had apparently crept into his prose. (*Female Persuasion*, p. 195).

19. McCord, "Review of F. Bastiat's 'The Right to Labor,' " *Southern Quarterly Review* (October 1849), p. 143.

20. *Ibid.*, pp. 143–44.

21. The following quotations are from McCord, "Carey on the Slave Trade," *Southern Quarterly Review* (January 1854), pp. 115, 118, 153, 141.

22. See articles listed in note 13 above.

23. McCord, "Carey," *Southern Quarterly Review*, p. 162.

24. *Ibid.*, p. 167.

25. McCord, *Caius Gracchus: A Tragedy in Five Acts* (New York: H. Kernat, 1851), p. 120.

26. Review of *Caius Gracchus, Southern Quarterly Review* (July 1851).

27. McCord, "Woman's Progress," *Southern Literary Messenger* (November 1853), p. 700.

28. *Ibid.*

29. Quoted in Ruth M. Baylor, *Elizabeth Palmer Peabody: Kindergarten Pioneer* (Philadelphia: University of Pennsylvania Press, 1965), p. 83.

30. Mrs. Peabody rendered Spenser's *Faerie Queene* into modern English for her students and published the work as *Holiness: or The Legend of St. George: A Tale from Spencer's [sic] Faerie Queene, by a Mother* (Boston: E. R. Broaders, 1836).

31. For a full account of Sophia's relationship with her mother, see Louise Hall Tharp, *The Peabody Sisters of Salem* (London: George P. Harrap), 1951.

32. Elizabeth Peabody to Sophia Peabody, 23 June 1822. Quoted in Baylor, *Peabody*, p. 651.

33. *Ibid.*

34. Ralph Waldo Emerson, "History," *Essays: First Series. The Selected Writings of Ralph Waldo Emerson*, Brooks Atkinson, ed. (New York: The Modern Library, 1940), p. 126.

35. Thomas Wentworth Higginson, *Cheerful Yesterdays* (Boston: Houghton Mifflin, 1898), p. 87.

36. Quoted in Baylor, *Peabody*, p. 72.

37. *Ibid.*, p. 71.

38. Edith G. Hawthorne, ed., *The Memoirs of Julian Hawthorne* (New York: Macmillan, 1938), pp. 44–47.

39. Peabody, ed., Preface, *Bettine and Günderode*. Margaret Fuller, trans. (Boston 1842). Quoted in Baylor, *Peabody*, p. 77.

40. Emerson, "Nature," *Selected Writings*, p. 15.

41. Peabody, *Lectures in the Training Schools for Kindergartners*. Quoted in Baylor, *Peabody*, p. 70.

42. Baylor's study of Peabody discusses Froebel's educational theory and practice and contains a valuable chronological list of the development of the American kindergarten, as well as an excellent bibliography of Peabody's writings in all fields.

43. Peabody, *Channing*, p. 261.

44. Lydia Maria Child, *The Progress of Religious Ideas, Through Successive Ages*, 3 vols. (New York: C. S. Francis & Co., 1855), 1:vii–viii.

45. *Ibid.*

46. Thomas Wentworth Higginson, *Contemporaries* (Boston: Houghton Mifflin, 1899), pp. 108–42. Higginson notes that Child, like her brother Convers, was "too good a compiler," adding that she had the "superior mind of the two."

47. Child, *Religious Ideas* 1:viii.

48. Elizabeth Peabody, "Female Education in Massachusetts; Reminiscences of Subjects and Methods of Teaching," *Barnard's American Journal of Education* 30:304.

49. *Ibid.*

50. Quoted in George W. Cooke, "Elizabeth Peabody," *An Introduction to The Dial* (1909; reprint ed., New York: Russell & Russell, 1961), pp. 146–47.

51. Peabody, *Chronological History of the United States, Arranged with Plates on Bem's Principle* (New York: Sheldon, Blakeman & Co., 1856).

52. For a detailed discussion of Mr. Peabody's strange career, see Tharp, *Peabody Sisters*.

53. Peabody, "Female Education," p. 308.

54. *Ibid.*, p. 309.

55. *Ibid.*

56. Peabody, "Emerson as Preacher," in F. B. Sanborn, ed., *The Genius and Character of Emerson* (Boston: James R. Osgood & Co., 1885), p. 155.

57. Quoted in Norman Holmes Pearson, "Elizabeth Peabody on Hawthorne," *Essex Institute Historical Collections* (July 1958), p. 270.

58. Channing's biographers often quote Peabody but no one has analyzed her memoir or noted its importance. See Jack Mendelsohn, *Channing: The Reluctant Radical* (Boston: Little, Brown, 1971), in which Channing is ludicrously made "relevant," almost a representative of Charles Reich's "Conciousness Three," in *The Greening of America*, and Peabody is once again dismissed as Channing's secretary.

59. Odell Shepard, *Pedlar's Progress: The Life of Bronson Alcott* (Boston:

Little, Brown, 1937), pp. 166–67. Shepard also declared that "so far as what is ordinarily called knowledge is concerned, she knew far more than Alcott did." (p. 128).

60. Peabody, *Record of Mr. Alcott's School, Exemplifying the Principles and Methods of Moral Culture*, 3d ed. rev. (1835; Boston: Roberts Brothers, 1874), pp. 7, 4, 243.

61. *Ibid.*, pp. 244, 296, 295–96.

62. *Ibid.*, p. 297.

63. *Ibid.*, p. 10.

64. Josephine E. Roberts, "Elizabeth Peabody and The Temple School," *New England Quarterly* 15:508. This excellent article is based on Peabody's letters to her sister Mary while the latter was teaching in Cuba. Called "the Cuba Journal," the manuscript is in the private collection of Mr. Horace Mann, Southwest Harbor, Maine.

65. Quoted in *ibid.*, pp. 508, 504, 506.

66. Peabody, *Channing*, p. 148.

67. *Ibid.*, pp. 444–45.

68. Quoted in *ibid.*, p. 38.

69. *Ibid.*, pp. 127, 141–42.

70. *Ibid.*, pp. 140–41.

71. *Ibid.*, p. 266.

72. William Ellery Channing, "On the Importance and Means of a National Literature," quoted in *Old South Leaflets*, 6:333.

73. Quoted in Peabody, *Channing*, pp. 180, 179.

74. *Ibid.*, p. 251.

75. Quoted in *ibid.*, p. 252.

76. *Ibid.*, p. 255.

77. *Ibid.*, p. 266. "Knowledge of Dr. Channing justified all the imagination and faith of my enthusiastic youth," Peabody declared. Although "a calumnous report," circulating in England and America, accused him of "exploit [ing]" her, "taking up all her leisure to write for and read to him," Peabody insisted that the rumor was unfounded. Channing was hesitant to ask her to copy out his sermons for him, afraid it would be an imposition, but Peabody told him she could easily copy them while he read to her from other works or when she was too tired for more laborious work. (pp. 8–11).

78. Peabody, "Ego-theism, the Atheism of Today," *Religious Magazine* (March 1859), pp. 165–74. Also in *Last Evening with Allston and Other Papers* (Boston: D. Lothrop & Co., 1886), pp. 240–52.

79. See John B. Wilson, "A Transcendental Minority Report," *New England Quarterly* (June 1956), pp. 147–58 for the best analysis of Peabody's views in contrast to those of other New England Romantics. This essay is the only serious treatment of Elizabeth Peabody as an intellectual by a contemporary historian.

80. Peabody, "Christ's Idea of Society," *The Dial* (October 1841), p. 216.

81. *Ibid.*, pp. 218, 220, 221.

82. *Ibid.*, p. 228.

83. *Ibid.*

84. Peabody, "The Dorian Measure, with a Modern Application," *Aesthetic Papers* (May 1849). (Gainesville, Fla.: Scholar's Facsimiles & Reprints, 1957), pp. 64, 69, 68.

85. *Ibid.*, p. 68.

86. *Ibid.*, pp. 96, 97.

87. *Ibid.*, p. 83.

88. *Ibid.*

89. *Ibid.*

90. The following quotations are from Peabody, "The Philosophy of History in the Education of Republican Men and Women," *The Una* (February 1855), pp. 29, 28, 29.

91. *Ibid.*, p. 29.

92. *Ibid.*, p. 29.

93. Peabody, "Lessons on God's Providence as it May be Traced in History," *The Una* 3:50.

94. *Ibid.*, p. 51.

95. Maria W. Chapman, ed., *Harriet Martineau's Autobiography* (Boston: Houghton Mifflin, 1877), 1:381.

96. The following quotations are from Elizabeth Ellet, *The Characters of Schiller* (Boston: Otis, Broaders & Co., 1839), pp. 7–8.

97. Lydia Maria Child, Journal, Lydia Maria Child Papers, The New York Public Library.

98. *Ibid.*

99. Margaret Fuller, "Genius," May 4, 1839. Quoted in Emerson et al., eds., *Memoirs of Margaret Fuller* 1:69–70.

100. Child, "What Is Beauty?," *The Dial* (April 1843), pp. 490, 492.

101. Lydia Maria Child to Maria White Lowell, 18 February 1854, Lowell Papers, The Houghton Library, Harvard. By permission of the Harvard College Library.

102. Elizabeth Oakes Smith, "Genius," manuscript copy, Elizabeth Oakes Smith Papers, The New York Public Library.

103. Lydia Maria Child to Sarah Blake (Sturgis) Shaw, 17 April 1858, Shaw Correspondence, The Houghton Library, Harvard. By permission of the Harvard College Library.

104. For characteristic examples of her method of questioning romantic thought, see Child, *Letters from New York*, 2d ed. (1843; New York: C. S. Francis and Co., 1844), pp. 2, 182–83, 214.

105. *Ibid.*, p. 168.

106. Lydia Maria Child to Francis George and Sarah Blake (Sturgis) Shaw, 18 July 1844, Shaw Correspondence, The Houghton Library, Harvard. By permission of the Harvard College Library.

107. Sarah J. Hale, *Ladies' Magazine* 2:142.

108. While discussing the much vaunted purity of the American woman

in *History of Women in All Ages and Countries* Child noted that being too "decorous" was both "vulgar" and "dull." 2:267.

109. Nathaniel Hawthorne, "The Custom House," *The Scarlet Letter* (Boston, 1850). Quoted in Stanley Bank, ed., *American Romanticisim: A Shape for Fiction* (New York: G. .P. Putnam's Sons, 1969), p. 250.

110. Margaret Fuller, "Lines," *Woman in the Nineteenth Century*, p. 355.

111. Quoted in Emerson et al., eds., *Memoirs of Margaret Fuller*, 1:99.

112. George W. Curtis to Sarah H. Whitman, 22 June 1845. Quoted in Caroline Ticknor, *Poe's Helen* (New York: Charles Scribner's Sons, 1916), p. 25.

113. *Ibid.*

114. *Ibid.*

115. Sarah Helen Whitman, "Emerson's Essays," *U.S. Magazine and Democratic Review* (June 1845), p. 598.

116. *Ibid.*, pp. 590–94.

117. *Ibid.*, p. 598.

118. *Ibid.*, pp. 591, 594.

119. *Ibid.*, p. 601.

120. Quoted in Ticknor, *Poe's Helen*, p. 290.

121. *Ibid.*, pp. 15, 282, 281.

122. Quoted in *ibid.*, p. 10.

123. Whitman's first poem, "Retrospection," was published in 1829 and signed "Helen."

124. See Ticknor, *Poe's Helen*, pp. 42–55.

125. *Ibid.*, p. 111.

126. Whitman, *Edgar Poe and His Critics*, 2d ed. (1860; Providence: Tibbitts and Preston, 1885), p. 54.

127. *Ibid.*, pp. 54, 56.

128. *Ibid.*, pp. 55, 64.

129. Quoted in Pearson, "Peabody on Hawthorne," *Essex Institute* (July 1958), p. 228.

130. Elizabeth Peabody, "Reviews of *The Blithedale Romance* and *The House of the Seven Gables*," *North American Review* (January 1853), p. 228.

131. *Ibid.*, pp. 230, 232.

132. Quoted in Baylor, *Peabody*, p. 73.

133. Peabody, "Last Evening With Allston," *Emerson's Magazine* (October 1857), pp. 500, 503.

134. Elizabeth Peabody to Samuel Ward, 13 September 1841. Quoted in Baylor, *Peabody*, p. 76.

135. T. W. Higginson, *Cheerful Yesterdays*, p. 86.

136. Peabody, "Prospectus," *Aesthetic Papers* (May 1849), p. iii.

137. See Joseph Jones's excellent introduction to the reprint edition of *Aesthetic Papers* cited above.

138. See Anne Firor Scott, *The Southern Lady: From Pedestal to Politics, 1830–1930* (Chicago: The University of Chicago Press, 1970). Curiously, given

the thesis of Scott's book, McCord's intellectual and political roles in antebellum America are ignored. She is cited only for her heroic nursing of wounded soldiers during the war.

## EPILOGUE

1. For fathers' professions, see Table 2, Appendix.
2. Sarah J. Hale, "An Authoress, No. II," *The Ladies' Magazine* 2:132.
3. Child's correspondence in the Loring Collection, New York Pubic Library, reveals her extreme financial difficulties throughout David's life. . . . His most visionary scheme, to raise beets in Northampton, Massachusetts—to prove them superior to sugar cane as a source for sugar was his way of offering a "realistic" alternative to slavery in the sugar trade—enslaved him and his wife, and the experiment was a financial disaster.
4. See Alma Lutz, *Created Equal: A Life of Elizabeth Cady Stanton.*
5. For religious affiliations of intellectual women, see Table 1, Appendix.
6. Elizabeth Oakes Smith, scrapbook entry, n.d., Elizabeth Oakes Smith Papers, New York Public Library.
7. See Jane Addams, "The Subjective Necessity for Social Settlements" (1892), reprinted in Christopher Lasch, ed., *The Social Thought of Jane Addams* (New York: Bobbs-Merrill, 1965), pp. 28–44.
8. Gertrude Stein, untitled speech, n.d., Gertrude Stein Collection, Beinecke Library, Yale University.

# Appendix

**Table 1.** Regional Background and Religious Affiliation

| | Region | Religion |
|---|---|---|
| Fuller<br>(1810–1850) | b. Cambridge, Mass.<br>Boston, Mass.<br>New York City<br>Rome, Italy | Unitarian |
| Child<br>(1802–1880) | b. Medford, Mass.<br>Cambridge, Mass.<br>Northampton, Mass.<br>New York City<br>Wayland, Mass. | Unitarian |
| Stanton<br>(1815–1902) | b. Johnston, New York<br>Boston, Mass.<br>Seneca Falls, N.Y.<br>New York City | Presbyterian to<br>no affiliation |
| S. Grimké<br>(1792–1873) | b. Charleston, S.C.<br>Philadelphia, Pa. | Episcopalian to<br>Quaker |
| Ellet<br>(1812–1877) | b. Sodus Point, N.Y.<br>Columbia, S.C.<br>New York City | Episcopalian to<br>Catholic |
| McCord<br>(1810–1879) | b. Charleston, S.C.<br>Philadelphia, Pa.<br>Washington, D.C.<br>Charleston, S.C. | Presbyterian |

**Table 1.** Regional Background and Religious Affiliation

|  | Region | Religion |
|---|---|---|
| Whitman (1803–1878) | b. Providence, R.I.<br>Boston, Mass.<br>Providence, R.I. | Unitarian to no affiliation |
| Peabody (1804–1894) | b. Billerica, Mass.<br>Salem, Mass.<br>Boston, Mass. | Unitarian |
| Smith (1806–1893) | b. North Yarmouth, Me.<br>Portland, Me.<br>New York City<br>Patchogue, L.I.<br>Hollywood, N.C. | Congregationalist |
| Brown (1825–1921) | b. Henrietta, N.Y.<br>New York City<br>Cincinnati, Ohio<br>Newark, N.J.<br>Somerville, N.J. | Congregationalist to Unitarian minister |
| Davis (1813–1876) | b. Bloomfield, N.Y.<br>LeRoy, N.Y.<br>Utica, N.Y.<br>Providence, R.I. | Presbyterian to no affiliation |
| Dall (1822–1912) | b. Boston, Mass.<br>Georgetown, D.C.<br>Boston, Mass.<br>Portsmouth, N.H.<br>Needham, Mass.<br>Toronto, Canada<br>Boston, Mass.<br>Washington, D.C. | Unitarian |
| Booth (1831–1889) | b. Millville, Long Island<br>New York City<br>(Brooklyn, Manhattan) | Episcopalian |

**Table 2.** Professions of Fathers and Husbands

| | Farmer | Lawyer | Politician | Physician | Banker | Merchant | Teacher | Other |
|---|---|---|---|---|---|---|---|---|
| **Father's Profession** | | | | | | | | |
| | Brown | Stanton | Stanton | Ellet | | Child | Peabody | Dentist—Peabody |
| | Davis | Grimké | McCord | | McCord | Whitman | Booth | Nightwatchman service—Booth |
| | | McCord | Fuller | | | Dall | | Ship captain—Smith |
| | | Fuller | | | | | | |
| **Husband's Profession** | | | | | | | | |
| | | Child | Child | Ellet | | Brown | | Dall—minister |
| | | Stanton | Stanton | | | Davis | | Smith—journalist |
| | | McCord | McCord | | | | | |
| | | Whitman | | | | | | |

# Selected Bibliography

## Manuscript Sources

Booth, Mary Louise. Booth Correspondence, The New York Public Library; Booth Correspondence, The Houghton Library, Harvard University.

Blackwell, Antoinette Brown. The Blackwell Family Papers, The Schlesinger Library, Radcliffe.

Child, Lydia Maria. The Ellis Gray Loring Collection, Child Correspondence, The New York Public Library; Francis George and Sarah Blake (Sturgis) Shaw Papers, Lydia Maria Child Correspondence, The Houghton Library, Harvard; Child Correspondence, The Schlesinger Library, Radcliffe.

Dall, Caroline Wells Healey. Caroline Dall Papers, The Schlesinger Library, Radcliffe.

Fuller, Margaret. The Fuller Family Papers, The Houghton Library, Harvard.

Peabody, Elizabeth Palmer. Peabody Correspondence, The Berg Collection, The New York Public Library; Peabody Papers, The Houghton Library, Harvard.

Smith, Elizabeth Oakes Prince. Elizabeth Oakes Smith Papers, The New York Public Library.

Stanton, Elizabeth Cady. Stanton Papers, The Schlesinger Library, Radcliffe.

## Nineteenth-Century Newspapers and Periodicals

*Aesthetic Papers; The Dial; Emerson's Magazine; Godey's Lady's Book; Graham's Magazine; Harper's Magazine; The Ladies' Magazine; The Ladies' Repository; Littell's*

*Living Age; New York Tribune; The North American Review; Peterson's Magazine; Putnam's Magazine; The Southern Literary Messenger; The Southern Quarterly Review; The Woman's Advocate,* Phila.: October 13, 1855 to December 6, 1856, vol. 1, no. 40 to vol. 2, no. 46 (incomplete file), microfilm courtesy Sophia Smith Collection, Smith College; *The Una: A Paper Devoted to the Elevation of Woman,* 1853–1855 (no extant file), microfilm courtesy Brown University; *United States Magazine and Democratic Review.*

## Sources (Books)

Booth, Mary Louise. *History of the City of New York.* 1867. 7 vols. New York: W. R. C. Clark, 1876.

Channing, William Ellery. *The Works of William Ellery Channing.* Boston, 1886.

Chapman, Maria Weston. *Right and Wrong in Boston.* Boston, 1836.

Child, Mrs. D. L. [Lydia Maria]. *The History and Condition of Women.* 2 vols. Boston: John Allen & Cox, 1835.

———. *Memoirs of Madame de Staël and of Madame Roland.* 1847. Rev. ed., Auburn, Me.: A. L. Littlefield, 1861.

———. *The Progress of Religious Ideas, Through Successive Ages.* 3 vols. New York: C. S. Francis & Co., 1855.

Coxe, Margaret. *The Young Lady's Companion.* Cincinnati, 1839.

Dall, Caroline W. H. *Margaret Fuller and Her Friends.* Boston, 1895.

———. *The College, The Market, and The Court: Or, Woman's Relation to Education, Labor, and Law.* Boston, 1859.

———. *Alongside, Being Notes Suggested by "A New England Boyhood" by Doctor Edward Everett Hale.* Boston: Thomas Todd, 1900.

Davis, Paulina K. W. *A History of the National Woman's Rights Movement.* 1871. Reprint. New York: Source Book Press, 1970.

Ellet, Elizabeth Fries Lummis. *The Characters of Schiller.* Boston: Otis, Broaders & Co., 1839.

———. *Domestic History of the American Revolution.* New York: Baker and Scribner, 1850.

———. *Pioneer Women of the West.* New York: C. Scribner, 1852.

———. *Women Artists in All Ages and Countries.* New York: Harper & Bros., 1859.

———. *Women of the American Revolution.* 2 vols. 4th ed. New York: Baker and Scribner, 1850.

Emerson, Ralph Waldo. *Selected Writings.* Edited by Brooks Atkinson. New York: The Modern Library, 1940.

———. *Journals.*

———. *Letters.*

Frothingham, Octavius Brooks. *Transcendentalism in New England: A History.* 1876. Reprint. New York: Harper & Row, Harper Torchbooks, 1959.

Fuller [Ossoli], Margaret. *At Home and Abroad*. Edited by Arthur Buckminster Fuller. Boston, 1859.

————, trans. *Correspondence of Fräulein Günderode and Bettine von Arnim*. Boston, 1842.

————, trans. *Eckermann's Conversations with Goethe*. Boston, 1839.

————. *Life Without and Life Within*. Edited by Arthur Buckminster Fuller. Boston, 1859.

————. *Margaret Fuller, American Romantic: A Selection from Her Writings and Correspondence*. Edited by Perry Miller. New York: Anchor Books, 1963.

————. *Memoirs of Margaret Fuller Ossoli*. Edited by Ralph Waldo Emerson, William Henry Channing, and James Freeman Clarke. 2 vols. Boston, 1852.

————. *Papers on Literature and Art*. New York, 1856.

————. *Summer on the Lakes*. Boston, 1844.

————. *Woman in the Nineteenth Century*. New York, 1845.

Fuller, Richard F. *Chaplain Fuller: Being a Life Sketch of a New England Clergyman and Army Chaplain*. Boston: Walker, Wise & Co., 1863.

Greeley, H.; Higginson, T. W.; and Parton, J.; eds. *Eminent Women of the Age: Being Narratives of the Lives and Deeds of the Most Prominent Women of the Present Generation*. Hartford: S. M. Betts & Co., 1868.

Greeley, Horace. *Recollections of a Busy Life*. New York, 1868.

Grimké [Weld], Angelina, and Grimké, Sarah. *Letters of Theodore Wright Weld, Angelina Grimké Weld and Sarah Grimké: 1822–1844*. Edited by G. H. Barnes and D. W. Dumond. 2 vols. New York: D. Appleton Century, 1934.

Grimké, Sarah Moore. *Letters on the Equality of the Sexes and the Condition of Women: Address to Mary Parker, President of the Boston Female Anti-Slavery Society*. 1838. Reprint. New York: Source Book Press, 1970.

Griswold, Rufus Wilmot. *The Female Poets of America*. 2d rev. ed. New York: James Miller, 1873.

Hale, Sarah J. *Woman's Record, or Sketches of All Distinguished Women from the Beginning till A.D. 1850*. New York, 1853.

Harper, Ida H., ed. *The Life and Work of Susan B. Anthony*. 3 vols. 1898–1908. Reprint. New York: Arno Press, 1970.

Hart, John S. *The Female Prose Writers of America*. 3d rev. ed. Philadelphia: E. H. Butler & Co., 1857.

Hawthorne, Edith G., ed. *The Memoirs of Julian Hawthorne*. New York: Macmillan, 1938.

Higginson, Thomas Wentworth. *Cheerful Yesterdays*. Boston: Houghton Mifflin Co., 1898.

————. *Contemporaries*. Boston: Houghton Mifflin Co., 1899.

————. *Margaret Fuller Ossoli*. American Men of Letters Series. Boston, 1894.

[Baronne de Staël-Holstein] Anne Louise Necker, Madame de Staël. *Corinne: or Italy*. Elizabeth Hill, trans. New York: A. D. Burt & Co., n.d.

Howe, Julia Ward. *Margaret Fuller (Marchesa Ossoli)*. Boston, 1883.

Martineau, Harriet. *The Martyr Age of the United States.* Boston: Weeks, Jordan & Co., 1839.

———. *Society in America.* 2 vols. New York: Sanders & Otley, 1837.

McCord, Louisa Cheves. *Caius Gracchus: A Tragedy in Five Acts.* New York: H. Kernat, 1851.

Parker, Gail, ed. *The Oven Birds: American Women on Womanhood, 1820–1920.* Garden City, N.Y.: Doubleday Anchor Books, 1972.

Peabody, Elizabeth Palmer, ed. *Aesthetic Papers.* Boston, May 1849.

———, ed. *Bettine and Günderode.* Margaret Fuller, trans. Boston, 1842.

———. *Chronological History of the United States, Arranged with Plates on Bem's Principle.* New York: Sheldon, Blakeman & Co., 1856.

———. *Last Evening with Allston and Other Papers.* Boston: D. Lothrop & Co., 1886.

———. *Lectures in the Training Schools for Kindergartners,* 1893.

———. *Record of Mr. Alcott's School, Exemplifying the Principles and Methods of Moral Culture.* 1835. 3d ed. rev. Boston: Roberts Bros., 1874.

———. *Reminiscences of William Ellery Channing.* Boston: Roberts Bros., 1880.

Poe, Edgar A. *The Literati.* New York: J. S. Redfield, 1852.

Smith, Elizabeth Oakes Prince. *Bertha and Lily.* New York, 1854.

———. *Old New York.* New York, 1853.

———. *The Sinless Child and Other Poems.* New York, 1843.

———. *Woman and Her Needs.* New York: Fowler & Wells, 1851.

———. *The Western Captive.* New York: 1842.

———. *Selections from the Autobiography of Elizabeth Oakes Smith.* Mary Alice Wyman, ed. Lewiston, Me.: Lewiston Journal Co., *ca.* 1924.

Stanton, Elizabeth Cady. *Eighty Years and More: Reminiscences, 1815–1897.* 1898. New York: Schocken Books, Studies in the Life of Women, 1971.

———. *Elizabeth Cady Stanton: As Revealed in Her Letters, Diary, and Reminiscences.* Theodore Stanton and Harriet S. Blatch, eds. 2 vols. 1922. Reprint. New York: Arno Press, 1970.

———. Anthony, Susan B., and Gage, Mathilda J., eds. *The History of Woman Suffrage.* 1881. 6 vols. 2d ed. 3 vols. Rochester: Charles Mann, 1889.

Swisshelm, Jane G. *Half a Century.* 1880. Reprint. Cincinnati: Source Book Press, 1971.

Wyman, Lillie B. Chace, and Wyman, Arthur C., eds. *Elizabeth Buffum Chace, 1806–1899; Her Life and its Environment.* Boston: W. B. Clarke, 1914.

## Authorities (Books)

Abrams, M. H. *The Mirror and the Lamp: Romantic Theory and the Critical Tradition.* 1953. New York: The Norton Library, 1958.

Anthony, Katherine. *Margaret Fuller, A Psychological Biography.* New York, 1920.

Ariès, Philippe. *Centuries of Childhood: A Social History of Family Life.* Robert Baldick, trans. New York: Alfred A. Knopf, 1962.

Baer, Helene G. *The Heart Is Like Heaven: The Life of Lydia Maria Child.* Philadelphia: University of Pennsylvania Press, 1964.

Bank, Stanley, ed. *American Romanticism: A Shape for Fiction.* New York: G. P. Putnam's Sons, 1969.

Barnes, Gilbert H. *The Anti-Slavery Impulse: 1830–1844.* New York: Harper & Bros., 1933.

Baylor, Ruth M. *Elizabeth Palmer Peabody: Kindergarten Pioneer.* Philadelphia: University of Pennsylvania Press, 1965.

Beach, Seth C. *Daughters of the Puritans.* Boston: American Unitarian Association, 1905.

Bell, Margaret. *Margaret Fuller.* New York, 1930.

Benson, Lee. *The Concept of Jacksonian Democracy: New York as a Test Case.* New York: Atheneum, 1964.

Bradford, Gamaliel. *Portraits of American Women.* Boston: Houghton Mifflin, 1919.

Brooks, Van Wyck. *The Dream of Arcadia: American Writers and Artists in Italy, 1760–1915.* New York: E. P. Dutton, 1958.

Cross, Barbara M., ed. *The Educated Woman in America: Selected Writings of Catharine Beecher, Margaret Fuller and M. Carey Thomas.* New York: Teachers College Press, Columbia University, 1965.

Dobrée, Bonamy. *English Literature in the Early Eighteenth Century.* The Oxford History of English Literature. New York: Oxford University Press, 1959.

Feidelson, Charles, Jr. *Symbolism and American Literature.* 1953. Chicago: The University of Chicago Press, Phoenix Books, 1959.

Fiedler, Leslie A. *Love and Death in the American Novel.* 2d rev. ed. New York: Stein and Day, 1966.

Filler, Louis. *The Crusade against Slavery: 1830–1860.* New York: Harper & Bros. 1960.

Flexner, Eleanor. *Century of Struggle: The Woman's Rights Movement in the United States.* Cambridge, Mass.; Harvard University Press, 1959. New York: Atheneum, 1968.

Fraser, Jessie Melville. *Louisa Cheves McCord: Woman, Patriot, Scholar.* Columbia, S.C.: University of South Carolina Press, 1919.

Froude, James Anthony. *Thomas Carlyle: A History of His Life in London.* New York: Charles Scribner's Sons, 1884.

Gay, Peter. *The Enlightenment: An Interpretation.* 2 vols. New York: Alfred A. Knopf, 1967, 1969.

Goodsell, Willystine, ed. *Pioneers of Women's Education in the United States: Emma Willard, Catharine Beecher, Mary Lyon.* New York: McGraw-Hill, 1931.

Gornick, V., and Moran, B., eds. *Woman in Sexist Society.* New York: Basic Books, 1971.

Grimes, Alan. *The Puritan Ethic and Woman Suffrage.* New York: Oxford University Press, 1967.

Harris, Neil. *The Artist in American Society: The Formative Years, 1790–1860.* New York: George Braziller, 1966.

Herold, J. Christopher. *Mistress to an Age: A Life of Madame de Staël.* New York: Bobbs-Merrill Co., 1958.

James, Edward T.; James, Janet W.; and Boyer, Paul S., eds. *Notable American Women, 1607–1950: A Biographical Dictionary.* 3 vols. Cambridge: The Belknap Press of Harvard University Press, 1971.

Kaul, A. N. *The American Vision: Actual and Ideal Society in Nineteenth-Century Fiction.* New Haven: Yale University Press, 1963.

Kraditor, Aileen S. *The Ideas of the Woman Suffrage Movement, 1890 to 1920.* Garden City, N.Y.: Doubleday Anchor Books, 1971.

————. *Means and Ends in American Abolitionism: Garrison and His Critics on Strategy and Tactics, 1834–1850.* New York: Random House, Vintage Books, 1967.

————, ed. *Up From the Pedestal: Selected Writings in the History of American Feminism.* Chicago: Quadrangle Books, 1970.

Lerner, Gerda. *The Grimké Sisters from South Carolina: Pioneers for Woman's Rights and Abolition.* New York: Schocken Books, Studies in the Life of Women, 1971.

————. *The Woman in American History.* Menlo Park, Calif.: Addison-Wesley, 1971.

Lovejoy, Arthur O. *The Great Chain of Being: A Study of the History of an Idea.* New York: Harper & Row, Harper Torchbooks, 1960.

Lutz, Alma. *Created Equal: A Biography of Elizabeth Cady Stanton, 1815–1902.* New York: The John Day Co., 1940.

Matthiessen, F. O. *American Renaissance: Art and Expression in the Age of Emerson and Whitman.* New York: Oxford University Press, 1941.

Meltzer, Milton. *Tongue of Flame: The Life of Lydia Maria Child.* New York: Thomas Y. Crowell Co., 1965.

Meyers, Marvin. *The Jacksonian Persuasion: Politics and Belief.* 1957. New York: Alfred A. Knopf, Vantage Books, 1960.

Miller, Perry. *The Life of the Mind in America from the Revolution to the Civil War.* New York: Harcourt, Brace & World, 1965.

————. *Nature's Nation.* Cambridge: The Belknap Press of Harvard University Press, 1967.

————. *The Raven and the Whale.* New York: Harcourt, Brace & World, 1956.

————. *The Transcendentalists: An Anthology.* Cambridge, Mass.: Harvard University Press, 1950.

Newcomer, Mabel. *A Century of Higher Education for Women.* New York: Harper & Bros., 1959.

O'Neill, William L. *Everyone Was Brave: A History of Feminism in America.* Chicago: Quadrangle Books, 1971.

————, ed. *The Woman Movement: Feminism in the United States and England.* 1969. Chicago: Quadrangle Books, 1971.

Papishvily, Helen. *All the Happy Endings.* New York: Harper & Bros., 1956.

Pattee, Fred Lewis. *The Feminine Fifties.* New York: D. Appleton-Century, 1940.

Peckham, Morse. *Beyond the Tragic Vision: The Quest for Identity in the Nineteenth Century.* New York: George Braziller, 1962.

———. *Romanticism: The Culture of the Nineteenth Century.* New York: George Braziller, 1965.

———. *The Triumph of Romanticism.* Columbia, S.C.: University of South Carolina Press, 1970.

Poirier, Richard. *A World Elsewhere: The Place of Style in American Literature.* New York: Oxford University Press, 1966.

Reigel, Robert. *American Feminists.* Lawrence, Kan.: The University of Kansas Press, 1963.

Schlesinger, Arthur M., Jr. *The Age of Jackson.* Boston: Little, Brown & Co., 1950.

Schneir, Miriam, ed. *Feminism: The Essential Historical Writings.* New York: Random House, Vintage Books, 1972.

Shepard, Odell. *Pedlar's Progress; The Life of Bronson Alcott.* Boston: Little, Brown & Co., 1937.

Sinclair, Andrew. *The Emancipation of the American Woman.* New York: Harper & Row, Harper Colophon Books, 1966.

Stern, Madeleine B. *Margaret Fuller.* New York, 1930.

Tanner, Tony. *The Reign of Wonder: Naivety and Reality in American Literature.* London: Cambridge University Press, 1965.

Taylor, Diane Greene. "Years of Transition: Margaret Fuller on the *New York Tribune.*" Master's thesis, The University of Texas at Austin, 1971.

Tharp, Louise Hall. *The Peabody Sisters of Salem.* London: George P. Harrap, 1951.

Thompson, Eleanor W. *Education for Ladies, 1830–1860: Ideas on Education in Magazines for Women.* New York: King's Crown Press, 1947.

Thorp, Margaret Farrand. *Female Persuasion: Six Strong-Minded Women.* New Haven: Yale University Press, 1949.

Tyler, Alice Felt. *Freedom's Ferment: Phases of American Social History from the Colonial Period to the Outbreak of the Civil War.* 1944. New York: Harper & Row, Harper Torchbooks, 1962.

Woody, Thomas. *A History of Women's Education in the United States.* 2 vols. New York: The Science Press, 1929.

## Authorities:
*Selected Recent Articles*

Baer, Helen G. "Mrs. Child and Miss Fuller." *New England Quarterly* 26 (1953).

Carter, Ray Cecil. "Margaret Fuller and the Two Sages." *Colby Library Quarterly* 6 (1961).

Hicks, Granville. "Conversation in Boston," *Sewanee Review* 39 (1931).

Hoyt, Edward A., and Brigham, Loriman S. "Glimpses of Margaret Fuller: The Green Street School and Florence." *New England Quarterly* 29 (1956): 87–98.

Lasch, Christopher, and Taylor, William R. "Two 'Kindred Spirits': Sorority and Family in New England, 1839–1846." *New England Quarterly* 36 (1963): 23–42.

Lerner, Gerda. "The Lady and the Mill Girl: Changes in the Status of Women in the Age of Jackson." *Mid-Continent American Studies Journal* 10 (1969): 5–15.

———. "Women's Rights and American Feminism." *American Scholar* (1971): 235–48.

Lutz, Alma. "Women Record History: 1784–1902." Address, Radcliffe Women's Archives Workshop, February 17, 1955. Alma Lutz Papers. The Schlesinger Library, Radcliffe.

Pearson, Norman Holmes. "Elizabeth Peabody on Hawthorne," *Essex Institute* (Mass.) *Historical Collections* (July 1958), pp. 256–76.

Roberts, Josephine E. "Elizabeth Peabody and the Temple School." *New England Quarterly* 15:497–508.

Rosenberg, Carroll Smith. "Beauty, the Beast and the Militant Woman: A Case Study in Sex Roles and Social Stress in Jacksonian America." *American Quarterly* 23 (1971):562–84.

Stearns, Bertha M. "New England Magazines for Ladies, 1830–1860." *New England Quarterly* (October 1930).

Stern, Madeleine B. "The House of the Expanding Soirées, 1846." *New York History Quarterly* (January 1942), pp. 42–51.

Wellek, René. "The Minor Transcendentalists and German Philosophy." *New England Quarterly* 15 (1943), pp. 652–80.

Welter, Barbara. "The Cult of True Womanhood, 1820–1860." *American Quarterly* 18 (1966):151–75.

———. "Anti-Intellectualism and the American Woman, 1800–1860." *Mid-America* 48 (1966):258–70.

———. "The Merchant's Daughter: A Tale from Life." *New England Quarterly* (March 1969), pp. 3–22.

Wilson, John B. "A Transcendental Minority Report." *New England Quarterly* (June 1956), pp. 147–58.

Wood, Ann D. "The 'Scribbling Women' and Fanny Fern: Why Women Wrote." *American Quarterly* 23 (1971):3–25.

———. "The Literature of Impoverishment: The Women Local Colorists of America, 1865–1914." *Women's Studies: An Interdisciplinary Journal* 1:3–47.

# Index